07/08

The Myth of Br

THE MYTH OF BRITISH MONARCHY

Edgar Wilson

Journeyman/Republic

First published in Great Britain
by the Journeyman Press Limited and Republic

The Journeyman Press Ltd, 97 Ferme Park Road
Crouch End, London, N8 9SA and
17 Old Mill Road, West Nyack, NY 10994, USA

paper 1 85172 025 1

First edition 1989
10 9 8 7 6 5 4 3 2 1

The publication of this book has been assisted by Republic. Republic is an
association of democratic republicans formed in London in 1983. Members of
Republic regard the ideas of hereditary office and privilege as both socially
divisive and morally repugnant. Republic has no party political affiliation. It
aims to promote Republicanism by peaceful, lawful, democratic means, and to
act as a focus for democratic republican opinion.
Republic may be contacted through the following people, who can provide
details of its activities, and a list of its local contacts:

Terry Liddle (Chairman), 83 Sowerby Close, Eltham, London SE9 6EZ

Colin Mills (Editor), 70 Chestnut Lane, Amersham
Buckinghamshire HP6 6EH

Albert Standley (Secretary), 8 Boone Place, The Grove
Witham, Essex CM8 2VE

Cover illustration reproduced with the kind permission
of Spitting Image Productions Ltd

Computer typeset from disc in Plantin by Wordstream Ltd, Poole
and printed in Great Britain by Billing & Sons Ltd, Worcester

TO THE MEMORY OF TOM PAINE

ACKNOWLEDGEMENTS

Personal thanks are due first and foremost to Ted Honderich of University College, London. He is not responsible for any of it and disagrees with some of it, including the tone, but he first encouraged it and tried hard to promote it from the outset in 1980. Vernon Pratt of Lancaster University and David Lamb of Manchester University also tried (alas, in vain) to promote it. David Webster and Mike Singleton commented on parts, to good effect. Heather Piper and Nicole Wilson volunteered valuable research assistance. Peter Doughty expurgated the entire text, and any barbarisms remain despite his efforts.

Republic has given all kinds of support, especially Philippa Gibson, Albert Standley, Peter Hunot, and Colin Mills, whose help with production was indispensable. Marjorie Foy and Linda Gross typed drafts. Sue Holland contributed her I.T. skills. Above all Paul Warsop made it finally possible with moral and financial support.

I have drawn, perhaps excessively, on the published work of others. It is all cited here: to acknowledge the debts; as substantiation; and for the benefit of those interested in pursuing their own inquiries.

I would like to pay special tribute to Peter Hunot, Honorary Treasurer of Republic, who died whilst the book was in press. His humanity and life-long devotion to the promotion of progressive causes were an example to all republicans.

CONTENTS

V THE MONARCHY AND DEMOCRACY

VI ALTERNATIVES TO MONARCHY

'People are still curiously deferential. It is a peculiarly English thing. It is because we are not really democratic. I mean, people despise democratic institutions in this country. If you look at the institutions that have the greatest public support, they are hereditary institutions. Peers are respected more than members of the House of Commons; the Royal Family is respected more than the peers. The further you are from the democratic process in this country, the more respect you have.'

William Waldegrave, Old Etonian and Conservative Government Minister, in Danziger (1988, p.285)

'If you see a nation decline, this is not because its government is bad; it is because this government, which is the best for the nation, dies like all human works, or rather because it is because the national character is worn out. Then nations must undergo a political rebirth or perish.'

Joseph de Maistre (1965, p.128)

'Once a people's customs are formed, once its prejudices have put down roots, any attempt to reform it is therefore a dangerous venture − and a futile one as well! It cannot bear to have anyone lay hands on its diseased parts, even to cure them − just as some foolish timid patients tremble at the sight of the doctor.'

Jean-Jacques Rousseau (1954, p.64)

'I am not one of those oriental slaves who deem it unlawful presumption to look their Kings in the face.'

Henry St John, Lord Bolingbroke (1949, p.41)

'People who write books ought to be shut up.'

King George V − quoted in Fulford (1970, p.176)

INTRODUCTION

It is three hundred years since the 'Glorious Revolution' of 1688 ended absolute monarchy, and Britain was established as a constitutional monarchy by the Revolution Settlement of 1689. Nevertheless, the British Monarchy remains a puzzle to foreigners and to perceptive students of politics and society. It is incompatible with democracy in principle, yet in practice, amidst widespread and caste based inequality, injustice and real deprivation, the ancient symbol and instrument of hereditary privilege remains unchallenged. It apparently even grows in popularity.

The main purpose of this book is to show that there is no good reason why the British Monarchy should be as popular as, apparently, it is. Also, that there is no argument from principle or any other basis adequate to justify it. This view, needless to say, is not often expressed in Britain. It is offered against the avalanche of wholly uncritical works produced by the royalty industry for popular consumption. In 1987, for example, there were approximately 240 books about the Monarchy in print of generally uncritical, inane, and sycophantic sorts, and just one critical work. If support for republicanism were even only approximately represented in print, there would have been at least 40 critical works. This shows the extent of the *taboo* protecting the Monarchy from healthy scrutiny.

There are a few classic critical texts. Above all stand Tom Paine's *Common Sense* (1776) and *The Rights of Man* (1791). Charles Bradlaugh's *Impeachment of the House of Brunswick* (1874) was published at the height of the 19th century republican movement. William Makepeace Thackeray's *The Four Georges* (1861) is a model of scatological irreverence.

In the forty-three years since the Second World War there have been astonishingly few essays in thorough-going criticism. Percy Black's *The Mystique of Modern Monarchy* (1953) is a broadly psychological study. Norman Birnbaum's article on 'Monarchists and Sociologists' (1955) deserves to be much better known. Kingsley Martin's *The Crown and the Establishment* (1962) condemns social and cultural aspects of contemporary monarchy but opines that the Monarchy could still be respected and loved. Willie Hamilton's *My Queen and I*

1

(1975) criticises personal and financial aspects. Piers Brendon's *Our Own Dear Queen* (1986) is a mainly historical critique in the same spirit as Thackeray's. Tom Nairn's various writings, notably *The Enchanted Glass – Britain and its Monarchy* (1988), address important cultural, political and constitutional issues from the perspectives of socialist theory. This list is virtually exhaustive. There is evidently ample scope for widening the public debate about the Monarchy.

The British Monarchy is an exceedingly complex phenomenon. One sort of complexity follows from the distinctions between: monarchy as a general idea; the various practical forms that monarchy can take; different dynasties; and present incumbents. Since each of these factors can be judged either favourably or unfavourably it follows that systematically there are, on this basis alone, sixteen different basic positions that might be taken on the British Monarchy today. The central strategy adopted here is to examine the Monarchy at the level of principle, because if it cannot be justified in principle then no other consideration will be sufficient to support it. For a different reason it is appropriate still to address other considerations: because people think them important or decisive. Personal matters are raised in some places, not because they are intrinsically important, but in order to give substance to matters of principle, and to dispel false beliefs that are materially relevant to principle.

A fully adequate study of the Monarchy would need to embrace a number of different perspectives, especially historical, political and cultural ones. This book offers a broadly philosophical perspective. What I have written should, therefore, be judged for what it is: as argument; that is by the truth or falsity and the rightness or wrongness of what is said, not from some other viewpoint entirely.

It will be helpful at the outset to explain what I understand to be involved in a discussion of the Monarchy at the level of principle. In order to do so it is necessary to distinguish two sorts of interest we may have in people's beliefs, and in social practices related to them.

First, we may be interested in reasons: in whether the beliefs are really true or right and in their justification; in short *why* people *should* believe. These are matters of evidence, argument, and other grounds for holding beliefs. This traditionally has been the interest of philosophers. Secondly, we may be interested in *causes*: in how people come to have certain beliefs, whether or not they are really true or right, and in the function that beliefs serve for individuals and societies: in short in *how* people *do* believe. These are questions for psychologists, sociologists and such like.

It is clear that the first sort of question, of whether a belief is true or right and warranted, and the second sort of question, of what causes people to have beliefs, and the results of holding them, are different sorts of questions. People may for instance have a belief in the Christian God because it was inculcated by parents and church at an early stage of their development. Also, people may be more or less happy, societies more or less cohesive, for holding the belief. But this tells us nothing about whether really there is a God, whether he is good, or whether people are adequately justified in believing these things. These are logically different matters entirely.

I am concerned mainly here with old-fashioned questions of truth and justification. These are the issues that exercised Tom Paine and others in that same radical tradition. In particular, I am not concerned with ideology, that is with the cultural formation of ideas and their function, except indirectly as it relates to my main concern. A study of monarchy from the perspective of the theory of ideology will be at least as interesting and important as the one I have attempted. But it would be a different study of different questions to mine. Other books can be written as well as this one. There is no reason to suppose that they would reach conclusions very different to mine.

The inquiry pursued here takes the following form, in outline. The central strategy is to see whether an adequate justification for the Monarchy is discoverable, that would solve the puzzle of its popularity. In Part One it is established, first, that well attested but not widely appreciated facts show that Britain is a grossly inequitable and unjust, that is immoral, society. Second, it is shown that the inequity and injustice are rooted in a system of unjustifiable hereditary social distinctions − virtually a caste system. The Monarchy in Britain, it seems, both exemplifies and sustains the caste system which in turn perpetuates repressive inequity and injustice. Thirdly, the Monarchy is shown to give rise to a variety of political problems because of the conservative effects of its influence and prerogative powers, and because it is unaccountable to the people. These problems raise the question of why the Monarchy remains popular despite its position in the unjustifiable social hierarchy and its repressive function. Possible justification is sought in two kinds of beliefs about the Monarchy.

In Part Two a number of influential popular beliefs about the Monarchy are considered. These are beliefs which turn out to be unexamined, largely untrue and largely irrelevant to an adequate justification of the Monarchy even if they were true. They are *petty myths* of popularity; hard work; good business; tradition; Commonwealth relations; moral example; powerlessness; and defence of liberty. The conclusion is reached that although these petty myths are widely influential in promoting popular support for the Monarchy there is no adequate support for them. Justification is then sought in more profound beliefs.

In Part Three the concept of *profound myths* is explained. These are beliefs which are supposed to provide a more or less profound and not necessarily obvious or widely understood justification for the Monarchy. This justification is typically and above all non-rational. Consideration is given, therefore, to the status of rationality and to whether an adequate rational appraisal of monarchy is possible. Against irrationalist and materialist objections it is shown that a rational appraisal of the profound myths of monarchy is both possible and necessary.

In Part Four, three main *profound myths* of monarchy are examined. The *myth myth* is the view that monarchy alone expresses something deep and mythic in human nature that is indispensable to a cohesive and stable society. It is concluded that even if some such myth is in general indispensable, the monarchy myth in particular demonstrably is not. Secondly, the *religious myth* is the view that there is something essential in human nature that is religious and that the Monarchy alone satisfies a need for such a religious aspect to the headship of state. It is established that there is no substance to this claim, and that the separation of Church and State is long overdue. Thirdly, the *psychology myth* is the view that monarchy alone satisfies an unconscious need for reassuring authority. Again, there is no adequate foundation for this either against other psychological theories or indeed against objections to any psychological theory. It is concluded that there is no adequate justification for the profound myths of monarchy. A justification is then sought in established social and political ideals and principles.

In Part Five the Monarchy is examined against the established democratic ideals of liberty, equality, justice and fraternity; and against the pragmatic ideal of utility. It is argued that monarchy is incompatible with liberty, because it is coercively persuasive; incompatible with equality, because it is essentially inegalitarian; incompatible with fraternity, because it is hierarchic, exclusive and requires deference. It is shown that whatever utility monarchy may have may be equally served by alternative institutions which are less objectionable. The Monarchy proves to be incompatible with the democratic ideals and serves no purpose that could not be served as well by other, less objectionable, institutions. The question is raised: whether there are practicable alternatives to the Monarchy in Britain.

In Part Six the question of constitutional change is considered. It is noted how questioning of the Monarchy is strangely *taboo* when most other constitutional issues are now openly discussed. The desirability of reform is considered on moral and constitutional grounds and a number of possible changes identified. Reforms on moral grounds include, among others, taxing royal income; and reducing prerogative powers. Reforms on constitutional grounds include, among others, transferring prerogative powers to the Speaker of the Commons, or to *informateurs*.

The abolition of the Monarchy is then discussed. Alternative institutions are mooted; of elective presidency and a bicameral arrangement including a re-constituted second chamber to replace the House of Lords. Finally the party-political context of possible change is discussed. It is considered that the prevailing *taboo* against discussing radical reform or abolition of the Monarchy is due to its supposed popularity which deters pragmatic politicians from considering the issue. The first step towards solving the problem of the Monarchy is to break the *taboo* and to dispel the myths that surround it and make it popular.

In all of this I am not suggesting that the Monarchy is the sole cause or even the principal cause of all of Britain's social and economic problems. It follows that I am not suggesting either that without a monarchy Britain's problems would be solved. What I am suggesting is that the Monarchy is both a significant manifestation and a substantial cause of a very great deal that is wrong with British society. I am also suggesting that the Monarchy does not help to solve any of the most serious problems of our society. At best it is a potent anodyne. Finally, I am suggesting that without the Monarchy Britain's problems would be very much more easily solved. At a minimum, an exercise of political will radically to reform or to abolish the Monarchy would be the most encouraging sign that Britons had abandoned antique fantasies in favour of a realistic, rational, and just view of the nation and its place in the world as we approach the twenty-first century.

PART I: THE PROBLEM

CHAPTER *1* THE MONARCHY AS PERNICIOUS MYTH

The British Monarchy works as a pernicious myth. It is pernicious because it is inherently immoral and unjustifiable, and yet deludes most British people into accepting a society which does not serve their best interests. It is mythic because it promotes widely held and influential prejudices which are related only remotely to the truth.

The simple truth is as follows. The Monarch in Britain has the status of head of state. The position is hereditary, the succession being in order of precedence of males, if any; if none, then of females. Heredity is legitimised by Parliament by an Act of Settlement which established the succession of the reigning Hanover-Windsor dynasty in 1714. The Monarch's official role in the 1980s is to be consulted by, to encourage, and to warn the government. Specific powers, largely dormant, include power to refuse dissolution of Parliament, and the power to invite a member of the House of Commons to form a government. The Monarch also bestows titles and honours. It is this simple truth that is surrounded by baroque myths.

Like every other great myth, whether benevolent or pernicious, innocuous or indispensable, of necessity the myth of British Monarchy is inexhaustibly rich and complex. It is sufficiently vague to permit an almost infinite variety of interpretations. Nevertheless, any account of the official ideology would include its status as a living personified symbol of the nation; its exemplification of the best standards of public and private morality; its superiority to the strife of political factions, castes, and classes; and its decisive contribution to political stability. So the official ideology and myth of the British Monarchy goes something like this.

First, the Monarchy provides tangible blood-ties to the tribal origins of the people and so a shared and proud tradition of 'ancient glories'. The monarch is thus a legitimate Head of State, and the elected democratic parliament governs in her name. According to Dermot Morrah, the monarch is the head of *every* major department of the nation's life, and therefore the symbol of the nation's unity.[1] A recent succession of monarchs, including Victoria, George V, George VI, and now Elizabeth II, have personified this ideal to perfection. So it is understandable that when the people honour the monarch they are, in a way, honouring themselves.[2]

Secondly, the monarch exemplifies, and so promotes by example, the highest standards of public and private morality. Selfless devotion to duty, justice, freedom, compromise, and tolerance are the virtues of public life. Equally important are the personal virtues of generosity, charity, loyalty, dignity, and respect for the individual. Since these values have sacred origins, it is fitting that the monarch is head of the established Church in England and leader of the nation's religious life. The values are most naturally expressed through the family, and so it is most fitting that a royal family is the model for personal, national, and even international relations, especially the Commonwealth.

Thirdly, the monarch does not rule, but rather reigns. This important distinction reflects the fact that the monarch exercises no political power. Indeed, the head of state defines a limit to political power. Strict political neutrality goes with a general posture of 'benevolent neutrality' in the social class struggle. One Labour spokesman boasted to the Russians that 'In England the King does what the people want. He will be a Socialist King.'[3] Some working class people even suppose that the Queen votes Labour 'like the rest of us ordinary people do'.[4]

Fourthly, political neutrality, among other things, allows the monarch to stabilise the political process. According to Bolingbroke's and Bagehot's constitutional formula, the monarch is consulted by the government, offers encouragement, and urges caution, which is calculated to prevent extreme and disturbing action. The *influence* exercised by the head of state in this way has tended to increase in proportion to the decrease of effective political power at her disposal.[5] Furthermore, the legitimacy of constitutional authority under the Crown is so unchallenged that it is a guarantee against illegitimate political and military adventures. As Kingsley Martin put it: 'If we drop the trappings of royalty in the gutter, Germany has taught us that some gutter-snipe (or house painter with a mission) may pluck them up.'[6] The experience of Spain in 1981, where parliamentary democracy was saved by the constitutional monarch, Juan Carlos, shows that this remains a vital safeguard.[7]

An institution which succeeds in embodying all of these virtues surely deserves popular respect; adulation, even. As Bolingbroke put it, a patriot king is a sort of 'standing miracle'.[8] It seems that in Britain we now live in miraculous times. The success of the British

Monarchy is measured by its universal popularity. Notwithstanding recurrent predictions about its decline and demise, in the 1980s numerous popular opinion polls confirm what the myth proclaims. Apart from a hand-full of puritans, egoists, cranks, and troublemakers, 85 per cent of the people, at least, consider the Monarchy to be an excellent institution, and prefer it by far to any sort of republican alternative.[9] It is sacrosanct. As one adulator says: 'Elizabeth is Queen ... because England would not be itself without her.'[10]

Surely there is something amiss here? British common-sense alone urges suspicion. How does something which is 'more to be wished for than hoped' [11] not only become an established fact, but remain so for generations, and become enshrined in the very constitution? Have the British learned to legislate miracles? Light begins to dawn if we consider another point of view.

The rhetoric of royal moral excellence is impossible to reconcile with the established facts of life in Britain. From a moral standpoint hospitals must always come before amusements, as Professor Flew reminds us.[12] Yet in Britain there is widespread deprivation among compatriots while the nation supports an hereditary royal family in a grand imperial style that is an affront to any impartial and morally competent observer. Far from providing the nation with exemplary moral standards, the Monarchy is itself intrinsically immoral. That is the moral problem of monarchy.

The idea that the King or Queen personifies one nation must be set against the notorious fact that in Britain there exist the most archaic entrenched systems of arbitrary social class and caste distinctions in the developed world. Disraeli first wrote of two nations in 1845, and in the 1980s they still persist. The pervasive and decidedly unfraternal inequities of British society are closely linked to these institutionalised, largely hereditary, distinctions. The Monarchy is set at the top of the social hierarchy, exemplifies it, and in a variety of ways legitimates and perpetuates it. That is the social problem of monarchy.

The official account of royal politics is, again, significantly at odds with well-attested facts. It would, indeed, be surprising if the political views of a family of hereditary billionaires were not politically reactionary. It would be equally surprising if the considerable covert influence such persons exerted were not generally in keeping with their personal views and interests. Contrary to the usual claims, the Monarch has substantial legal powers, which in emergencies can override even parliament and the constitution, such as it is. Yet the head of state is not elected or accountable to anyone. The 'stabilising' function of monarchy itself may be against the common good, because it perpetuates the exercise of power by an established hereditary *élite*, providing constitutional safeguards only for the interests of that establishment.[13] That is the political problem of monarchy.

It is evident that the widely received official ideology of British Monarchy is substantially at variance with the truth. Precisely how far, and in which ways, requires further elaboration that will be undertaken presently. What is already clear is that the Monarchy successfully promotes a false picture of British society, itself included.

CHAPTER *2* THE MORAL PROBLEM

Great differences in human condition exist in most countries, and they are usually linked to great differences in wealth, power and privilege. Most of these countries are not monarchies. From this it is sometimes inferred that, therefore, deprivation and inequities in Britain are not especially remarkable or anyway that they are not due to the Monarchy, but would exist without it. Such reasoning is mistaken. The existence of inequities in Britain is not made acceptable by the existence of inequities elsewhere. Neither is the moral affront of the British Monarchy diminished by such facts, because the Monarchy pretends to special moral excellence and responsibility for the general welfare. Nor does it follow from the existence in other countries of inequity without monarchy that in Britain inequity is not related to monarchy. And Britain is where we live. Most significantly, other countries do not enshrine arbitrary hereditary privilege in their constitutions. That difference alone is sufficient to distinguish Britain from most other nations. It remains to be seen what is the nature and extent of the deprivation and inequity in Britain, and whether and how they might be related to the Monarchy. So let us now consider these questions in more detail.

To begin with, it is important to be clear about one thing. The intention in taking a sober look at the material and social conditions of Britain is not merely to establish whether or not the cost of maintaining a monarchy on the grand imperial scale is an indecent extravagance. All things being equal the justification of such things is a matter of taste in pomp and pageantry. Morally sensitive people are liable to see such things as frivolous, and to see the people who want them as frivolous too, but that is a dispute about inessentials and can be left aside here. What is relevant is the extent to which there is real material deprivation on a morally objectionable scale; whether this is systematically determined by an inequitable and arbitrary social caste hierarchy; and finally, the extent to which in Britain the Monarchy reflects and even sustains caste systems and thereby the deprivation and inequity. The Monarchy cannot be regarded as an institution isolated from the rest of society, because it is the apex and the very symbol of an arbitrary social hierarchy. As we contemplate the prevailing state of affairs in Britain, we may recall Edmund Burke's observation that 'to make us love our country, our country should be lovely'.[1]

The statistics of such things date rather quickly, but in Britain the over-all picture persists remarkably unchanged. There is available substantial but not widely appreciated evidence from a wide variety of studies which establishes what simple observation suggests: that Britain is a very inequitable and unjust society. Chronic deprivation coexists with obvious and unjustifiable privilege. The stresses of inequity and social injustice from the cradle to the grave are well documented. The strains are more evident every day in the incidence of ill-health and mortality; in education and career opportunity; in wealth and income; even in the administration of justice under the law.

First consider the most elementary matters of health and life-expectancy. The Department of Health and Social Security report of 1980 on *Inequalities in Health* established that there are 'marked differences in mortality rates between the occupational classes, for both sexes and at all ages. At birth and in the first month of life, twice as many babies of unskilled manual parents (class V) die as do babies of professional class parents (class I).'[2] 'The extent of the problem may be illustrated by the fact that if the mortality rate of class I had applied to classes IV and V during 1970-72, 74,000 lives of people aged under 75 would not have been lost. This estimate includes nearly 10,000 children and 32,000 men of working age.'[3] 'A class gradient can be observed for most causes of death ... Available data on chronic sickness tend to parallel those on mortality. Thus self-reported rates of long-standing illness ... are twice as high among unskilled manual males and two and a half times as high among their wives as among the professional classes.'[4]

The explanation for these inequalities is that there are corresponding inequalities in the utilisation of health services which are the result of under-provision in working-class areas and of costs of attendance.[5]

The writers of the report stressed the importance of differences in material conditions of life.[6] Some of these differences are specific to socio-economic environments (such as work-accidents and over-crowding). Others are the more diffuse consequences of social class structure: poverty, working conditions and deprivation in its various forms.[7] The illness and deaths would be avoidable if the same provision were to be made for all compatriots in similar need. Other research shows that in the 1980s with more than four million of the working age population unemployed, and with unemployment unevenly distributed along class lines, the attendant psychological stresses lead further to illness and suicide.[8]

More recent evidence shows that in the late 1980s there is a strong trend toward even greater inequalities in health. In its report of 1987, *The Health Divide*, the Health Education Council concluded that: 'All major killer diseases now affect the poor more than the rich ... Those at the bottom of the social scale have much higher death rates than those at the top. This applies at every stage of life from birth through adulthood and well into old age.'[9]

Typically these findings have not been widely publicised officially, let alone acted upon. The Black Report is made available by a public spirited commercial publisher.[10] The report on *Unemployment and Health in Families* commissioned by the D.H.S.S. was virtually unannounced and suppressed; only 200 copies were produced. The way that such bad news is treated in Britain is typical of the secrecy that abets the national vices of humbug and complacency. In the late 1980s official evasion of the facts about the social roots of health inequalities has become obsessional. When the facts are not virtually suppressed[11] their obvious implications for policy are denied or rejected by Conservative governments.[12] By 1988 the historic practice of classifying data on health according to social class had been discontinued.

If we turn next to matters of education and life-chances, we find a similar picture. The reality in Britain over forty years after the 1944 Education Act is no more impressive than the reality of the National Health Service proves to be. Against widespread complacency about such things, two most recent studies clearly show that, after the war, education had negligible effect on making life chances more equal in different social classes. Halsey and his co-workers have established that access to effective schooling, the ability to stay at school long enough to benefit from it (in terms of academic qualifications, and access to university) have all been crucially determined by the material conditions and the class background of pupils.[13] This much would be expected perhaps, but more unexpected and illuminating findings are reported. There seems to have been no connection between 'family [cultural] climate' and success at school: class, not culture, is important.[14] Perhaps most interesting of all for delusions of social justice is the Oxford researchers' discovery that measured intelligence was 'surprisingly unimportant'. Its effects on the likelihood of educational success were quite small compared to other factors, overwhelmingly the effects of social class stratification.[15] In human terms, all of this means that, for example, even on the most illiberal interpretation of the measured intelligence of working class pupils, 6,000 children have been excluded from their 'meritocratic due' of selective schooling every year.[16] Innumerable children who could have obtained A-levels did not stay at school long enough. And there were many others who obtained A-levels but who could not find a university place.[17] In the years since the data for the studies was collected the situation has not been changed by comprehensive schooling. Recent years of Conservative government have, if anything, turned the clock back further.

The view has often been expressed that class differences are a thing of the past in Britain. Leonard Harris, for example, said in 1966 that class barriers raised by birth had almost completely gone.[18] This popular delusion that British society is open to all the talents is dissipated by John Goldthorpe and his co-workers. After studying data of half a century they conclude that, despite supposedly favourable circumstances of expanding economy and educational provision, no significant reduction in class inequalities has in fact been achieved.[19] The illusion that class barriers have been raised was created by statistics that showed upward mobility of people born into the lower social order. This however was due only to the expanding number of 'service-class' jobs, which could only be met by recruitment from 'below'.[20] This is by no means the same as an open society. Quite the opposite. The Goldthorpe studies confirm that, in Britain, the transmission of social status is a kind of closed circuit.[21] Apart from the mobility explained by expansion alone, there is a 'situation of no-change in relative mobility chances (as between different class origins) ... in which the inequalities in such chances that prevail are of a quite gross kind ... it is here that the reality of contemporary British society most strikingly and incontrovertibly deviates from the ideal of genuine open-ness.'[22] The fact was that in Britain at the outset of the 1980s the social structure prevented individuals of certain social origins from realising their full potential as citizens, or even as human beings.[23] Since Goldthorpe's findings were published three terms of Conservative government have done less than nothing to improve matters. It is instructive to recall in this connection the wise remarks of Adam Smith who observed that:

> The difference of natural talents in different men is, in reality, much less than we are aware of; and the very different genius which appears to distinguish men of different professions, when grown up to maturity, is not so much the cause as the effect of the division of labour. The difference between the most dissimilar characters, between a philos-

opher and a common street porter, for example, seems to arise not so much from nature, as from habit, custom and education. When they come into the world they are perhaps very much alike ... after, they come to be employed in very different occupations ... the difference of talents comes then to be taken notice of and widens by degrees, till at last the vanity of the philosopher is willing to acknowledge scarce any resemblance.[24]

Political philosophers of every complexion from Plato on have emphasised that there should never be too great disparities in the distribution of material wealth, otherwise the different social conditions so caused will prove detrimental to society. The radical Rousseau said that 'the social condition is a benefit only when all own something, and none owns the least bit too much'.[25] The arch-Conservative Hobbes compared extreme wealth-concentration to a 'Pleurisie' of the body politic causing 'Inflammation, fever and painful stitches'.[26] It is unsurprising, therefore, that the social problems facing Britain in the 1980s are associated with gross inequities in the distribution of material goods of various kinds.

Establishing an accurate economic map of British society is extraordinarily difficult; one imagines rather like mapping fog. Apart from the intrinsic technical complexity involved, the simple fact is that the most wealthy and powerful groups and individuals deploy all of their considerable resources to frustrate or evade such inquiries. Nevertheless a reliable and instructive picture emerges from the best efforts reported by the Inland Revenue, the Diamond Commission and academic researchers. In the matter of income the most reliable estimates put the share of the top 1 per cent at about 5 per cent of all income, and that of the top 10 per cent at 24 per cent of all income. The effect of Conservative government in the 1980s has been further to transfer from those with the lowest incomes to those with the highest incomes.[27] These are not at first shocking disparities, until we consider that individual differences between top and bottom incomes of workers range upwards of fifty to one hundred-fold. For example, at 1988 rates, the basic annual income of members of the National Union of Public Employees was £5,750, compared to the salary paid in 1985/6 to Mr William Brown of Walsham Brothers, of £1,268,583. These are not the extremes of income. At 1988 rates, the basic income for 'UB-40s' – unemployed people – was £1,456, compared to dividend income alone paid to Mr David Sainsbury of £13,374,706.[28] (Differences in taxation are more than offset by substantial extra perquisites for those on the highest incomes. Plato, in

The Laws, suggests an order of difference in income compatible with class concord of not more than four between those in 'painful poverty' and the wealthy. In Britain today we have a difference as great as 9,186:1 and as much as 221:1 even between incomes from employment. So far as income is concerned economists provide ample evidence to support de Jouvenel's point that powerful people simply take more for themselves.[29]   Not to mince words, they are greedy.

Disparities in income, however, are as nothing compared to disparities in wealth. Again, the problems of sleuthing and the technicalities of computation are forbidding, but the basic picture is indisputable. The richest 1 per cent of the population owns (at least) 21 per cent of marketable wealth, and the richest 10 per cent, 53 per cent.[30]   In 1984, the poorest 50 per cent of the population owned just 6 per cent of wealth.[31]   Although there has been a trend to redistribute wealth from the richest 1 per cent, this has not benefited the worse-off. The redistribution in this century has not been between the rich and the poor, but between successive generations of the same families.[32]

By 1981 the share of the worst-off 75 per cent dropped to just 16 per cent of marketable wealth.[33]   The most striking differences appear in the distribution of private holdings in company stocks and shares, and of land. According to 1981 Inland Revenue statistics, the wealthiest 1 per cent of private shareholders owned 75 per cent of the value of private shares, and only 20 per cent of adults in Britain were shareholders.[34]   Similar proportions hold for land: with the wealthiest 10 per cent owning 84 per cent; the top 5 per cent owning as much as 75 per cent of land. Forty-two per cent of all land is still owned by the old landed aristocracy, with some individual holdings of almost unbelievable extent. The Duke of Buccleuch, for example, possesses personally over 268,000 acres.[35]

This picture goes with a corresponding picture of poverty, both absolute and relative. All authorities readily accept that there is a hard core of 2 million people below the supplementary benefit level, and not in receipt of benefit. Bad though this seems, the real extent of poverty is much worse. According to Townsend's definitive study published in 1979, various defensible criteria put the number in poverty at from 3.32 million (at or below the supplementary benefit level) to 12.46 million (by the deprivation standard of ability to participate in the normal life of the community), and up to as many as 17.5 million (by the standard of supplementary benefit, plus 40 per cent) on the margins of poverty, that is about one third of the entire population.[36]   In 1987 estimates by the Child Poverty Action Group, based on assessment of the income of low-paid workers and the unemployed, are substantially higher, at 19 million,[37] and Rentoul suggests it is higher still at 20 million.[38]

Some comparisons with other industrialised countries, again show Britain in a bad light. In 1970, for example, the top 1 per cent in Britain held 30.1 per cent of the wealth compared with the United States (25 per cent), Canada (22 per cent), Germany (19 per cent) Sweden (16 per cent), France (12.5 per cent), and Australia (9 per cent).[39]

It is wrong to suppose that the great differences in wealth in Britain are due to extra-ordinary thrift, ability, or enterprise. Thrift could in theory explain how some richest 10 per cent might accumulate 30 per cent of the wealth by life-long saving,[40] but tells us nothing at all of how in reality the richest 1 per cent owns 25 per cent.[41] Again, there is little evidence that ability, however defined, is a requisite for wealth. Such evidence as exists correlates education with wealth. But since wealth buys education, this only shows in another way that the conclusions of Goldthorpe and others are correct: the transmission of social status through wealth is largely a closed circuit. There is an enormous discrepancy between the chances of people from different social class origins which must be presumed to reflect real inequalities in opportunity in Britain.[42] Finally, it is simply not true that very wealthy people are especially enterprising. Inheritance remains the factor of paramount importance in the distribution of wealth.[43] The *sources* of great inherited wealth and of heritability, are rarely questioned. They need to be, because they include a catalogue of conquest, exploitation, expropriation and chicanery.

It is commonly presumed, even by radical reformers, that although there are disgraceful inequalities in health, education and general social conditions related to wealth, at least there is equality before the law in Britain; that is the bedrock of Britain's legendary personal liberties. This presumption has been shown to be as deluded as the complacent estimates of the other social conditions.[44] As with everything else, the gross maldistribution of wealth leads to uneven justice under the law. The system of legal aid for defendants without substantial personal wealth operates very unevenly. Whether or not an accused person has proper legal advice and representation, depends very much upon the arbitrary discretion of individual magistrates in granting legal aid, and this varies very widely from place to place. For example, in 1979 in Allertonshire, Yorkshire, over 44 per cent of applications for legal aid were refused, compared to just 1.4 per cent in Ripon. At Highgate 67.6 per cent of applications for aid in relation to non-indictable offences were refused, compared to nil in Waltham Forest.[45]

In personal terms, the effects are predictable and sometimes catastrophic. For example, in one case, Mr George Lindo was not allowed costs of a solicitor's services, but only for representation by counsel. Largely as a result of this Mr Lindo spent six months in prison for a crime he did not commit.[46] Against this background the then Lord Chancellor, Lord Hailsham, expressed the view that the system of legal aid is getting out of hand because it costs too much. In Britain today we are not prepared to pay to have equality before the law.

Another source of uneven justice in Britain is the extremely narrow background of the legal profession. Their experience and natural affinities distance them from most of the people with whom they deal and so make equitable judgement far more difficult. Whereas the working class comprises 66 per cent of the population only 16 per cent of people admitted to law school are from working class backgrounds. By contrast over 80 per cent of High Court and Appeal judges have attended public schools where only 2.6 per cent of people are educated.[47] As Levinson says, academic agility, intellectual independence and political querulousness do not make for a lawyer well able to fit in the network of patronage, nepotism, and political reliability within which legal practice operates.[48]

Griffith has shown that in Britain the judges are neither strong defenders of liberty nor supportive of social reform. In 1977 he wrote:[49]

> It is demonstrable that on every major social issue which has come before the courts in the last 30 years concerning industrial relations, political protest, race relations, government secrecy, police powers, moral behaviour — the judges have supported the conventional established, settled interests. This conservatism does not necessarily follow the day-to-day political policies currently asociated with the party of that name. But it is a political philosophy nonetheless . . .

> To expect a judge to advocate radical change, albeit legally, is as absurd as it would be to expect an anarchist to speak up in favour of an authoritarian society. The confusion arises when it is pretended that judges are somehow neutral in the conflict between those who challenge existing institutions and those who control those institutions. And cynicism replaces confusion whenever it becomes apparent that the latter are using the judges as open allies in those conflicts.

Experience in the 1980s has only reinforced these points.

There can be no doubt that Britain is a profoundly unequal and inequitable society in most matters essential to the basic wellbeing of its citizens (and that the worst off suffer privations, absolutely). The questions remain of how to understand and explain the deprivation and inequalities; in particular to understand the relationship between basic inequalities and other social circumstances.

CHAPTER 3   THE SOCIAL PROBLEM

A consideration of the theme of class consciousness and conservatism in the legal profession leads to a more general consideration of the hierarchy of status and privilege in British society, and its relationship to the Monarchy. That important issue has arisen directly from a consideration of the social conditions which obtain in Britain in the 1980s. It is clear that there are gross differences separating a privileged minority of 'haves' from the majority of 'have-not' compatriots. Now, it is not unusual for masses of people to be subordinated by a privileged minority. Indeed it is commonplace. What is peculiar and in need of explanation is how in Britain the mass of people seem resigned to their subordination, and many acquiesce to it. In order to understand this it is necessary to understand that Britain is basically a caste society, still moulded by conquest. The sociologists' idea of class, a system based on occupation and wealth, must in Britain be linked to the system of caste, a system based on heredity. In Britain class and caste are linked much more than in other industrialised societies.

A catalogue of the data of social inequality, inequity, and injustice in Britain is not altogether different from those of other advanced industrial nations. But British society can not be understood simply in terms of a social class system built on a sub-structure of late capitalist economic relations. A class hierarchy is a structure of social relations based on systematic distinctions between individuals and groups. The distinctions may be both social and personal. Differences in role and authority, responsibility and accountability are a natural basis for social hierarchy. Differences in personal competence, accomplishment and character (intelligence, initiative, skill, courage, integrity, diligence and 'charisma') likewise form a natural basis for elite hierarchies. A social class system may be egalitarian, equitable and just, if it has equal regard for the different interests of its individual members, if its distribution of goods is in fair correspondence to desert and need, and if social arrangements generally do not distinguish arbitrarily between people. It is not necessary to deny the naturalness of hierarchies of this sort, or to embrace a Marxist conflict theory of class hierarchy based on economic production and ownership, in order to

22

question and reject the existing social hierarchy in Britain, where we clearly have a *caste* system. Class and caste systems are both hierarchies based on distinctions, but class systems permit mobility up and down the scale according to personal capacities and accomplishments, whereas caste systems are based on hereditary relations between castes which are virtually incapable of change and closed to mobility.

The differences in social conditions in Britain are largely related to wealth and social position. These in turn are 'closed' The rich and privileged remain rich and privileged from one generation to another. Notwithstanding the odd rags-to-riches story that proves the rule, the poor and deprived remain poor and deprived from one generation to another. This has remained so in spite of changes to the educational and welfare systems intended to open the social hierarchies.[1] The pervasiveness of caste obstacles to social mobility and equity is what distinguishes Britain from other industrially advanced capitalist countries. It is unsurprising therefore that Britain is also uniquely distinguished by a monarchy on the grand imperial scale.

Nothing more clearly exemplifies the caste-nature of British society than the double standards that systematically apply to low caste ('have-not') groups and high caste ('have') groups of which the Monarchy is the epitome. British caste standards are derived from a potent residue of ancient aristocracy whose values are transmitted to the groups identified in the Registrar General's 'upper professional classes' I and II, and progressively downwards for the falsely-conscious consumption of the lowest orders.

Beginning with basic equality under the law, it is clear that great wealth is almost as effective a guarantee of privilege as the aristocratic exemptions of the *'Ancien Regime'*. When radicals, such as Labour politicians and trades unionists, are falsely slandered in the gutter press, they have no redress because they have no money to pursue justice through the courts. High caste personages are treated differently. The selective class bias of the legal profession in general, and senior judges in particular, guarantees partial and privileged comprehension at the very least. This is brought forcefully home to those who presume to question caste privilege. For example, when Simon Winchester sought to publish established but unpalatable truths about members of the aristocracy, he was effectively suppressed by an avalanche of legal writs. The head of the Monarchist League, the Marquis of Bristol, invoked the menace of his personal friend, the Attorney General, Sir Michael Havers, in order to suppress publication of established facts that called into question Bristol's fitness to participate in the legislative processes of the Lords.[2] What is true of the aristocracy is even more true of the Monarchy. The self-imposed silence of the media about dubious royal affairs is encouraged by the knowledge that unwanted disclosures will be suppressed with all the resources at the disposal of the state. When in 1981 it was thought that the contents of an innocuous royal conversation might be published the whole panoply of law and the state apparatus of the Government, the Diplomatic Service, the judiciary, and the police was invoked to suppress it.[3] It is understandable, therefore, that in matters of moment, there is legalised silence, dissimulation and even mendacity worthy of any Orwellian Ministry of Truth.

A prime example of this is the case of King Edward VIII's flirtation with Hitler and Nazism. Alistair Cooke ventures the opinion that there is little doubt that Edward entertained the idea of returning to England as a puppet king under a Nazi occupation.[4] William Shirer, in his book *The Rise and Fall of the Third Reich*, gives details of the former King's dealings with Nazi diplomats during his wanderings about fascist Europe. Amongst farcical elements there seems to be substantial evidence from published Nazi diplomatic records that Edward disapproved of the war, and that he contemplated resuming the throne with his wife as queen after a Nazi conquest. After the war there was a public denial, and a formal Foreign Office disclaimer.[5] But in 1983, five or six secret service files on the British fascist, Oswald Moseley, were withheld from the general release of papers under the Thirty Year Rule. It is likely that these files contain Moseley's statement about the former King, and some of his relatives. If these corroborate the records in Nazi files, they would explain why Edward was banished by Churchill to Bermuda for the duration, and why the security services and the Foreign Office undertook a royal cover-up.[6] Cover-ups are are in the long tradition of Masonic secrecy which is a continuous feature of the reign of the Hanover-Windsor dynasty.[7] Prince Charles could be the first king since George I not to be a member of 'The Mafia of the Mediocre'!

A difference in the levels of zeal with which the law is prosecuted among different social groups has been especially striking in the 1980s. Whereas the comparatively minor problem of social security fraud resulted in an increase in the number of inspectors from 2,400 to 3,000, at the same time the number of Inland Revenue staff preventing tax evasion was cut by 14,500. In 1986 the number of wages inspectors enforcing low-pay legislation was reduced from 120 to 71, prompting the Low Pay Unit to comment: 'The poor now know that the law will be used against them if they are unemployed, but it will not be used to protect them when they are in work.'[8]

It goes almost without saying that there are double caste standards applied to health care. At one extreme most people consider themselves privileged to be serviced by any doctor at all; the patients are patronised by their doctors. At the other extreme, wealthy patients can call upon all the best care that private money can buy. Members of the medical profession are positively honoured to serve persons of high caste; the patients patronise the doctors.

Education shows the unmistakeable double standards of caste, also. For example, low-caste pupils must demonstrate measured intelligence of a subtantially higher order than high caste pupils, for admission to the same level of education. One informed estimate puts the 'I.Q. handicap' of lower caste pupils at 6.6 points at age 18, and 10 at age 16. At age 11 public schools require low caste boys to have I.Q.s 11 points higher than high-caste pupils.[9] Similar dual standards apply to the required standards in A-level school leaving certificate examinations, for admission to the high caste universities. It is not unusual for 'Oxbridge' colleges to require 4 'A' grades at A-level as a condition for admitting low caste applicants. For high caste applicants the requirements are substantially lower. A prince of the realm can gain admission to Cambridge University with A-level grades so low (1 D, 2 Es for Edward Windsor in 1983) that he would hardly be considered qualified for higher education at all if he were a low-caste person.

The greatest caste difference of all, however, with respect to education, is that persons of the highest caste have no need of it and often a frankly expressed contempt for it. The need for low caste brain-labour has given rise to the myth that it is necessary to be highly intelligent and well educated in order to succeed in life. Low-caste pupils strive for academic success in order to qualify for the most menial, undemanding, often transient work, if it is paid. They and their teachers are vilified by Right politicians when they do not succeed against all odds. High caste personages, however, experience no difficulty in conducting their lives and discharging their (often supposedly onerous) duties with no education to speak of, and very little hard evidence of native wit either. One conspicuous example is the Duke of Westminster. After receiving the best education that money can buy, he succeeded in obtaining just two passes at O-level G.C.E. His native wit is so slender, that he failed to pass the map reading test required for his high caste army commission.[10]

Nevertheless, conspicuous lack of the usual evidence of either intelligence or education is no obstacle to him presiding over estates worth hundreds of millions. How different it is for even the brightest low caste persons seeking any sort of paid employment, who do not have the shoulders of ancient conquerors to stand upon.

The irrelevance of education and ability to high caste privilege in Britain is perfectly exemplified by the Monarchy itself. Prince Philip has frequently expressed the view that the value of higher education is vastly overestimated. On one occasion he said: 'I'm one of those stupid bums that never went to university, and a fat lot of harm it did me.'[11] As Andrew Duncan observed, the trick which Philip carried off was to marry the Queen of England. British monarchs have never been required to have, and certainly have rarely in fact had, high intelligence or learning. But the Hanover-Windsor dynasty qualifies as the 'Dunciad', as H.G. Wells called it, even by the very modest standards of the British Monarchy. George V, the present Queen's grandfather, was a notorious dunce. His father's educational aims for him were no higher than the average standard of schoolboys of leaving age; in this he did not succeed.[12] George V was ranked 68 out of 68 at Osborne School, at age 14, and 61 out of 67 at Dartmouth at age 17.[13] He had much in common with another great and privileged dunce, Lord Douglas Haig. One result of caste solidarity among dunces was the loss of countless British lives in the First World War. The King kept Haig in command of attritional slaughter, against Prime Minister Lloyd George's bitter opposition.[14] In the face of popular adulation of George V, only Keir Hardie had the moral courage to tell the truth, that he was a man 'destitute of even ordinary ability, who if born into the ranks of the working class, his most likely fate would have been that of a street corner loafer.'[15]

George VI was his father's son, and a typical Hanover-Windsor. His unfortunate stammer partly reflected the fact that like many of his predecessors he found his position intellectually stressful. As Christopher Hibbert has observed, 'George VI would not himself, of course, have risen to greatness through his own merits, which he well knew were limited.'[16] He had a great deal to be modest about. It seems likely that his tendency to outbursts of bad temper, rudeness, and obsessively finical attention to the trivial minutiae of formal dress, were not merely inherited from his German ancestors, but were natural expressions of his feeling of intellectual inferiority.

Queen Elizabeth II sets her official adulators a difficult task for the same reasons. Dermot Morrah explains how: 'when it became apparent that Princess Elizabeth would never progress beyond the simplest elements of mathematics, it did not worry the Duchess [her mother] at all.' This was because the main ingredients of the reigning monarch's 'education' were 'Open Air, Good Manners and Art Appreciation, and only after that, as much book learning as might prove to be within her capabilities.'[17] As Morrah points out, 'this was the normal upbringing of any children born into a comfortably situated family of private station.' It is small wonder therefore that the Queen has expressed exasperation that she wasn't educated.[18] What is surprising is that such meagre abilities are apparently adequate to sustain the great burden of the wise counsel of state that she supposedly dispenses to her ministers. Be that as it may: the fact is that the British Monarchy is exceptionally unburdened with intellectual curiosity or education. Even its friends remark on its philistinism.[19] This is all in sharp contrast to the demands increasingly made upon even the ordinary members of the lower castes in the way of intellectual development and educated competence. The case of the Hanover-Windsor dynasty provides impressive support for those theories which attribute a greater part of manifest intelligence to heredity, not environment.

The qualities and competences of high caste individuals in Britain, the Monarchy included, reflect the merely hereditary basis of their positions and the structure that locates them. We should, therefore, no more expect to find effective hereditary leaders or social *elites* than we expect to find hereditary Olympic champions or hereditary Nobel Laureates. As a consequence we suffer from 'the British Disease': a well documented unique national affliction compounded of incompetence and inertia, complacency and conflict. In particular, Britain has never been comfortable with industrialism.[20] The cultural values of the nation are archaic caste values, in which status is attached to caste and consumption, not merit and production. David Hume argued in 1741 against monarchy that it is a system in which birth, titles and place must be honoured above industry.[21] The Duchess of Argyll demonstrated in 1986 that the British establishment has changed very little in two hundred and fifty years when she said: 'You've got to think of rank as rank .... eminence... that's just brains, which is very nice to have but it doesn't count.'[22]

In the matter of income, the all-pervasive dual caste standards are stated more clearly than anywhere else. For low caste occupations, pay is set by 'market forces'. Revealingly these market forces are made to apply to such professional occupations as teaching, social welfare work and engineering, as well as to the more plebeian jobs. Nothing could more clearly demonstrate the specious nature of the evidence for class mobility than this. White collar work is still paid according to the old low caste market standards, of interchangeable 'hands'. With technological change, we now simply have instead interchangeable 'heads'. For persons of low caste, whatever their accomplishments, income is the minimum possible. Minimal competency is the measure presumed. By contrast, high caste occupations, such as judging and politics, have 'remunerations' based on considerations totally other than market forces. Maximal competency is the measure presumed. Judges, we are told, would deteriorate in judgement if they weren't paid a lot.[23] A 'labouring' judge is worthy of his hire. To high caste standards of equity and merit money, is added prestige money. Typically, the then Conservative leader of the House, Mr St. John Stevas, explained to the Commons in 1979 that if MPs became a deprived class financially, in the long run their status would be undermined.[24] The 'law' of supply and demand that 'naturally' determines low caste incomes does not apply to high caste positions, although there is no evidence that the supply of competent would-be judges, senior civil servants, field marshals, or monarchs would dry up if the remuneration were determined by the minimalist criterion, of how little some barely-adequately qualified person would accept.

Bernard de Jouvenel argues that an opulent life style is indispensable to maintaining a proper sense of high caste dignity.[25] The matter of the income for the top position in the caste system, the Monarchy, is so dignified that open discussion of it is treated as *taboo*. Even parliamentary select committees are expected automatically to endorse regular increases without demur.[26] The most 'dignified' of all aspects of royal income is that it is exempt from income tax and the undignified process of Inland Revenue scrutiny of private income. Lord Blake has argued that it would demean the Queen to hire tax accountants and high powered lawyers, to avoid taxes like any other high caste person.[27] It is interesting that he does not doubt that she would, if necessary. As it is, the Queen simply refuses to demean herself by answering questions about the extent of her private income, even when she is asked by parliamentary select committees to do so.[28] How different this all is from the indignities of Pay As You Earn taxation exacted at source from low caste incomes. Such things are the basis of castes; they are not simply consequences of them.

The grotesque maldistribution of wealth in Britain has already been alluded to, and also the fact that heredity remains the main basis for it. Here more than anyhere else, caste-differences assert themselves. High caste persons deploy their resoures to avoid payment of death duties, so that revenues from that source are negligible in the 1980s. As Atkinson has explained, such redistribution of wealth as has occurred in this century is between successive generations of the same families. This is the caste system at work. Recent studies have shown that 'new' money from early industrial enterprise, made little difference to the composition of the high caste social structures. Even intermarriage has been much rarer than is commonly supposed.[29] The situation in Britain in the 1980s, therefore, with regard to wealth distribution and power, is remarkably little changed since the industrial revolution.

One way to appreciate the real significance of this is to recall that 43 per cent of all land is still owned by the old aristocracy. Land-ownership was the basis of the fortunes made in the first industrial revolution from mining and transport. Fortunes so made were then invested in the manufacturing industries of the early capitalist phase of industrial development, the entrepreneurial phase. Many commentators suppose that the change in patterns of ownership in late capitalism, to the corporate phase, has significant implications for questions of wealth and power,[30] but this is not really so. It is wrongly supposed that since public corporations have replaced private ownership, the wealth and power of the high caste has been reduced. In reality, however, the old high caste retains control of wealth and its deployment, even while, nominally, ownership is distributed more widely. By means of personal connections between the directorships of Merchant Banks, Commercial Banks, and Insurance Companies, wealthy individuals of high caste maintain the powers and privileges they have always exercised. As Ceri Thomas has said, 'perhaps the continuance of degrees of inequality almost unparalleled in the industrial world may be explained by the considerable powers of resistance which the privileged may call upon to defend their property and position ... The rich, given the way our society is structured, tend to benefit from a combination of benign neglect, mystique and ignorance.'[31]

The importance of wealth to caste differences is threefold. Firstly, it provides a basis of personal security. Secondly, wealth provides power over one's own and, more importantly, *others'* means of livelihood. High caste persons have power and control, low caste persons do not. Thirdly, wealth is a means of expressing caste status, by 'conspicuous consumption' as Thorstein Veblen memorably put it. High caste persons can afford to spend profligately, especially in pursuit of leisure, whereas low caste persons can not. They may, however, imitate high caste practices as a kind of sympathetic magic, as they fantasise about living a high caste life. When a typist with low earnings *recognises herself* in the 'big wedding' of royalty, the process of deluding the low caste with high caste mystique is complete.[32]

Nothing is more secure than the wealth of the Hanover-Windsor dynasty. Although its origins in conquest and expropriation are obscure or ignored, its substance is easy to discern in its public aspect at least. There are five palaces, paid for by the Exchequer. The Exchequer also pays for extensive household services, maintenance and repairing, running costs, and transport (by land, sea, and air). High caste status is reflected in the perquisites. Conspicuous among these are personal incomes from the Duchies of Lancaster and Cornwall, audited in 1983 at £1,225,000 and in 1985/6 at £1,462,573 respectively.[33] The most notable perquisites of all, however, are the exemptions from income tax and estate duty on personal wealth. For example, the Queen pays only 2.8 per cent income tax on her personal revenues from the Duchy of Lancaster. Her personal wealth is a state secret, as befits her caste status. It was conservatively estimated at £53 million shortly after her accession to the throne, and if so, must in the late 1980s be at least of the order of £300 million. One informed recent estimate by *Fortune* magazine puts it as high as £4.5 billion.[34] So long as the Queen maintains a dignified silence on these matters there will remain an element of pure speculation about the extent of private royal wealth.

A reliable general guide to such speculation is the amount spent on conspicuous consumption in sporting and leisure pursuits. The high caste pursuits shared by the royal family absorb almost incredible sums, compared to the absolute and relative deprivation and poverty experienced by low caste compatriots. The British Field Sports Society, for example, reported in 1981, that British hunts alone spent over £4 million. Almost four thousand people were employed on hunting and coursing. Game shooting was worth £100 million annually. At least that amount again was spent on other forms of shooting. Thirty thousand jobs are dependent upon shooting. The riding 'industry' was turning in over £500 million annually by 1981.[35] One form of expenditure on conspicuous high caste consumption, 'horsiculture', has had dire effects on home counties land that remind us of the Highland Clearances of the nineteenth century. Tens of thousands of acres of prime farmland in Hertfordshire, Berkshire, Surrey, Sussex, Essex, Oxfordshire, Buckinghamshire and Suffolk are being turned over to horse riding, while the cost of basic foods continues to escalate. At 1970 rates, wealthy equestrians were prepared to pay up to £3,000 per acre for grazing land, compared to the price of £1,000 for farm land.[36] Not content with wealth and incomes which support these activities, the British Equestrian Association, on behalf of its members, in 1980 argued that the horse is an agricultural animal and the sale of riding horses for leisure should be exempt from V.A.T. altogether, or at least charged at the carcase price for dead horses.[37]

This in a nation where there are an estimated 67,000 avoidable premature deaths every year among working people, and where in one London hospital alone, 97 children die avoidably each year purely because (supposedly) we cannot afford £7,000 each for necessary operations.[38] The Duke of Edinburgh, who contributed a supportive foreword to the *Case for the Riding Horse*, reports the royal view that it is the responsibility of the government to make provision for the sick.[39] But as we know, governments set their priorities by the standards and priorities prevailing in the nation, and depend upon tax revenues to provide for the sick. The Duke is a devoted polo player, and so is his son Charles. In the early 1980s five million pounds was invested in Britain in polo ponies alone, by only 550 players.[40] The cost of a patron's polo could then be over £100,000 per annum, though this apparently included the cost of 'hired assassins' and Argentine *paramours*.[41] This sort of expenditure is regarded by Prince Charles himself as a little 'extravagance' he permits himself, which he would drop if there were 'immense criticism'.[42] The Queen is a racing woman, with 22 horses in training. The average cost in 1981 of keeping a horse in training was £7,500. That represented an annual royal expenditure of, at the very least, £165,000 on race horse training alone (enough at that time for twenty-two life-saving operations on children at the Westminster Hospital). The Queen is one of 16,000 owners, who together spend over £110 million per annum training race horses, and in 1981 paid prices of £500,000 and more for a single animal.[43] By 1988 it is not uncommon for race-horses to fetch £1 million or more at sale, while the dole is £1,500 per year for an adult. What is difficult to discover about wealth by more direct inquiry is thus manifest in the expenditure on conspicuous consumption: high caste status is demonstrated by extravagance on a gross scale.

It is clear that in Britain the prevalence of real deprivation goes with a social system in which different standards apply to different classes of citizen. Some compatriots are in real need of the necessary basis for a civilized life, such as hospitals, while others indulge in enormously expensive amusements.

Caste, Democracy and Monarchy

A caste society and caste attitudes are ill-fitted to democracy and democratic institutions. Democracy presumes the basic equality of individuals, as autonomous moral and political agents. A caste society is based on the presumpion that some people have heritable rights, privileges and precedences that others do not. In Britain, castes doggedly persist despite recurrent pronouncements of their demise. In the 1980s, Britain remains a land where hereditary lords are still created, to join the antediluvian ranks of Monarchs, Escorts, Princes, Dukes, Marquesses, Earls, Viscounts, Barons, Knights and Baronets, to mention only the ancient aristocratic hierarchy still with us.

We are impressed but not surprised therefore to learn, for example, that someone rejoicing in the titles, Major General Sir Evelyn Dalrymple Fanshaw, a former High Sheriff of Northamptonshire, felt that he had 'a moral right to live what he deemed was a proper life for a retired officer and a country gentleman'. This entailed keeping a horse, hunting three or four times a week, employing a groom and a valet, and, as President of the Hunter Improvement Society, travelling extensively in England and abroad. Unfortunately he did not earn the money with which to pay, so it was necessary for him to make an arrangement with someone prepared to relieve him of financial concerns until the end of his days.[44] In contrast to this, elitists such as Mr Paul Johnson believe that the trouble with Britain these days is that people, that is low caste people, go around mistakenly thinking that they have *rights* of all sorts, such as rights to work, housing, and, for ethnic minorities, racial equality of esteem.[45]

Not only does a full-blown caste system persist in Britain; many commentators believe that it is becoming even more entrenched.[46] Some people, like Lord Blake, argue that most people actually want it to persist.[47] Whether or not they do, most people appear to accept the caste system, including the Monarchy, as an inevitable, even a *natural* phenomenon. Predictably, the Duke of Edinburgh believes that 'Castes ... are not the product of ideologies; [they] are creations of human nature.'[48] Appearances, however, are deceptive. In reality, the social differences of Britain's caste system are not as widely accepted as complacent apologists suggest. In reality, there is perpetual trouble caused by entrenched social inequality and inequity.

These are manifested most obviously in chronically bad industrial relations; in industrial disputes and strikes; in race and class rioting and in crime, vandalism and hooliganism.

This is widely understood by people in Britain. For example, in 1980 a *Times* survey showed that 43 per cent of people recognised that Britain suffers from class-snobbery, or are undecided, and almost half (47 per cent) would like to see the class / caste system swept away. A large majority, 71 per cent, believe that Britain's problems are completely or at least partly due to social caste / class distinctions.[49] The widely recognised facts of class conflict in Britain have led some observers to conclude that British society sustains a mere semblance of stability, because the lower classes are coerced by the combined forces of the law, the courts, the police, and the penal system, together with 'the dull compulsion of economic relations'.[50] Such analyses presuppose that Britain is like other advanced capitalist societies where the 'dominant ideology' is capitalist, and basic values economic ones: property, market relations, and profit. It is imagined that the subordinate classes have competing values of equality, community, and equity which are maintained despite coercion.

What such analyses neglect is the very peculiar caste nature of British society which is nationalist, not capitalist. In Britain the values of patriotism, place and pragmatism are at least as potent as the supposedly dominant capitalist values. This explains a very peculiar and remarkable finding of the *Times* survey. Although 71 per cent of people attributed Britain's problems to the class system, 86 per cent disagreed that abolition of the Monarchy would have any effect on that system. Now this is a most peculiar thing because both royalists and anti-royalists can agree that the Monarchy not only exemplifies caste and class privilege but is its very apotheosis.[51] How the recognised source and symbol of arbitrary social distinctions comes to be detached in the public mind from the chronic problems that such distinctions give rise to is a matter that calls for further explanation. That it *is* so detached seems to be an established fact.

Significantly, however, the Monarchy seems to be detached only from the damaging consequences of the system it exemplifies and promotes. Unless it were detached, its mythic prestige would not be effective, positively to sustain and promote socially damaging distinctions. It seems obvious, as Bagehot already recognised in 1867, that it does promote them.

The apparent rulers of the English nation are like the most imposing personages of a splendid procession: it is by them that the mob are influenced; it is they whom the spectators cheer. The real rulers are secreted in second-rate carriages; no one cares for them or asks for them, but they are obeyed implicitly and unconsciously by reason of the splendour of those who preceded and eclipsed them.[52]

Two systematic studies strongly support Bagehot's thesis. At the time of the investiture of the Prince of Wales in 1969, Blumler found a significant correlation between positive attitudes to the Monarchy and conservative views about moral and social issues, various forms of social protest and, most significantly, deferential criteria in the choice of leaders from different social backgrounds.[53] Similar findings were reported in 1976, by Rose and Kavanagh: a majority of pro-monarchists (61 per cent), that is a majority of people, believe that some people are born to rule.[54] Patriotism and the conviction that some compatriots are born to rule; these things have the same practical effect as law, police and prisons in subordinating masses of 'have-nots'. They have the additional advantage of being bloodless and inconspicuous.

The influence of the Monarchy in holding together an inequitable society can be explained as follows. The modern state is always in danger of losing its legitimacy by failure to reconcile the conficting fiscal imperatives of cumulative private wealth and public expenditure for the common good, especially that of the worst off. There are also difficulties in rationally realising coherent social policies even if they exist because of the complexity of the state apparatus. The state thus stands in danger of losing legitimacy in the eyes of its citizens, unless there is some way of containing the potentially disruptive tensions. In Britain, the means of achieving this is to trade on the 'decaying remnants of the traditional status criteria of the gentlemanly meaning-system of the nineteenth century'. As Scott explains: 'This meaning-system is itself an integral part of a framework of traditional ideas which encompasses much of British life. At the heart of this system of ideas is the institution of the monarchy, which brings to a focus the political activities of the state and the criteria of social status which legitimate these activities.' Whilst there may be no moral consensus in Britain, there is a dominant meaning-system based on the Monarchy, which legitimates arbitrary social differentiation. 'Inequalities are accepted by people in a factual, not a moral way, just as they accept the weather – there is apparently nothing they can do about it. These inequalities, however, are justified by those who are privileged in terms of particular vocabularies of motive, and those who are less privileged will voice similar justifications when required to make some general statement about their perceptions of stratification.'[55]

A significant aspect of the prevalent social outlook is essentially anti-democratic. Characteristically, the Duke of Edinburgh has limited regard for democratic institutions, as shown in his observation to a Brazilian government official: that there wasn't much wrong with a system in which only certain people were allowed to vote, because there was no guarantee the majority were always correct.[56] This is a perennial caste view of the world, expressed most revealingly by one arch-monarchist, Sir Charles Petrie, as follows:

Reason, philosophy, fiddledum, diddledum,
Peace and fraternity, higgledy, piggledy.[57]

Petrie held the view that a dictatorship is probably the only effective method of repairing the evil wrought by democratic administration.[58] The direction in which such caste attitudes ultimately leads is clearly marked by Petrie who in 1933 wrote: 'In marked contrast with the mediocrities who are at the head of affairs in so many states is Signor Mussolini, the greatest figure of the twentieth century, and he is a convinced monarchist.'[59] Britain's inequitable hierarchical social system has at its tap-root the Monarchy. Its significance lies not only in its diffuse social influence, but is also more precisely political and constitutional.

CHAPTER *4*   THE POLITICAL PROBLEM

The political and constitutional problems of the Monarchy are numerous, and have become increasingly pressing. First: the Monarch is unelected, and so, despite the propaganda to the contrary, really represents nobody but herself, although she is a key part of the executive. It is said that in Britain, ministers of the government are the Queen's ministers. They are not delegated power from the electors through their representatives in parliament. Such an idea, it is said, derives from the French Revolution and does not fit in with our institutions.[1]

Secondly, the Monarch retains considerable prerogative powers. Apart from the well known powers to dissolve parliament and appoint a prime minister, there are emergency powers which in certain circumstances over-ride parliament.[2]

One authority on the constitution, Lord Simon, has expressed the view that the monarch would be justified in using her legal 'unconstitutional' powers, if necessary to maintain and restore the constitution.[3] As head of the armed forces, these powers are considerable in an emergency, and there is a need to ensure that their use is accountable.

Thirdly, the nature of the royal prerogative powers is very imprecise, in the absence of a written constitution. Bagehot says that 'there is no authentic explicit information as to what the Queen can do, any more than of what she does.'[4] Powers to dismiss ministers and dissolve parliament have not been used, as a matter of mere convention. But Lord Simon has explained that 'a rule of English Common Law, once clearly established, does not become extinct merely by disuse; it may "go into a catatonic trance", but like Sleeping Beauty it can be revived "in propitious circumstances".'[5] There is a need, therefore, to ensure that the nature and scope of royal powers is more precisely defined. The often cited need for 'flexibility' in the constitution is not an excuse for a royal *carte-blanche*.

Fourthly, there is no reason in principle or from past experience to expect that the monarch will always exercise the existing prerogative powers judiciously. It is, to say the least, unlikely that an hereditary billionaire with executive political powers will act against the established interests of the rich and privileged in favour of the poor and the underprivileged. William IV dismissed Lord Melbourne's government in 1834 and the Monarch's legal powers have not been changed since. Ramsay MacDonald was kept in office by the King in 1931 for the purpose of dole cutting without the support of his own Labour Party. In 1954 the Governor General in Pakistan dissolved the elected assembly, and the courts held that this was legal because the 'law of civil necessity' governed the situation. This judgement is said to apply as well to the United Kingdom.[6] In 1975 Gough Whitlam's Labour Government was dismissed by Sir John Kerr, the Queen's Governor General in Australia, with the authority of the royal prerogative. Royal partiality was informally expressed against the leader of the Mineworkers' Union in the bitter strike of 1984-85.[7] The impartiality of the head of state can not be presumed in exercising its executive function. It was Disraeli who remarked that 'the principles of the English Constitution do not contemplate the absence of personal influence on the part of the sovereign; and if they did, the principles of human nature would prevent the fulfilment of such a theory.'[8] Since the exercise of royal prerogative power and influence is inevitably partial and unavoidable, it is necessary in a democracy to ensure that they are not abused. Perhaps they should be curtailed or even abolished altogether.

Fifth, the circumstances in which royal prerogative powers, including unconstitutional ones, may be exercised, became in the 1980s increasingly likely to arise in so far as there was a significant redistribution of electoral support. Only the inequities of the British electoral system have rescued the nation from democracy and permanently hung parliaments. If the once expected breaking of the established mould of two-party politics were ever to occur, then even the monarch's traditional rights to nominate the prime minister, to grant dissolution and prorogation of parliament and to approve ministers would take on a renewed practical importance. Also, with accelerating decline of the economy and growing social unrest, emergency powers to maintain social order are no longer vestigial, but could be vital to future social stability. It is inappropriate that such powers are vested in an unelected, unrepresentative hereditary and partial head of state.

Sixth, the Monarchy fails to represent and defend the national interest against misgovernment. The most serious political and constitutional problems revealed in the 1980s have not been related to hung democratically elected parliaments, but to 'strong' government by an unrepresentative minority led by a species of elected dictator. Although various commentators have affirmed that the monarch has a legitimate role in protecting the nation from constitutional misgovernment [9], in practice a combination of partiality and concern for self-preservation prevent an hereditary high caste head of state from exercising this function decisively. Although a significant majority of the electorate did not support the Conservative Party in 1979, 1983, or 1987, and although there has been no mandate sought or given for specific controversial policies, these policies have nevertheless been implemented at heavy cost to millions of the most disadvantaged compatriots. Another sort of head of state, who was less partial and less concerned with self-preservation, would be in a position to exercise restraint on 'conviction' politicians who do not command the support of a majority of the people. For example, a truly representative and effective head of state might, in the national interest, be empowered to require a referendum on particularly controversial legislation before approving it.

Seventh, attempts to reform British society, especially the economy, are hampered by outmoded political institutions including the Monarchy. Far-reaching reforms of an antiquated structure of goverment are an essential prerequisite for economic and social regeneration. It is ironic, therefore, that the heir to the throne, the most antique institution in the land, should publicly decry the fact that Britain is struggling against an out-of-date industrial culture and going on in the same old way. It is even more ironic that he should hold up as an example the thrusting individualistic culture of the U.S.A., a republic.[10] The emergence of a rational, self-confident republican spirit would signal the emergence to political maturity of the British people and provide the necessary basis for economic regeneration.[11]

The common view that the British Monarchy is above and beyond politics is clearly mistaken, for all the reasons enumerated here. It is appropriate at this point to take stock of the problems reviewed so far. The picture that clearly emerges from a study of British society is that there is in Britain real material deprivation on a morally objectionable scale. This is directly related to an inequitable and arbitrary social caste hierarchy. The Monarchy symbolises, and to a significant degree sustains, the hierarchy, and so the deprivation and inequity. There is also a variety of problems of a political and constitutional sort related to the Monarchy's unique role. An extra-ordinary feature of the picture remains to be explained: that is, how the Monarchy, which is the apotheosis of arbitrary caste privilege and power, becomes, in the public consciousness, detached from the effects of the caste system, which are well-established and deplorable. This brings us, at last, to the myth of the British Monarchy.

The myth of the British Monarchy turns out to be a cluster of myths. There are two main sorts of myth. First, there are *petty myths*. These are widely held beliefs which form the main basis of popular support for the Monarchy. Although they are widely believed and influential, they are largely unexamined, largely untrue, and, most significantly, typically irrelevant to the question of whether the Monarchy is justifiable. The petty myths are the myths of popularity; hard work; good business; tradition; moral example; accumulated wisdom; impartiality; Commonwealth relations; powerlessness; and the defence of liberty. Secondly, there are *profound myths*. These are beliefs and feelings supposed by those who have and hold them to provide a more or less profound, and not necessarily obvious or widely understood basis for the Monarchy, which is, typically and above all, non-rational. The profound myths are the myth of nation; the religious myth; and the psychological myth.

It should be remembered here, what is at issue. We are concerned with the beliefs people hold about the Monarchy, and which persuade them that it is an admirable thing. The questions raised are to do with whether the beliefs are right, or true, or justifiable. For if they are not, then people are mistaken in their positive view of the Monarchy, in so far as it depends on these beliefs. How the beliefs are acquired, and the functions they perform, personally or culturally, are matters not directly pertinent to the questions at issue.

PART II: TEN PETTY MYTHS

CHAPTER 5   POPULARITY

The myth of the *popularity* of the Monarchy is the one most closely related to the simple truth. Many polls suggest that about 85 per cent of people favour the Monarchy. But the whole truth turns out to be far from simple. The first thing to be said about popularity is that in itself it is no basis at all for an institution, unless the popularity is both genuine and warranted. As de Jouvenel explains, 'majority opinion derives its authority not from majorities alone, but from majorities found in a climate of liberty of opinion.'[1] Certainly crowds turn out to ogle and adulate royalty: but Cromwell wisely remarked of adulating republican crowds, that they would even more readily turn out for his execution.[2] Those people who are impressed by the magnitude and sincerity of the crowds that adulate royalty would do well to watch newsreels of Adolf Hitler's triumphant tours in pre-war Germany. The size of the crowds and the sincerity of their adulation of Hitler are undeniable, but that, surely, is no argument for National Socialism. Those impressed by statistics of polls showing overwhelming support for the Monarchy should recall that on 19th August 1934 in a plebiscite with a 95.7 per cent turn out, 90 per cent of voters endorsed Hitler as both Chancellor and President. On the evidence of polls Hitler was even more popular then than the Monarchy is now in Britain.[3]

Though there is no reason to doubt the authenticity of most support for Hitler in Germany in 1934, it is true that if necessary he was not averse to coercion by S.A. stormtroopers. Not all coercion is so crude and overt, however. There is coercive persuasion. The extent of the apparent popularity of the Monarchy in Britain should be related to the fact that there is constant saturation propaganda in favour of it throughout all media, the education system, and society at large. Dissent from the popular view is rarely broadcast and never treated as a basis for serious reform or change. The pro-monarchy bias of the media, despite boasts about impartiality, is unmistakable and overwhelming. As the inventor of the B.B.C.'s legendary impartiality, Lord Reith, confessed to his diary: 'They know they can trust us not to be really impartial.'[4] In view of the pervasiveness of pro-Monarchist propaganda it is surprising that there is not more fervent support for it and less scepticism. Most researchers agree with Leonard Harris' view that the Monarchy is tacitly accepted, like the weather, rather than actively supported.[5] This can very quickly turn sour, as it did in 1936 during the abdication crisis when a poll showed that half the British people wanted then to abolish the Monarchy altogether.[6] One curious and interesting research finding is that those who have done military service are less likely to see the need for a Queen. As Rose and Kavanagh remark: 'The patriotic risk of dying for Queen and Country appears to have a slightly negative effect upon those experiencing them.'[7]

Scepticism about the Monarchy is indeed much more widespread than the simplest statistics suggest. One reason why the true picture is obscured in some reports is that the surveys upon which they are based are very inadequate. A survey conducted by telephone from London is unikely to reach the parts that the mystique of monarchy does not reach.[8] That would explain how Marplan concluded in 1979 that only 10 per cent of British people were more or less opposed to the Monarchy, whereas a more thorough survey by Mass Observation Limited reported in 1965 that 31 per cent of all people had more or less negative attitudes towards the Monarchy ranging from entirely unfavourable (10 per cent) to uninterested (11 per cent).[9]

Different groups' attitudes to monarchy vary very widely indeed. The Mass Observation research showed that almost 60 per cent of all men had more or less negative or indifferent attitudes.[10] Another survey conducted in 1971 by the *Daily Mirror* showed that among people within the 16 − 26 age group, 36 per cent were opposed to the Monarchy altogether.[11] A survey of specifically working class attitudes in London's dockland in 1968 found that 50 per cent were against retaining the Monarchy, and 60 per cent were against retaining the Lords.[12] There is then good evidence to suggest that even the factual basis for the myth of the popularity of the Monarchy is very shaky. There has been, as well, growing evidence that anti-monarchist feelings are more likely to find overt expression. In 1981, two incidents threatening the Queen's life threatened also to dispel the myth of the unchallenged popularity of the Monarchy. In May 1981, the Queen was the target of a bomb attack at Sullom Voe Oil Terminal in the Shetlands and only delays in the official schedule kept her away from the explosion.[13] In June of the same year an unemployed youth, Marcus Sargeant, of whom nothing has been heard since, fired blanks on the Queen during her official birthday parade up The Mall.[14]

It is most likely that the myth of the popularity of the Monarchy is straightforwardly the result of incessant, universal and insidious monarchist propaganda. A century ago Karl Marx recognised the potential of modern media to promote myths of this sort. In 1871 he wrote:

> Up until now it has been thought that the growth of the Christian myth during the Roman Empire was possible only because printing was not yet invented. Precisely the contrary. The daily press and the telegraph which in a moment spread inventions over the whole earth fabricate more myths ... in one day than could have formerly been done in a century.[15]

Leonard Woolf has explained how the British Establishment resorted to coercive persuasion by monarchic myth after electoral reforms of the late 19th century rendered its overt and direct exercise of political power difficult and unreliable.[16] The covert and indirect coercive persuasion by the myth of monarchy, which was so perceptively and accurately described by Bagehot, has been amplified to entirely higher orders of distorton with the advent of radio and television. George V has been credited with enhancing the popularity of the Monarchy immeasurably through his radio broadcasts. According to myth, the reality of monarchy was conveyed all the more effectively by radio. It is much more likely that the new medium was amplifying whatever was around to amplify. In Britain it was the Monarchy. In the U.S.A. Roosevelt achieved the same effect, and he was president of a republic. The same was achieved by Hitler in Germany, and he was a dictator in a tyranny. There is no reason at all to believe that the Monarchy, or George V in particular, exercised any special hold on the popular imagination that couldn't as well have been exercised by almost anybody else in any other political system, using the same means.

The case of George V raises another important issue. Keir Hardie described him as no better than a street corner loafer. George Lansbury described him as 'a short tempered, narrow minded, out of date Tory with a tendency to interfere in matters which the crown had had no business with for two hundred years'.[17] The popular view of this man, as the kindly, loving, impartial monarch for all his people was largely manufactured by the media, especially radio. We are now in a position better to understand the persuasive power of the media for better and worse, good and ill. A carefully manufactured myth can be quickly dissipated by uncontrolled exposure to the realities embroidered by the myth-makers. All of this is well recognised by the Keepers of the Royal Myths, who religiously follow Bagehot's injunction never to let daylight in upon the Monarchy.

With that crucial proviso, however, the resources of modern communications media for popular image promotion are very considerable. They are deployed systematically and resolutely to sustain, enhance and promote the popularity of the Monarchy. If a royal personage seems to be attracting criticism for sins of sloth or anger, there will be an orchestrated programme of exposure on television and the other media, showing the miscreant diligently occupied in new-found good works. If a royal prince betrays his native oafishness and venality with *ex tempore* acts of vandalism and over-public displays of promiscuity, then there will be a penitential programme of exposure of the culprit suitably sober, and airing such worthy platitudes as can be articulated with the aid of a teleprompter. By such manipulative means, and by keeping the daylight away from the reality of monarchy, the myth and its popularity are secured.

CHAPTER 6   HARD WORK

The myth of the hard-working monarch is among the most widely accepted and effective in sustaining royal popularity among ordinary people. It is edifying to notice, first of all, that some monarchists of a less credulous and obsequious turn of mind concede, ruefully one supposes, that the royal family doesn't really work very hard, compared to most ordinary people, and by ordinary standards. One royalist, B.A. Young, brashly revealed in 1957 'the fact ... that the royal family do not have a very hard life compared with most of their subjects ... The royal family have plenty of time on their hands; thirty-odd public appearances in ninety days is hardly a back-breaking programme for a company whose principal *raison d'être* is the making of public appearances.'[1]

The myth is created partly by the incessant publicity, not to say propaganda, about what *is* done. An impression is created that royalty is always doing something official. Another way in which a misleading impression of relentless toil is created is the form in which the statistics of royal activities are presented. Work-rate is measured mainly by the number of 'engagements' fulfilled and, until recently, the number of miles travelled. Almost any royal contact outside of the immediate royal household may count as an engagement, no matter how brief, or undemanding. A 'reception' counts as an engagement, in fact the most common form of all (there were eighty-six in 1981). But a reception may in reality typically mean nothing more than a fairly brief encounter with a passing diplomat. The average company director, public relations executive, or professional person has numerous such 'engagements' every day. Many other official royal engagements would not be counted as work at all by any ordinary standards. Young even calls them 'Relaxation Engagements'. Such events include flower shows, variety performances, picnics, Crufts Dog Show, and above all horse-racing, especially Ascot.

The long time practice of measuring royal activities in miles travelled is suitably archaic. It may have been a hangover from horse and carriage days when travelling was extraordinarily difficult, and a mile travelled was a measure of real hardship, doggedness and even risk. But when the principal mode of overseas travel is now luxury turbojet airliner, mileage is just a bizarre way of attempting to create the impression of 'a lot' of something or other. For example, sitting for an average of two hours per day for two weeks in a royally appointed and serviced VC-10 airliner does not sound very arduous, especially when it is touring the West Indies and Mexico in the middle of an English winter (February 1975). However, since a VC-10 travels at over 600 miles per hour, the *distance* covered is over 15,000 miles. That seems like a lot of something (hard work?), and that is what is reported by the Palace. The impression is created that the Queen is constantly travelling abroad to represent Britain. The bald fact is that she travels abroad surprisingly little. In the ten year period from 1971 to 1980 for example, she spent a total of just 328 days abroad; on average less than five weeks annually, including three weeks, on average, each year visiting Commonwealth countries.[2] This is not awe-inspiring by any standards. There is, too, another little recognised feature of royal work on official overseas tours. These are usually arranged to warm parts and to coincide with the British winter. The royal progress goes like this: the Pacific (March 1970); Turkey (October 1971); the Far East (March 1972); Australia (October 1973); the Pacific again (January – February 1974); Indonesia (March 1974); the West Indies and Mexico (February 1975); the Pacific (February – March 1977); the West Indies (October – November 1978); the Middle East (February 1979); North Africa (October 1980); the Pacific and Sri Lanka (October 1981); the Pacific, yet again (October 1982); the West Indies and Mexico (February – March 1983); Kenya, Bangladesh and India (November 1983); Jordan (March 1984); the West Indies (October – November 1985); New Zealand and Australia (February – March 1986).[3]

Lord Altrincham, another constructively critical royalist, has pointed out that the royal holidays are very long by normal standards.[4] Here is the root of the matter. In the royal year recorded by Andrew Duncan in 1968-69 the Queen was engaged on official duties on only 110 days.[5] In the calendar year 1981, official duties occupied only 166 days. The Queen has no official engagements at all on 94 weekdays of the year compared to the national average of about twenty. That is, she has thirteen weeks, or three months, holiday *more* than most people, who have just four weeks. Apologists will say that the monarch is never *really* on holiday; 'red' boxes of official papers follow her everywhere. (Not exactly everywhere. They do not follow her overseas.[6]) The idea is put about that the Queen turns to her tedious boxes at the end of a long hard day.[7] Her private secretary told a parliamentary select committee that this occupied two to three hours daily.[8] In reality she spends about one hour and a half daily on the boxes, between six p.m. and seven thirty.[9] And she meets the prime minister for a half-hour each week.

Official embarrassment about the lightness of the royal workload typically takes the form of paltry and lame excuses. For example the Arundel Herald Extra-Ordinary and Fellow of All Souls' College, Oxford, Dermot Morrah, with reference to the extraordinarily long vacational absences of the monarch from London, fatuously explains: 'If the Queen spent Christmas in London she would find it deserted of most of the people she needed to see. And if she visited other parts of the counry during the summer she would disrupt the holiday arrangements of public functionaries.'[10]

The royal workload must also be set in the context of the very considerable staff establishment which supports the monarch's activities. The English household alone in 1983 numbered 323 or more persons, including 172 working courtiers, mostly in the Private Secretary's Office (23); the Department of the Privy Purse (27); the Lord Chamberlain's Office (77); and the Royal Mews Department (34). There is no reason to doubt that the present Queen works considerably harder than did most of her predecessors. But that is not to say a great deal by ordinary standards. Victoria took 'French leave' from public engagements for fifteen years after Albert's death. Edward VII and George V were well known sloths. When Lord Clark visited George VI and the Queen at Windsor in 1938 he was reported to have been shocked at how little the Queen, and the King as well, did with their days. She never rose before 11. There were hardly any guests.[11]

It is obvious that British royalty does not produce and never has produced the Stakhanovite labours of popular mythology. The importance of this is not a question of how hard, or little, the monarch works. Perhaps ritual Heads of State should not work very hard by ordinary standards. It is a question of whether or not people have a totally mistaken view of what the monarch does in the way of work, and how a mistaken view helps to sustain a myth of monarchy which is otherwise insupportable. The process by which the myth of hard work is generated is typical of the manufacture of misleading monarchist publicity.

CHAPTER 7 BUSINESS

The myth of hard-work goes with the myth that the Monarchy is good for business, foreign trade and especially tourism. The head of a U.K. trade delegation to Australia, for example, expressed the common view that: 'The Royals are the spearhead of our commercial attack on the world — we simply can't afford to get rid of them.'[1] A Mass Observation poll showed that a majority of people believe that the Monarchy is better than a republic would be at encouraging trade with other countries.[2] The belief that the Monarchy is good for tourism is even more widespread. One survey showed that no less than 90 per cent of people believe that the Monarchy is good for the tourist trade.[3]

The view that it is fitting for the head of state to promote trade is supported by the most distinguished theories of monarchy. Bolingbroke, for example, equated the effectiveness and success of the head of state with the flourishing of the nation's trade and commerce.[4] James Frazer in *The Golden Bough* traces the anthropological roots of the view to ancient beliefs that a whole nation's prosperity is bound up with the personal capacities, effectiveness and well-being of its monarch. The Shilluk of the White Nile killed off their kings with due ceremony when the prosperity of their country seemed in jeopardy.[5] On this view, and in the light of Britain's chronic economic decline since the 1870s, all British monarchs, starting with Victoria, would have been clear candidates for regicide. The catastrophic collapse of Britain's position in international trading and commerce since 1953 would, by Shilluk standards, leave Elizabeth II with no case to argue. Far from promoting economic prosperity, the British Monarchy seems to provide the nation with its greatest solace in failure, a fantasising nostalgia for past glories.

The basic problem with the myth of good business is that commercial sales promotion is no basis for organising a great nation's political constitution and social structure. It is not even good business, as H.G. Wells argued in 1939.

> If that is the sort of use kingship is put to by Britain, the sooner we clean up kingship the better. Englishmen like myself, who follow the

high republican and intensely English tradition of Cromwell, Milton, George Washington and so forth, will have to intervene to save not only the kingly idea but also the reputation of British goods for selling on quality rather than personal charm, from the unseemly grossness of such vindicators.[6]

This would be true even if the Monarchy proved to be an effective spearhead of commerce. But there is not the slightest reason to believe that it is. All the available evidence proves that it is not. Andrew Duncan pointed out in 1970 that royal visits have no impact on trade figures but, typically, no notice was taken. After a state visit by the Queen to Brazil in 1968, exports to Brazil fell and imports increased in the months following the royal visit. The Board of Trade described these facts as merely 'seasonal'. Similar trends were recorded after tours by Prince Philip of New York in 1960, and again of the U.S.A. in 1966.[7] It is just possible that Duncan's evidence was inadequate. In fact a closer and more extensive examination of the effect of official royal visits overseas on Britain's trade shows that the picture is even worse than he supposed. The effects of royal visits should be assessed against a universal and general trend towards greater volume and dollar value of trade. Also, it is more realistic to consider the effects of a visit on trade for a period of up to two years following the visit, to account realistically for 'lead-times' on the deliveries of major capital equipment. Taking both of these things into account, a simple and unbiased look at official trade figures, together with a record of royal visits for the fourteen year period from 1971 to 1984, shows that royal visits are more likely than not to be counter-productive in one or more of four different ways.

First, there are cases, such as Brazil in 1968, where the gross value of exports actually drops significantly after a state visit by the Queen. Such was the case after the visit to Yugoslavia in May 1972. Exports, valued at £62 million in 1971, fell to £50 million in 1972, and remained below the 1971 level during 1973 at £56.3 million. The same thing happened after the state visits to New Zealand in 1974, Tanzania in 1979, Belgium in 1980, Italy in 1980, Switzerland in 1981, Australia in 1982 and India in 1983. Secondly, there are cases where an established trend of increasing exports is significantly slowed down following a royal visit. Such was the case in Indonesia, where a royal visit in 1974 reduced by nearly half the annual rate of increase in exports: from 55 per cent in 1972-74 to 29 per cent in 1974-76. The same thing happened after state visits to Mexico in 1975, the U.S.A. in 1976, Canada in 1976, 1977 and 1978, and Denmark in 1979. In a third set of cases, increased exports following a state visit are more than offset by even greater increase in imports from the country visited; thus adversely affecting the balance of trade. Such was the case following the visit to Japan in May 1975: exports which had fallen by a value of £10 million betwen 1974 and 1975 rose by £5 million and £109 million in the two years following the visit; however imports from Japan rose far more; by £124 million and £263 million in the same two years. A similar pattern followed royal visits to France in 1972, West Germany in 1978, Algeria in 1980, Norway in 1981, New Zealand in 1981, the U.S.A. in 1983, and Kenya in 1983. Royal visits can do more to promote imports from the countries visited than they do for British exports! In a fourth sort of case a royal visit does have the effect of both increasing the exports to, and improving Britain's balance of trade with the country visited. Unfortunately, such countries are as likely as not to be developing Third World or Commonwealth countries which can ill afford an adverse balance of trade with Britain. Such was the case following a state visit to Zambia in May 1979. In 1980 exports to Zambia increased by £11 million (13 per cent) and imports from Zambia fell by £14 million (14 per cent); a nett worsening of the balance of trade, to a developing Commonwealth country, of 27 per cent.[8] A similar thing happened after a state visit to Mexico in 1983.

Even the exceptions are not clear cut, and throw further light on the matter. There were increases in exports and a positive balance of trade with Australia after royal visits in 1980 and 1981 totalling together £220 million. These, however, were largely reversed after the royal Tour of 1982 for the Commonwealth Games, which was followed by a nett fall of £173 million in 1983. After royal tours of Canada in 1982 and 1983 exports did increase significantly by 14.2 per cent and 21.5 per cent compared to less than one per cent in the previous year. However, there was an increase of the same order in 1981 of 12.4 per cent with no royal tour at all in 1979 or 1980. After a state visit to Sweden in 1983 there was an improvement both in exports (21 per cent) and the balance of trade (41 per cent), to a country which could afford it. However, there was an even greater increase in trade with Sweden in 1976 of 27 per cent but without a royal visit. Finally, there is the interesting case of the visit by the Duke of Edinburgh specifically to the Helsinki Trade Fair at the end of September 1970. Britain's exports to Finland after that fell by £5.2 million in 1972, and imports from Finland increase by £31.3 million.

A study of foreign trade statistics and royal tours overseas shows many other interesting things. During the ten year period 1971-1980 Britain's trade with the old British Commonwealth increased by a factor of two. In the same period trade with Europe increased by a factor of eight. Even trade with the U.S.S.R. increased by a factor of five. By contrast, trade with Jamaica fell by a disastrous 23 per cent. During the same period the amount of time devoted to state visits by the Queen was almost a precise reversal of the order of the increase in trade to the places concerned. Royal visits to the old Commonwealth totalled 116 days, compared to just 33 days to E.E.C. countries. The Queen spent five days in Jamaica, and no time at all in Russia. One obvious inference to be drawn from all of this, is that the less involvement there is with British royalty, the better the prospects for Britain's export trade. Another is that the trade of Commonwealth countries does not conspicuously benefit from the sharing of the same royal sovereign as head of state.

The conclusion to be drawn in the end, however, is really that international trade is affected by a wide variety of factors, to which the Monarchy is largely irrelevant. There is no evidence for the view that monarchy is good for trade. There is, on the contrary, very sound evidence that, if anything, it could be bad for trade.

As with trade, so with tourism: it might well be questioned whether the British constitution should reflect the values of Ruritanian or Toy-Town spectacle. A nation's proud history may well provide, incidentally, engaging spectacle. But it is surely a sign of national decadence that the mere spectacle itself should be promoted as a substitute for the authentic objects of pride themselves. What have the Guards come to, when their principal function degenerates to one of satisfying tourists' curiosity?

Still, suppose that tourism were an acceptable basis for monarchy; does the Monarchy in fact promote tourism? On the face of it, it seems very unlikely. At the times when most tourists visit Britain, royals are either abroad themselves, or else vacationing in the remoter parts of their private country seats. Tourists never see them. And as a tourist attraction Buckingham Palace has no more need of a monarch than does the Palace of Versailles.

Even a brief study of the facts is enough to establish that the Monarchy has little or no discernible effect on promoting tourism. *The Tourism Compendium*, published by the World Tourism Organisation, provides evidence for a very different picture.[9] Measured in gross income from tourism for 1980, both Italy ($8,914 million) and France ($8,232 million) among European countries earned more money from tourism than Britain ($6,982 million); and they are both republics. A more realistic assessment is on the basis of annual *per capita* income from tourism. On this basis in 1980 no less than eleven other countries earned more than Britain ($132): Austria ($860), Switzerland ($484), Denmark ($260), Spain ($188), Norway ($188), Greece ($186), the Netherlands ($181), Belgium ($180), Italy ($157), and France ($150). Notably, half of the 'top ten' earners are republics, including the most successful by far: Austria and Switzerland.

Another interesting picture emerges from a comparison of the number of tourists visiting various countries *per capita* of population. In 1985, for example, the following order was recorded: Austria (2.2), Switzerland (1.46), Ireland (0.734), Greece (0.71), France (0.69), Portugal (0.50), Italy (0.44), the United Kingdom (0.27), and West Germany (0.21). Not being a continental nation might explain the United Kingdom's lagging behind most European republics, but it doesn't explain why Ireland is more successful in attracting tourists. Even among monarchies, Britain lags behind Spain (0.742), Belgium (0.72), Denmark (0.70), and Norway (0.47).

Income from tourism should not be considered apart from *expenditure* on tourism. There is a 'balance of tourism' to be accounted for. A positive balance of the tourism account occurs when a country's income from tourism is greater than its expenditure on foreign travel. On this basis, it is illuminating to compare republics and monarchies on the basis of positive and negative balances of tourism accounts. Of ten relevantly comparable republics, nine have positive balances (Austria, Finland, France, Ireland, Italy, Greece, Switzerland, Czechoslovakia and Yugoslavia) and just one has a negative balance – West Germany. Significantly the republic with a negative balance is also the most wealthy country. By comparison, of nine comparable monarchies, seven have negative balances of tourism (Belgium, Denmark, the Netherlands, Norway, Sweden, Canada, and Morocco), and just two have positive balances (Spain and Britain). Spain has a warm climate which explains its position, with no need to invoke monarchy at all. Britain's singular positive balance of tourism might be construed as evidence to support the case for monarchy as a tourist attraction. But this would be to ignore the weight of all the evidence. The fact is that the trend has increasingly been for Britons to spend more abroad. By 1980 income from tourism, at $6,982 million, was very little more than expenditure on travel abroad ($6,454 million). We might as well infer from this that, increasingly, Britons have been driven abroad by the repulsion of monarchy, as infer that income from tourism is attributable to the attractions of monarchy.

Prominence is given to the myth that monarchy is a tourist attraction, but there has been little effort to establish positively whether, in reality, it is. Official Home Office immigration statistics for 1985 showed that apart from Business (20.78 per cent) and Study (3.09 per cent) a large group (20.01 per cent) come simply to visit friends and relatives. Only a minority (46.00 per cent) came for holidays or recreation. It is not easy to establish the extent of the effect of the Monarchy on this minority, though it is unlikely to be great, for the reasons already given. One survey of incoming tourists conducted by the British Tourist Authority does give some reliable information however. Only 12 per cent of people who chose Britain first to visit even *mentioned* royalty, the Palace, or the Changing of the Guard. All of these things put together ranked royalty only ninth out of ten attractions, behind scenic country, historical places, visiting friends, castles, friendly people, cultural events, way of life, and general sightseeing. Only night-life ranked lower, and that by just 1 point (11 per cent).[10] The most celebrated recent grand imperial royal spectacle, the wedding of the heir to the throne, Charles, and the future queen, Diana, took place in 1981, in which year the number of tourists slumped by almost one million to 11.5 million, from 12.5 million in 1980.[11] Even if it were true that the Monarchy is a major tourist attraction, that would not be a very good reason for having it. As it happens there is little or no substance in the belief that the Monarchy is a major tourist attraction. Since they are never to be seen during high season for tourism that is only to be expected.

Finally, there is evidence that the direct costs of maintaining royal tourist attractions are greater than the income generated. Department of Environment estimates showed in 1988 that it costs up to £16 million a year to run the royal palaces, but the income generated is as little as £8 million.[12] In conclusion, there is no reason to believe that the Monarchy in fact is good either for business or tourism. There is sound evidence to show, if anything, the very opposite. It is, of course, unnecessary, and even undesirable that a head of state should have such a role. In Britain, however, the belief that such a role is fulfilled does serve to bolster support for the Monarchy. Since the belief is evidently false it goes to show how much support for the Monarchy is based on myths.

CHAPTER 8   TRADITION

The myth of tradition has, perhaps, the widest popular appeal, engaging as it does some of the best human sentiments of loyalty, integrity, and warranted pride. It is the most impressive achievement of the Hanover-Windsor dynasty that it has succeeded in convincing British people that the Monarchy is virtually identical with the nation and its best traditions. This goes a long way to explain the popularity of the Monarchy.

The Queen's household itself in the 1980s is a fascinating fossil of archaic traditon, with its Ladies of the Bed-chamber, Women of the Bed-chamber, and Extra-women of the Bed-chamber; Secretary to the Private Secretary to the Queen; Gentleman Usher to the Sword of State; Bargemaster; Keeper of the Swans; Apothecary to the Queen; and Harbinger. Where else, outside of the Gothic fantasies of Mervyn Peake, is the Head of State served by acolytes called Leach, Leech, Lowe, Batten, Butler and Grafton? Where else are the purse-strings held by Wimpenny, Mintram and Blewitt? Where else are there chaplains called Caesar and Vicary? Where else would bed-chamber ladies Hussey and Baring, and secretary Perfect, meet steward Dickman, secretary Titman and canon Carnell? And where else outside the world of Bertie Wooster could you hope to meet Sir Hugh Lockhart-Mummery and Sir Archie Little Winskill? Is it any wonder that Britain leads the world in jokes and lags in micro-chips?[1]

On tradition as such, Winston Churchill perceptively remarked that the traditions of the British Navy are rum, sodomy, and the lash. For, of course, there are traditions and traditions: the question is whether the traditions are beneficial, admirable and justifiable. The fact is that most British people are mistaken about their own traditions. They are not told, they do not understand, or else they forget that the most honourable British tradition of all is a radical tradition: the tradition of questioning traditions. The freedoms that ordinary British people prize (such as they are) have been won only after long and often violent struggle against the forces of conservatism and reaction. Not least among these forces have been the parade of royal dynasties, from the Normans to the Hanover-Windsors. Typically William IV, when Duke of Clarence, argued in the House of Lords strongly against the abolition of the slave trade, saying: 'I assert that the promoters of the abolition are either fanatics or hypocrites, and in one of these categories I rank Mr Wilberforce.'[2] The fittest objects of national reverence and pride are the humane radicals such as John Ball, John Lilburne, Tom Paine and Keir Hardie. Republicanism has also inspired some of the most illustrious names in British letters, such as Milton, Blake and Shelley. What a travesty, therefore, that today so many people should fondly believe that it is the reactionary and philistine family 'Hanover-Saxe-Coburg-Gotha' (now Windsor) that represents our best traditions, for that is approximately the opposite of the truth.

Since the Norman conquest, British monarchs have been noteworthy as much for their rapacity, murderousness, bullying, insanity, incompetence, imbecility, vaulting ambition, mendacity, pride, venery, pettiness, laziness and general unworthiness as for any great virtues.

Not even strict legitimacy has been maintained throughout a succession of royal knaves and fools. In proposing *The Impeachment of the House of Brunswick* in 1874, Charles Bradlaugh was able to appeal to the fact that, out of thirty-three monarchs in the succession from William the Conqueror to Victoria, only thirteen had succeeded by straightforward hereditary right.[3] Students of constitutional law at Oxford used to be entertained by Maitland's demonstration that the House of Saxe-Coburg-Gotha had no legal title to the throne of England. Only by changing the rules could it be legitimated.[4] One monarchist, Charles Petrie, recognises that the present dynasty, 'the Hanoverians, were usurpers ... depending upon the minority whose fortunes were linked to theirs, for both in 1715 and 1745 the English people had shown in no uncertain fashion that it was not prepared to lift a finger to keep them on the throne.'[5] Not that legitimate succession of hereditary monarchy is any great thing. Another admirer and advocate of monarchy has described the later history of the Hanover dynasty preceding the recent era as 'long years of a pathetic rambling-invalid old King [George III], of the Regency and then the reign of a self-indulgent dissolute prince [George IV], followed by a King so blandly foolish that he kept the official world in perpetual apprehension of a new imbecility he might utter in public [William IV] — these make but a poor and undignified succession.'[6] Critics found much stronger things to say.

As to the Britishness of the Monarchy, that is a black joke. Geoffrey Bocca has interestingly pointed out that the present Queen is the first

British sovereign to have British blood in her veins; and that through her Scottish mother.[7] The dynastic name 'Windsor' was chosen only in 1917 at the height of the First World War by the Hanover-Saxe-Coburg-Gothas, not to signify a new management, but to deflect anti-German feeling. When the Kaiser heard that his cousins had changed the family name, he commanded a performance of 'The Merry Wives of Saxe-Coburg-Gotha'.[8] Prince Philip was so concerned with tradition that he abandoned his traditional family name of Schleswig-Holstein Sönderberg-Glücksberg for similar reasons of public relations expediency in 1947, and assumed the name Mountbatten – which is just an Anglicisation of Battenberg anyway. This was carefully calculated to make him a more plausible incumbent in the Dukedom of Edinburgh, the Barony of Greenwich, the Earldom of Merioneth and the Knighthood of the Garter. So much for the Monarchy and British traditions! The simple fact is that ever since the Revolution Settlement of 1689, the British Monarchy has been the instrument of the plutocratic establishment of Britain, which has been successfully deployed to legitimise an unjust and inequitable social structure. For this purpose it has always been more convenient to have mediocre and tamed foreign princelings, 'Hanoverian Mercenaries', on the British throne. That is the real tradition of the Monarchy in Britain.[9]

For many people the traditions of the Monarchy go with, and are virtually the same thing as, the material trappings of office and the rituals of public ceremonial. These are believed to be of ancient origin and to have survived because of the profound significance they have for ancient and modern Britons alike. The truth of the matter is that most of the things that now count as typical royal traditions were invented in the recent past by royal public-relations persons. As David Cannadine has shown, until almost the end of the 19th century, the British were renowned for trying to make their ceremonials great – and for failing. At the funeral of Princess Charlotte in 1817, for example, the undertakers were drunk. At George IV's coronation pugilists had to be employed as 'bouncers' for unruly guests.[10]

It was with unintended symbolism that for the investiture of the Prince of Wales in 1969, Lord Snowdon had the giant coats of arms fashioned from expanded-polystyrene boards painted to simulate substantial regal gold figures.[11] The popular image of the traditions of the British Monarchy is bogus and has little or nothing to do with either the truth or the national traditions which are beneficial, admirable or justifiable.

CHAPTER 9 MORALITY

A desirable, even if misleading, myth of monarchy is the myth of personal moral impeccability. Bolingbroke recognised the need for effective monarchs to exemplify in their personal demeanour and actions, the highest standards of decency, grace, and lack of affectation.[1] The vast majority of people believe that these standards of personal morality are set by the British Monarchy: for example, in one poll 80 per cent of those asked agreed that the royal family is a marvellous example to everybody of good family life.[2] It is supposed that the example set by the Monarch permeates from the Court to the nation at large.[3] Even those otherwise critical of recent British Monarchs have conceded that their morality is beyond reproach. 'Chips' Cannon said of the Windsors that they had 'no wit, no learning, no humour . . . no vices'.[4]

The morality myth claims both too much and too little at the same time. From the point of view of the ordinary person it seems extravagant to laud a monarch for standards of morality which most people who have not the social and economic privileges of high caste status normally sustain as a matter of course, even now in a cynical and permissive age. *Reynold's News* once asked whether it was really so meritorious for the Queen to live the life of a respectable woman. If, for example, anyone were to compliment the chastity of a mother, wife, sister, or daughter, would we not actually take violent offence? 'To exalt the Queen's chastity, therefore, as something remarkable, is really to affirm that hardly anything short of a miracle can prevent a royal lady from falling below the most ordinary standard of female virtue − a very doubtful compliment to the institution of royalty.'[5]

On the other hand, if the Queen sets impeccable moral standards, they have not been contagious enough. Even members of the immediate royal family depart from the best standards. The departure of Princess Margaret's behaviour from the best standards has been excused by royal apologists on the grounds that '. . . to expect not only the occupant of the throne but the entire royal family to provide a perpetual example of moral perfection is to ask too much, and would be to ask too much even in a society which was clearer than ours is about what constitutes these ideals'.[6] But if the monarch's example is not expected to influence even immediate blood-relations, what sort of exemplary effect can it reasonably be expected to have on fifty-six million total strangers? Perhaps we have here another example of the double standards that apply to different castes.

It must be said that even the Monarchy's critics concede that the present incumbent, Queen Elizabeth II, has extra-ordinary virtues; especially devotion to duty as she herself conceives it. But unqualified adulation of the ubiquitous guff and gush variety needs to be set against a more realistic assessment of the moral example set by the Monarchy in some detail. Morality is too often equated in the public mind with sexual chastity, so that the great variety of moral vices is overlooked. There are traditionally seven deadly sins: Pride, Covetousness, Lust, Anger, Gluttony, Envy and Sloth. There is also the national sin of the Jews, Idolatry. And there are sins that cry out to heaven for vengeance, including oppression of the poor and defrauding a labourer of his wages. Which of these does the Monarchy commit?

Gluttony and Envy are not conspicuous defects of British Monarchy now, though they have been in its history. Sloth is more prevalent among royalty than the myth of hard-work suggests, as has been already shown. Apart from these, there is something more to be said about each of the other sins.

First there is pride. It is well known that Queen Elizabeth II, and her heir Charles, Prince of Wales, subscribe to the antique belief that 'divinity doth hedge a king [and queen]'.[7] Despite attempts at humanising by walkabouts and such like, there is no question that, by the standards of humility set by, say, Mother Theresa of Calcutta, the Queen and her family display a pride that is neither divine nor required by their offices. Andrew Duncan in his book, *The Reality of Monarchy*, refers to numerous observed instances of the Queen demonstrating her superior status to those deemed deficient in deference.[8] Tom Baistow has explained how the royal charm is deceptive and can lead to painful snubs. The faintest hint of familiarity produces an instant freeze.[9] One typical episode occurred in 1984 during a tour of Canada when the Queen became furious with a folksy Canadian Minister because he repeatedly held her elbow as he guided her.[10] Windsor-pride extends to the rest of the family. Charles disappointed his mentor at Cambridge, Lord Butler, by for three years confining his circle of friends to the polo playing fraternity and public schoolboys from the country gentry, rather than the grammar school products who comprised three quarters of his college's population.[11] The morally corrupting effect of royal privilege is exemplified most notoriously by Princess Margaret. One biographer has spoken of how 'her royal pride asserts itself ... [and of how] she is used to getting her own way and to being treated with the respect due to a Royal Highness. Some people who know her well describe her as snobbish, bordering on arrogant, and say she can be withering if she senses any lack of deference.'[12] Only by the mindless standards of obsequious adulation can British royalty be regarded as a model of humility.

Second is covetousness. The most conspicuous moral defect of the Hanover-Windsor dynasty is its inordinate desire for money. This extends to a refusal to divulge its personal wealth and a porcine refusal to forego its unique tax concessions. The origins of the family's personal wealth probably lie in Queen Victoria annually defrauding the Treasury of enormous sums. By the Civil List Act the Monarch is required to return to the Treasury the difference between payments made and costs incurred. Charles Dilke estimated that at least £100,000 per annum was saved by Victoria on tradesmen's bills. As *Reynolds News* put it: 'She defies the Act of Parliament, and impudently robs the nation of £100,000 a year.'[13] *Reynolds News* escaped prosecution for publicising these facts, but Charles Dilke's political career was sabotaged by Queen Victoria personally. The present Queen's father, George VI, was involved in a similarly unedifying episode which is not widely publicised. During the Second World War, official royal activities were, for obvious reasons, reduced to a minimum. The King accumulated and kept a considerable nest egg during these years. Nevertheless in the 1947 estimates he made heavy demands on the Civil List provision with no regard to the post war circumstances of Britain. Only hard opposition by leading members of the Labour government forced a revision. It was then necessary to dissemble, making a virtue of necessity. The public were told of the King's magnanimous action in using 'his' savings to supplement the Civil List payments. The Chancellor of the Exchequer, Hugh Dalton's, opinion as recorded in his diary, was that George VI's demands were ill-considered and excessive, and he was not at all satisfied with the King's proposals.[14]

Greed and mendacity still prevail in matters of royal wealth and income. The most remarkable feature of this is that the very considerable private income and wealth of the monarch is wholly exempt from income tax and death duty (or capital transfer tax). The Hanover-Windsor fortune thus increases in geometric proportion. Richard Crossman has set out an unanswerable case against the present situation based on the clear distinction between money granted to the monarch for official purposes, and royal income from private wealth which is exempted from taxation. In 1987 the Civil List Grant to the monarch was £4,326,000. A further total of over £1,335,200 was paid to other members of the royal family. This does not include the Prince of Wales, whose income from the Duchy of Cornwall is substantially more than £1 million per annum.

Income from private wealth cannot be estimated, since private wealth is not disclosed. At present the monarch receives *both* tax free grants, adjusted annually to match inflation, *and* tax free income from personal wealth. As Crossman has argued, either one provision or the other would be royal enough concession for people with an ordinary sense of moral proportion. But the Queen insists on retaining both the massive Civil List income (plus the other abundant perquisites provided by government departments), and the tax exemptions on very considerable income from a huge private fortune, of approximately £4.5 billion. As Crossman politely puts it, that is a truly regal cheek.[15]

The avariciousness of these arrangements is veiled by dissimulation. Both royal and Government sources have typically fostered the untruth that the Queen pays taxes on her private income. Authors of approved adulatory texts retail it with the knowledge and agreement of Palace and Government offices. For instance: Dorothy Laird in her book *How the Queen Reigns* acknowledges the full and extensive cooperation of royal household staff and Government departments, including the highest experts in their fields, in preparing her text.[16] But this does not prevent her from perpetuating the untruth that 'Income from the Queen's private estates *and so on* is liable for tax.'[17] Official sources collude directly in the same untruths. The Central Office of Information booklet on the Monarchy, of 1969, perpetuated them.[18] It was corrected in later editions only after MP Willie Hamilton persistently campaigned to have the truth told.[19] Again, Palace officials disingenuously disseminated the information that the Queen's private income is subject to tax under the Crown Private Estates Act, 1862. What they knew perfectly well, but did not tell, is that both forms of tax specified in the Act are obsolete.[20]

Apologists, such as Lord Blake, argue that the monarch is not like anyone else: there is only one Queen of England, so why not treat her as unique?[21] There are a number of good reasons why not. First, the non-payment of tax by any prominent and very wealthy persons is a conspicuous disincentive to others to pay. Secondly, the tax due to the Inland Revenue is likely to be very considerable, and could finance much needed good works, instead of race horses. Thirdly, above all, it is precisely *because* the Queen is different, or rather in the way she is different, that she *should* pay tax as a private citizen. As head of state she has an extra-ordinary responsibility to set the best moral standards. Isn't that supposed to be one of the monarch's main functions, according to the myth? As it is, the example that is set is a very low standard of covetousness and disingenuousness. Such an example is all too easy for other high caste plutocrats to follow. An object lesson was the case of the Vestey family.

A scandal was caused in 1980 when the Vesteys — peers of the realm and polo-playing friends of the royal family — were discovered to have been exploiting tax loopholes for more than 60 years.[22] In 1978 the family business yielded profits of £2,300,000 and had paid just £10 in tax. But the Vesteys attained really royal standards of tax avoidance in 1979, when on profits of £4,100,000 they paid no tax at all. The moral standards were commented upon by Viscount Simon in a similar case as follows: 'There is, of course, no doubt that they are within their legal rights, but that is no reason why their efforts, or of the professional gentlemen who assist them in this matter, should be regarded as a commendable exercise of ingenuity or as a discharge of the duties of good citizenship. On the contrary, one result of such methods, if they succeed, is of course to increase *pro tanto* the load of tax on the shoulders of the great body of good citizens who do not desire, or do not know how to adopt these manoeuvres.'[23] The moral bankruptcy of grand tax-dodgers was clearly expressed by the head of the family, Edward Vestey, who expressed his belief that 'we're all tax dodgers, aren't we?' In the royal circles he moves in, no doubt. Understandably, therefore, the Chairman of the Conservative Party, Lord Thorneycroft, wished them all 'good luck'.[24] The British Monarchy sets a positively bad moral example in the matter of covetousness and dissimulation.

Lust does not taint the Queen's personal image of family life, but her predecessors, especially those of her own dynasty, have been notorious fornicators. Prince Charles' racy public image before his marriage in 1981 may not have been warranted, but his brother Andrew's widely publicised liaisons with pornographic movie actresses and models is in the long tradition of the Hanover-Windsors: a fine example to us all. The dual standard that required Lady Diana Spencer's uncle to testify to her virginity before her marriage is a recent innovation. Her noble lineage included Georgina Spencer, whore to George IV, Fox and Grey the Whig politicians, and also to the Duke of Bedford, while she was married to the cuckold Duke of Devonshire. Georgina's sister, Henrietta Spencer, was pleased to record that even at 51 years of age she had sexual affairs with four different men.[25] The sexual conduct of British royalty has rarely in the past set an impeccable moral example, and it does not in the 1980s.

Anger is the original dynastic sin of the Hanover-Windsors. For example, it is said of Princess Margaret that she is 'highly strung, unpredictable and volatile, with a temper reminiscent of both her father [George VI] and her grandfather George V.'[26] Some critics have suggested that royal anger can turn to spite. This is how L.G. Pine describes the treatment of the Duke of Windsor by the royal family, who ostracised the Windsors for over thirty-five years.[27] It may, however, be that they had good reasons, which were the subject of a royal cover up, after the war. In either case, there is no moral example to be had.

Britain undoubtedly commits the national sin of idolatry where the Monarchy is concerned, as numerous commentators have observed. Leonard Woolf, writing in 1935, spoke of the irrational and uncritical attitude towards the monarch and the royal family which people are encouraged to assume; and how children are taught that they cannot be good and loyal patriots unless they approach political questions in the flag-waving, incantatory, medicine-man frame of mind.[28] Kingsley Martin wrote: 'The danger of monarchy lies in its magic, in the ease with which the deep-seated tendency to substitute worship for respect, to substitute personal homage for rational acceptance of a symbol, may be utilised for class or party purposes.'[29] Malcolm Muggeridge has written of the Monarchy providing a sort of *ersatz* religion.[30] And Antony Sampson has drawn the inference that 'it would be surprising if there were not some price to be paid ... The national habit of mind which enjoys the suspension of disbelief on royal occasions, can easily spill over into a suspension of realism towards the working of the administration.'[31] All of this was understood very well by Oliver Cromwell who was offered the Crown during the *interregnum* of the English Republic in 1658. He replied: 'Royalty is but a feather in a man's cap; let children enjoy their rattle.'[32]

In so far as the Monarchy sustains the inequitable caste and class systems which lead to the absolute and relative deprivation of compatriots, and avoids taxes, then it connives instrumentally in the oppression of the poor, and defrauding labourers of their wages; sins that cry out to heaven for vengeance.

The dubious moral example of the Monarchy extends to racism, and blood sports. One of the most hypocritical aspects of the Monarchy's morality is the way that racial tolerance is constantly preached, though in practice the royal family does nothing about it, even things that could easily be done. People from 'coloured' races do not find work with the Queen's Household.[33] There are no black faces at high table. Nor do they easily find accomodation in royal properties.[34] The Duke of Edinburgh's response to a pointed question about this put to him by Willie Hamilton, was that it had nothing to do with modernising the Monarchy.[35] It has a great deal to do with moralising the Monarchy, however; because ethnic minorities need the support of the major institutions of British society. The bad example set by the royal practice of racial discrimination goes with its unedifying patronage of controversial blood sports, especially fox hunting and game shooting. This has led even such a noted royal adulator as Spike Milligan to denounce the royal 'hunting junkies' as hooked on blood sports.[36] Brutality in this instance goes with hypocrisy as well, since members of the royal family practice blood sports at the same time that they patronise animal welfare organisations.

Apologists for the Monarchy will say that a myth of royal moral excellence is beneficial because it serves at least to set a standard which produces good effects. The error of this view is best shown by an example. Two severely mentally handicapped cousins of the Queen were discovered in 1987 to have been living in an institution for many years after their deaths were first recorded in *Burke's Peerage* in 1963. One, recorded as having died in 1940, really died in 1986. The other, who was recorded as having died in 1961, was still alive in 1987. Neither cousin was visited by members of the royal family. The case raised particular interest because the Queen Mother was both their aunt and the patron of MENCAP, the Royal Society for Mentally Handicapped Children and Adults. In that capacity she had campaigned for the end of such institutions. The official explanation given was that the women's mother, the Hon. Fenella Bowes-Lyon, was extremely vague in filling in forms, and the Queen Mother, who presumably relied on *Burke's Peerage* for news of her nieces, did not know of their existence. Mental handicap and mental illness of various kinds is known to exist in the royal family itself, in the Bowes-Lyon family from which the Queen Mother came, and in the Trefusis family from which the royal cousins' mother was descended. Sir Brian Rix, the secretary general of MENCAP, expressed the view that it was commonplace in the past for wealthy families to follow the standard medical advice in such cases, to 'put them away and forget about them'. It had, he said, been common among families to cease to refer to hospitalised mentally handicapped children and frequently this was taken by others to mean they were dead. *'Between lying and not contradicting an impression I would say there is a great difference '*, he said.[37]

This example raises a variety of moral problems. First, it illustrates how claims to hereditary distinction based on 'natural' superiority and the purity of 'blood-line' are false. Royal and aristocratic families have the same genetic histories as any other. If anything, aristocratic in-breeding aggravates common genetic problems. Secondly, because the claims to power, wealth and status by aristocracy, especially royalty, depend so much upon pretensions to purity of blood line, there is a strong incentive for such people to conceal inconvenient facts about their ordinary humanity. Concealment by deliberately creating, or omitting to correct, false beliefs is in such cases morally wrong in itself. Not to correct a false impression, with the knowledge that the false impression will have significant consequences for those who are mistaken and deceived, is a form of lying: lying by omission. The consequences of false beliefs create more moral problems. Ordinary people who are persuaded that the royal family personifies an ideal may come desperately to feel defective and immoral by comparison with the ideal, which is really practically unattainable and false. It is obvious that deception about other matters of fact may have other sorts of undesirable consequences for the deceived. As the remarks of Sir Brian Rix clearly show, those who defend the Monarchy may distinguish between avoidable false impressions and lies, and that is the basic moral problem at the root of all the petty myths of monarchy.

Reasonably objective scrutiny of the matter shows that the morality myth of the British Monarchy has far less foundation than is usually assumed. It too, like everything else about the Monarchy, is largely a fantasy of public relations. The myth can even be positively harmful.

CHAPTER 10 COMMONWEALTH

The Commonwealth myth is that the Monarchy sustains a unique global association of familial English speaking nations. The Commonwealth, it is supposed, is an invaluable institution, and the British monarch is its indispensable head. As Dermot Morrah puts it: 'To each independent nation, and indeed to each independent colony, she can be and is a symbol of unity, of the ideas common to all of the British allegiance concerning justice, tolerance, liberty, the love of peace, the fundamental decencies of family life ... they can all see their ideals symbolised in the person of the Queen.'[1]

Another legitimate view of the Commonwealth is that it is the 'Cheshire Cat' remnant of British colonial power. As such it is reassuring to British chauvinism when all else is failing. To the 'old' Commonwealth it is a reminder of colonial subservience. To the 'new' Commonwealth, it is a reminder of colonial exploitation. The values of subservience and exploitation, and their continuing affirmation, cannot easily be eradicated by mere proclamations of fellowship, and some worthy foundations with limited effect. The British Empire meant economic exploitation on an unprecedented global scale. Expanded trade meant debt and bankruptcy for colonial nations, and immense fortunes for colonialist nabobs. Entire industries were destroyed. The Indian cotton industry, for example, once the largest producer and exporter in the world, was during the nineteenth century reduced by the effects of British tariffs virtually to nothing. British 'liberty' frequently took the form of vigorously suppressing dissent against criminal exploitation. As late as 1937 the governor of Trinidad was dismissed from office because he supported impoverished oil workers who organised for redress against employers who were distributing dividends of 23 per cent, and paying in wages only one third the sum paid in dividends.

British 'justice' frequently took the form of draconian suppression of native colonials. As late as 1938 men were sentenced by British West African courts to 10 years gaol for stealing two shillings' worth of yams, and the sentences confirmed by Appeal Courts.[2] Nothing so became the British as the way that the Labour Government of 1945 proceeded, on principle, to dismantle the colonial empire, but the old imperial attitudes and activities are a long time in dying. Morrah expresses the old British view when he boasts that Britain introduced an 'admittedly higher civilization to Africa'.[3] More recently prime ministers, including Harold Wilson, Edward Heath, and Margaret Thatcher, have infuriated Commonwealth leaders by the patronising, churlish, arrogant attitudes they have shown towards those they regarded as insignificant upstarts.[4]

The new Commonwealth countries have increasingly found it most useful to turn for political support to other countries, to Scandinavia, China, and Eastern Europe, and the United States is now the principal source of economic aid. Trade and commerce have developed on the basis of value-for-money without the coercive constraints imposed by British rule. Japan and other nations are providing what the former colonies need, more effectively. The continuing association with Britain through the Commonwealth is now established on the utilitarian basis of political and economic advantage. As this has become clearer, the allegiance of the new Commonwealth has become tenuous. In any case it has little or nothing to do with the Monarchy.

There are two outstanding difficulties facing Commonwealth countries − racism and poverty. It is extremely unlikely that the Commonwealth and the Monarchy can do anything about either of them. The problem of racism is most acute in South African *apartheid*. Since South Africa left the Commonwealth over this issue, only concerted external pressure and influence can be brought against it, but concerted efforts are virtually impossible. British capitalists have over £6,000 million invested in South Africa. Unsurprisingly the British government continues to support South Africa. In 1971 the Commonwealth Conference almost collapsed because of Edward Heath's proposals to supply South Africa with arms. In 1981 Britain vetoed a United Nations Security Council resolution to apply sanctions against South Africa because of its annexation of Namibia. The Commonwealth Secretary General, in his 1981 report, argued 'This appearance of pardoning *apartheid* is becoming harder to dispel by mere declarations to the contrary.'[5] Attempts have been made to influence South Africa by the application of a boycott on sport, under the terms of the Gleneagles agreement. This too has failed, because some countries have continued to permit sports exchanges. Most notably, New Zealand has continued officially to sanction exchanges of rugby tours.

The Commonwealth Games of 1986 were the occasion for a major dispute when Black African nations led a substantial boycott. This was in protest against the United Kingdom government's singular refusal to join the other governments of the Commonwealth in imposing sanctions against South Africa. This was followed by reports of the Queen and the Prime Minister being at odds over the issue, which clearly threatened the continued existence of the Commonwealth. In this situation, the Conservative M.P. Enoch Powell expressed the view that 'the title "Head of the Commonwealth", and the contraption of the Commonwealth itself are ... essentially a sham, something we have invented to blind ourselves to the reality of the position ... The people of the United Kingdom have outgrown the need for the self-deception of the Commonwealth. They are at best indifferent, at worst even allergic to its continuance.'[6] This view was widely endorsed. The approval by a chorus of conservative voices ranging from the *Spectator* and the *Telegraph* to the *Sun*, demonstrated the power of unsentimental financial interests in the heart of the British Establishment, and how the Monarchy is ultimately subservient to those interests.

The issue of poverty, and specifically the gross inequalities in wealth between industrialised nations and the developing countries has proved to be no more amenable to Commonwealth initiatives than has *apartheid*. Although no less than seven of the twenty-two nations convened in Mexico in 1981 to discuss the matter were members of the Commonwealth, there was no significant concerted initiative. Britain did not even show interest. At the Commonwealth Conference in Delhi in 1983, the British Prime Minister directly opposed the proposals of the chairwoman, Mrs Gandhi, to boost Third World development.[7] When the Queen, in her speech to the Commonwealth at Christmas 1983, identified the greatest problem of the world today as the gap between rich and poor countries, the only result was controversy. Her suggestion that nationalism was an obstacle to recognising interdependence, was attacked by Mr Enoch Powell on the grounds that the Queen's speech was excessively partisan towards poor, developing countries, and was speaking against Britain's interests which were the monarch's first and proper concern. Powell argued that 'The place of the Crown in the affections of the people would be threatened if they began to sense that the Crown was not in that unique and exclusive sympathy with the people of the United Kingdom which their mutual dependence ought to imply.'[8] That his view was an expression of true British chauvinism was shown by the endorsement of the *Sunday Telegraph*, which said: 'On her home ground which is Britain, the Queen cannot put a foot wrong. Instinctively she is in tune with her people. Such concentration of concern cannot survive too much dilution without losing its essential magic.'[9] Nothing could more clearly demonstrate the flimsy and illusory nature of the claims that Britain is the head of a commonwealth of nations mutually devoted to the common welfare of each. The real position of the Queen, even within Britain itself, is again clearly shown, and the real limits of her authority and influence. (No one, of course, mentioned the fact that the moral authority of a tax-avoiding hereditary multi-millionairess calling for a reduction in the poverty gap, is approximately nil.)

These difficulties are well recognised by the Crown even while the Commonwealth myth is assiduously promoted. Sober opinion recognises that the Monarchy's responsibilities will diminish 'as the Commonwealth becomes less, even a shadow of reality'. The Palace itself hopes for no more than that the old Commonwealth can be retained.[10] It is unlikely that even this minimal hope will be recognised. Canada has progressively disposed of all its constitutional links with Westminster, so that by 1982 no anachronisms remained: except, that is, for the Queen as official head of state. This last vestige is virtually irrelevant. Canada's population is so varied that it makes nonsense of claims that Elizabeth II is the personal symbol of the shared traditional values of its Italian, Greek, Polish, Hungarian, and numerous other ethnic groups. Above all, in political importance, is the view of the large minority of French-Canadians, of between 25 and 30 per cent of the population, very many of whom enthusiastically repudiate the idea that the Queen of England is their Head of State. Only delusion disguises the schizophrenia of a 'Royal Canada'. Both British flag and anthem were dispensed with long ago for the sake of federal unity. The Republic of Canada already exists in all but name.

Despite earnest endeavours to preserve Royal Australia, it is likely that the Republic of Australia will also be proclaimed. By one Palace estimate it is already overdue.[11] Even someone described as the most conservative man on the continent, Judge Sir Garfield Barwick, has said publicly that 'a monarch has now no part in the constitutional affairs of Australia – this is 1982, not pre-1900 colonial days.'[12] The transition to republicanism was accelerated by a notorious episode in 1975 which showed the unacceptably subservient nature of Australia's relationship to Britain. The Queen's representative in Australia, Sir John Kerr, actually dismissed the elected Prime Minister, Gough Whitlam. This controversial action casts light, not just on the constitution of former colonies, but also on the residual powers of royal prerogative in Britain. One Australian National Opinion Poll showed that 58 per cent of Australians thought they did not need the Queen, and that, of those under the age of twenty-five, 74 per cent thought the Monarchy was redundant.[13]

New Zealand is the most conservative member of the old Commonwealth, but even the extremely conservative former Prime Minister of that conservative country, Robert Muldoon, was cynical about the Commonwealth and its function. Speaking at a Commonwealth Heads of Government conference in Melbourne in 1981 he said: 'We come here and drink Scotch and have dinners, but I don't see how the poorer countries in Africa and Asia could see anything effective coming out of it ... Anyway it's all up to the Americans in the end, and they're not here ', then he wondered out loud why the Melbourne meeting was being held at all.[14]

The United States have proved to be entirely immune to the myth of the Commonwealth. In 1984 the Americans invaded Grenada and deposed the (to them) unacceptable left-wing government without any reference to the Queen as head of state. In 1987 the elected government of Fiji was ousted by a coup almost certainly inspired by the American C.I.A. for military reasons. Again, the Queen as head of state, and her Governor General, were disregarded.

In so far as there are shared problems which nations of the former British Empire can solve by concerted action, then there is substance to the notion of a commonwealth. If there are not shared problems, then a common head of state is irrelevant. If there are, then no special significance attaches to the symbolic head, monarch or any other, since it is the problems themselves and the pursuit of solutions which provide the substantial basis of common activity. In that case, a rotating headship or chairmanship would serve the Commonwealth as well as anything else. The argument against this idea put forward by the then Commonwealth Secretary General, Arnold Smith, confirms the view that the Commonwealth serves mainly as a 'Cheshire Cat' British empire. Addressing African ministers on the subject he said: 'Such a change would deeply upset British opinion at a time when Britain [is] still going through the neurosis of diminished relative power in the world. They should realise ... how important a role the Queen was playing in helping take Britain ... through this problem period.'[15] There we have the unvarnished truth about the Commonwealth, from someone in the best position to know.

CHAPTER *11* CONTINUITY

It is repeatedly said that hereditary monarchy uniquely provides continuity throughout continual changes in government. A notable advantage of this is that the monarch is able to accumulate wisdom, so that a mature monarch will be much better informed than any prime minister. This is the continuity myth.

It is true that constitutional monarchy is one possible way to secure continuity, but it is by no means the only way or the best way, though this is often implied. Lewis Namier has pointed out that the Civil Service also gives continuity in change.[1] The departments of the Civil Service are staffed by persons specially selected for their qualities of high intellect, integrity and industry, who pursue careers in the service which provide them with a life time of accrued experience. It is more than likely that the continuity and wisdom provided in this way exceeds in quality and usefulness whatever wisdom accrues to an hereditary monarch. This is to say the least. Tom Paine put the real point with characteristic force. 'What is this office which infants and idiots are capable of filling? Some talent is required to be a common workman; to be a King nothing more is needed than to have a human figure, to be a living automaton.'[2]

The point, of course, is that by the hereditary principle there is no necessary reason to expect that the inheritor of the office has the necessary competence and motivation. Edward VII, for example, acceded to the throne in 1901 at the age of sixty with virtually no knowledge at all of State affairs. George VI came to the throne in 1936 with no knowledge or experience of the monarch's duties. Even the most careful upbringing and education will not compensate for innate deficiencies of intelligence, temper, or character. Marcus Aurelius was among the wisest and best Roman emperors, for instance, yet his son Commodus was one of the worst. As Gibbon recounts it:

> Nothing was neglected by the anxious father, and by the men of virtue and learning whom he summoned to his assistance, to expand the narrow mind of young Commodus, to correct his growing vices and to render him worthy of the throne for which he was destined. But the power of instruction is seldom of much efficacy, except in those happy dispositions where it is almost superfluous ... Marcus himself blasted

the fruits of this laboured education, by admitting his son, at the age of fourteen or fifteen, to a full participation in the Imperial power.[3]

If Britain has enjoyed two or three hereditary reigns without calamitous consequences, then that is undoubtedly more a matter of luck rather than an occasion for self-congratulation! As for the accumulation of wisdom, that could only apply to a mature monarch, and there is no reason always to expect one.

Even popes are selected from among those who have demonstrated the development of the necessary capacities and character throughout a lifetime of experience, and there is no serious question raised about the continuity of the papacy, or the wisdom of individual popes. The good and perfectly obvious reasons why there are no hereditary popes apply just as much to presidents, and they apply just as much to monarchs also. It is sheer delusion to suppose otherwise.

CHAPTER 12 IMPARTIALITY

The effectiveness of constitutional monarchy depends above all on the impartiality myth: the belief that the head of state is above factional disputes and party politics. According to Bolingbroke, the monarch 'will distinguish the voice of his people from the clamour of a faction, and will hearken to it. He will redress grievances, correct errors, and reform or punish ministers.'[1] The British Monarchy has succeeded in promoting the belief that it is suitably impartial. As Charles Douglas-Home has said, 'Its authority is based on an illusion that it is what the people want; that as an aggregate of their wishes it represents the power of the people.'[2]

Illusion it is, however, despite strenuous efforts to disguise it. Sometimes illusion is piled on illusion, apparently to induce self-delusion in some royalists. Dermot Morrah persuaded himself that 'leaders of all parties are accustomed to meet in [the Queen's] house as her friends, and are therefore friends of one another. This tradition of personal good-will between political opponents is strongly rooted in the British tradition and is displayed in the social life of Parliament as well as that of the Royal circle.'[3] The truth is more likely to be that, as the head of the top caste, the monarch regards all politicians as more or less equal, and more or less of equally little account.

There are obvious reasons why British hereditary monarchs would not be really impartial. Their position at the peak of a precipitous social caste hierarchy ensures that their knowledge of, and acquaintance with the lives of most of their subjects is several removes from the reality. Efforts to explain this away only serve to show how much it is true. One apologist, eager to assure us that the Queen is just as interested in the ordinary fellow as she is in great statesmen, recalls the story of how, during a portrait sitting, she occasionally became so interested in the people she saw in the Mall through the curtains, that she craned her neck and unconsciously changed her position to get the last glimpse of some little incident which caught her interest.[4] This fatuous tale unintentionally captures the nature of the Monarch's relationship with her subjects. Almost equally fatuous is the following argument by a *Times* writer: 'The Queen and her son Charles have solved with reasonable effectiveness the problems of class. They belong to the upper classes, but familiarity with policy and the contacts, however perfunctory, during provincial visits with other classes, give an impression of wider sensitivities which neither the horses nor the allegations of immense untaxed wealth ... appear to annul.'[5] Impressions and appearances notwithstanding, it beggars belief that mere acquaintance with policies, together with perfunctory and entirely artificial contacts can convey to British royalty anything like a full and clear understanding of the lives of the people. (Typically, Prince Charles inquired of a local woman in a Welsh pit village whether she was the nanny of two local boys he had spoken to.[6]) Enormous disparities of wealth and conditions of life have the same distancing effect as caste. Prince Charles, for example, can only admit lamely, 'I have never been unemployed ... not being one of them it's terribly hard to know ... It's so hard when you're not living in a deprived area. I can't give anybody any advice.'[7]

Invincible ignorance of the real conditions of others' lives naturally fosters partiality towards oneself and one's high caste. The story is told of how during the miners' strike of 1926, King George V castigated Lord Durham who had called the striking miners 'damned revolutionaries'. The King is reported to have said 'Try living on their wages before you judge them.'[8] in the established form of impartial royal rhetoric. However, the same King, in 1931, persuaded Labour Party leader Ramsay MacDonald to lead a government to pass legislation cutting workers' wages and dole by 10 per cent because of a 'national' crisis due to a budget deficit.[9] This was at a time when the richest 1 per cent of the population owned 62 per cent of the wealth, and no less than 91 per cent of all wealth was owned by just 10 per cent of people.[10] Even Winston Churchill regarded this as George V's most despicable action. Not only did it deprive the poorest people of basic livelihood; it also split the Labour Party, which expelled MacDonald for his collusion with the establishment against the people whose interests he should have been protecting. Sir Charles Petrie, writing shortly after the events, could not have been more explicit (or satisfied). He says: 'The Socialist party had proved itself so inimical to the national interest that it had become the duty of the Monarch, the living embodiment of the nation, to cripple its power of mischief.'[11]

In addition to social caste and economic differences, differences in related privileges also serve to distance the Monarchy from ordinary people. Nothing exemplifies this better than the way taxes are exacted from income at source for most people, whereas the monarch knows no taxation and receives a substantial index-linked state income. It is, again, difficult to imagine how such privileged royal persons are supposed to regard these matters impartially. The truth is revealed by Prince Philip who has said that 'Perhaps one of Marx's worst miscalculations was to forget that if you threaten people with ... expropriation of their property they ... may well fight back.'[12]

History bears out what common sense tells us. People whose every social, cultural and economic value, experience, interest and practice lie with high caste privilege will instinctively identify with the common interests of the caste to which they belong. Impartial public pronouncements and seeming even-handedness in judgement can at best be cosmetic self-delusion, and at worst hypocrisy and dissimulation. British monarchs are no exception. For Queen Victoria, a Conservative government was the natural order of things. For her, Liberalism was subversive. She wrote: 'Mr Campbell-Bannerman forgets the danger of increasing the power of the House of Commons and having no force to resist the subversive measures of the so-called Liberals, but better called destructives.'[13] Among the 'subversive' measures she objected to were national compulsory elementary education, reduced working hours for children, and votes for women. In 1892 she wrote from Balmoral, after some slight insubordination among the Life Guards: 'Something must be done to prevent the non-commissioned officers from getting demoralised by socialists.'[14] It has been said that if Gladstone had publicised even just a part of the truth, Britain would have become a republic before the start of the twentieth century.[15]

Edward VII shared his mother's loathing of socialists: he banned the first Labour leader, Keir Hardie, from royal garden parties, saying: 'We don't want that bloody agitator among us.'[16] He liked Liberals no better. Lord Esher, in a letter to his son during a constitutional crisis in 1910 over creating hundreds of Liberal peers, let slip the truth: 'If the King says yes, he mortally offends the whole Tory party to which he is naturally bound.'[17] As one biographer has put it: 'He was a strong conservative and a still stronger jingo. He feared that "continental socialism" was threatening all that he held most dear ... He went to his death bed believing that his son [George V] would be the last King of England.'[18] He underestimated the power of conservative British inertia.

George V was supposed to be impartial, but the truth was really otherwise. When the general election of January 1924 produced no overall parliamentary majority, but returned Labour as the largest single party, he is reported to have fled from the decision to invite

Ramsay MacDonald to form the first Labour government, as if he were avoiding the plague. He intrigued against it, trying to cobble together an anti-socialist coalition of Tories and Liberals.[19] It was only after he realised that MacDonald would 'have to' form a government that he was invited to do so. But MacDonald still thought that the King's resistance to socialism had to be overcome, so he virtually capitulated on Labour's programme even before he took office. He undertook to try to satisfy the King's wish to abolish the dole, which George V thought was exercising a pernicious effect, especially among the young, who he thought were growing up to dislike work and to live upon the State.[20] This, in a country where the richest 10 per cent owned 91 per cent of all wealth!

Edward VIII showed briefly some signs of genuine impartiality during his time as Prince of Wales. In the 1920s he took unprecedented trouble for a royal person to learn at first hand about the conditions of the people who would be his subjects. His personal visits to the pit villages in depressed areas of the North East and Wales, in particular, were well remembered long afterwards. So too was his conclusion that 'something must be done'. He publicly expressed his view that 'some of the things I have seen in these gloomy, poverty stricken areas make me almost ashamed to be an Englishman.'[21] The *Manchester Guardian* in 1935 reported his view that the housing problem was a slur on civilization.[22] Such sentiments openly expressed proved to be unacceptable to the establishment, and there were informed people who were sure that the real reasons why Edward VIII was an unacceptable monarch for Baldwin and the establishment, had more to do with his dangerous ideas about the state of the country than with his choice of bride.[23] In any case, the first monarch openly to express sympathy with the conditions and aspirations of the working class, was forced to abdicate before he was crowned.

His brother George VI was cast in the same conservative mould as his father. In private he was consistently pro-Conservative and anti-socialist. The 'Red' Countess of Warwick reported how court gossip, including talk with Tories, was anti-socialist. He had doubts about the Labour cabinet's ability to govern, saying 'Thank God for the Civil Service.'[24] In 1948 he commiserated with Vita Sackville-West about the transfer of her ancestral home to the National Trust in payment of death duties; her son reported how the King raised his hands in despair, saying 'Everything's going nowadays. Before long I shall have to go.'[25] None of this is widely publicised, or discussed. It is concealed behind a facade of official impartiality and royal prudence.

As Thomas Hale has explained: 'The House of Windsor is naturally Tory and anti-socialist in outlook. The royal family has generally gone to great lengths to keep their political opinions from being publicised, but their party preferences are known.'[26] This is just as true of the present royal family as it was of their forebears. Discussion of the matter is almost *taboo*, and the myth of impartiality is promoted now more assiduously than ever, but the truth can scarcely be suppressed. The Queen herself has succeeded in avoiding reportable expressions of partiality since she responded to the news of the Labour Party's landslide victory in the 1945 election with the revealing utterance 'Oh, bother!'[27] In 1967, her conservative instincts were, however, roused to overt action, unnecessarily as it turned out, to stop Emrys Hughes' bill to abolish the present honours system.[28] The Duke of Edinburgh's antipathy to politically radical views is more widely known than that of any other royal person. In August 1973 during an address to the University of Strathclyde, he said 'I regret to say that it was Nationalism and Socialism which produced Nazis and Fascists.'[29] The Scottish Nationalist and Labour Parties must remain unpersuaded of the impartiality of the Monarchy. The learning of the Duke is, of course, par for sea-dogs. Prince Charles' reputation as a thoughtful and diffident chap, belies the fact that in private he shares most of his father's political prejudices. Andrew Holden reports, for example, how in private Charles is an 'inveterate and impassioned union-basher', and that 'his political views on this as on most economic and industrial issues are considerably to the right of centre.'[30]

The impartiality myth has been preserved because there has been no attempt at revolutionary change in Britain for centuries. All political parties are basically conservative. This has enabled the Monarchy to sustain an image of impartiality whilst in reality being as partial as can be.[31] The simple fact is that hereditary monarchs are not chosen for their impartiality, on the basis of proven moral integrity. They are not chosen at all. On the contrary, they are born into an exclusive and immensely privileged high caste position, and everything in their experience and preferred station conspires to make them partial to their caste. It is preposterous to suppose that an hereditary British monarch comprehends, let alone promotes the interest of most people, especially those worst off, when those interests conflict with high caste interests, as they inevitably do. We might as well expect an hereditary Yorkshire pitman impartially to adjudicate the interests of that 5 per cent of the population which owns 73 per cent of the land and 47 per cent of investment income.

An important factor in sustaining the Monarchy against potential opposition is the disarming effect of the powerlessness myth. It is commonly assumed that the power of the monarch has been progressively eroded since *Magna Carta* in 1215, so that by the 1980s nothing remains but a vestigial facade. Every schoolboy knows that, if the Queen were required by parliament to sign her own death warrant, constitutionally she would be obliged to do so. A list of many of the powers ostensibly remaining to the royal head of state serves only to heighten the impression of vestigial antiquity. By the constitution, the monarch may: disband the army, and dismiss all the officers; sell off all warships and provisions; sue for peace by sacrificing Cornwall; make everyone a peer; and establish every parish as a university.[1] Nobody believes for an instant that any of this is really possible, or even legitimate. The presumption that the Monarchy is politically neutral and anyway really powerless, politically, has been a necessary condition for tacit acceptance of the institution by many politicians and the radical parties. An interesting and revealing version of the powerlessness myth has been offered by a former editor of *Paris Match*.

'There [is] one decisive argument to convince us that the Windsors will never commit, unless unwittingly, any act which might compromise their reign: namely, the humility which springs from the sense that they have been singled out and pledged to one particular task: representing their country. England was not created by them: she owes none of her basic structure to them, socially or economically. The Windsors are *imported* Kings and for this reason they are less likely to succumb to the intoxication of power, or the dynastic pride of family whose ways of thought, whose life's blood, makes up the very texture of the land.'[2]

It is a simple and gross mistake, however, to suppose that the British Monarchy has no real power. First of all, the monarch may determine events indirectly through advice, force of personality, and the prestige attached to the office.[3] Secondly, and more specifically, the monarch occupies *ex officio* roles which have great power. Some of the powers may be dormant but not extinct in the offices of Head of the Executive, Chairman of the Privy Council, Head of the Judiciary, Commander in Chief of the Armed Forces, and temporal head of the Church of England. The monarch's functions, discharged legitimately under the constitution, include: the summoning, prorogation, and dissolution of parliament; the enactment of laws; making appointments to offices of state, the judiciary and the armed forces; and the awarding of honours.[4] Most notably, the monarch has powers to appoint the prime minister and to refuse a dissolution of parliament.[5] There is little room for doubt about the royal view of this. Dermot Morrah wrote his book on *The Work of the Queen* from the position of Arundel Herald Extraordinary. He explained how 'scarcely a page could have been written without continual recourse to the information and advice of the private secretaries and other confidential secretaries of the Queen.'[6] In the book he claims that: 'Even when her government and her parliament are in agreement with one another, she is still entitled, acting on no-one's advice, to dismiss the government or to dissolve parliament.'[7]

In the 1980s the residual constitutional powers of the monarch have taken on a new, revived and very real importance. If, as seemed possible, the two-party system no longer obtained, and there were no automatic choice of prime minister, then the choice devolves to the monarch.[8] Already in this century three prime ministers have been appointed by the monarch who were not leaders of their parties, and who were unlikely to have been elected as leader: Lloyd George in 1916; Ramsay MacDonald in 1931; Winston Churchill in 1940.[9] MacDonald was expelled from his party for accepting the King's controversial invitation to form a government. In two other cases, it was by no means obvious that the persons appointed prime minister would have otherwise been elected leader of their party: namely, Harold MacMillan in 1957, and Alec Douglas-Home in 1963. It is possible easily to envisage a situation developing in the future where the monarch again, as in the past, selects the prime minister and so the sort of policies that a government would pursue. Significantly, in 1931 the policies were to cut wages for workers and dole for the unemployed. The royal influence has also been exercised in the selection and, more importantly, the exclusion of politicians from ministerial office. Most conspicuously, unrepentant and over-vociferous republicans have little chance of achieving high office. Charles Dilke was obliged publicly to recant his republicanism as a condition for achieving office. John Burns, who was unrepentant, became 'Labour's Lost Leader'.[10] George Lansbury was probably excluded by George V for his anti-monarchist remarks. His eventual acceptance was, like Dilke's, conditional upon recantation.[11] In more recent times, it is more than likely that Willie Hamilton has been excluded from office for saying publicly what many of his colleagues prudently have left unexpressed.

The more draconian powers of dissolution have also been exercised, and exercised too recently to be counted among the obsolete constitutional curiosities. In 1939 the Governor General of South Africa, the King's representative, Sir Patrick Duncan, refused a dissolution of parliament requested by the Prime Minister, General Herzog. Herzog wished to call a general election on the issue of whether South Africa should enter the Second World War, after his party had been defeated on the issue in parliament. By refusing to allow an election, South Africa was brought into the war under Jan Smuts' leadership, but without the contentious issue being put to the South African people. More recently, in 1975, the Governor General of Australia, Sir John Kerr, dismissed the government of the Labour Party majority led by Gough Whitlam. Whatever the responsibility of Buckingham Palace, if any, it is clear that constitutional powers based in the Monarchy are alive today, and more likely than not to be used against radical parties and politicians in order to resist social and constitutional change.

The most draconian powers imaginable still devolve to the monarch in a crisis. The royal prerogative includes, under the provisions of the Defence of the Realm Act 1914, and the Emergency Powers Acts 1920 and 1964, the power to issue Orders in Council under the authority of 'the Queen in Council'. These powers extend to arrest and imprisonment by courts of summary jurisdiction (that is, without juries). Proclamations under the Acts may be made without the consent, or even the knowledge of parliament.[12] At least one monarchist, Sir Charles Petrie, has gone so far as to argue that the exercise of these powers ought to be considered as a *first*, not a last resort in an emergency. 'What is wanted now is an assurance that the aid of the Crown will be forthcoming, not in the last but in the first resort, and that the Monarch shall be able to intervene before things have reached such a stage that only a miracle can avert disaster.'[13] In fact the 1964 Act provides for just this power, when it states: 'Her Majesty may by proclamation declare that a state of emergency exists if at any time *it appears to her that there* have occurred or *are about to occur* events of such a nature as to be calculated to deprive ... any subtantial proportion of the community of the essentials of life.'. Once such a state of emergency is declared, then it is lawful for the Queen in Council to impose such powers as are deemed necessary for any purposes essential to public safety and the life of the community.[14] Clearly it is intended that the monarch should be empowered to *anticipate* problems on the basis of how events appear to her. It is evident that these provisions could lead to the establishment of despotism, unless the head of state is responsible to parliament. Harold Nicolson takes a sanguine view because, he says, the Government is ultimately responsible for all Royal acts and all delegated legislation.[15] This could prove to be mistaken, in practice. The Emergency Powers Acts 1920 allows the proclamation to stay in force for one month, without prejudice to the issue of other subsequent proclamations. Also, regulations made under states of emergency are to be laid before parliament only *'as soon as may be after they are made'* (Section 2(2)). A requirement that emergency regulations shall not continue in force more than seven days applies only *'from the time when they are . . . laid before parliament'*. Clearly, regulations may not be laid before parliament at all, if 'as may be', it does not appear convenient to Her Majesty in Council.

There seems to be no doubt that the monarch has very considerable legal powers of prerogative in states of emergency. It seems at present inconceivable that they would ever be used. It is certainly inconceivable that they would be used to defend a legitimate radical-left government against reactionary treason. They are more likely to be used to defend establishment interests against attempts at radical social reform that might well appear to an hereditary monarch to threaten the *spirit* of the constitution.[16]

The view that the monarch is powerless is a myth 'on stilts'. A leading authority, Lord Blake, has argued that the powers remaining to the Monarchy are indispensable to its prestige and continuing importance. More portentously he has pointed out that occasions may arise when dormant powers need to be used.[17] Lord Simon has expressed the view that the monarch would be justified in using 'unconstitutional' powers if necessary.[18]

CHAPTER *14* LIBERTY: THE PRACTICE

The final petty myth of monarchy is the liberty myth: that the monarch is the ultimate trustee of liberty and democracy.[1] According to this myth the Monarchy stands between the British people and would-be upstart demagogues, tyrants and 'elected dictators' who are denied legitimate authority so long as an hereditary monarch reigns. The most plausible support for this myth is provided by the example of King Juan Carlos in Spain. Twice in 1981 he pre-empted attempts at right-wing *coups*. In February he persuaded ambivalent military commanders to oppose right-wing rebel units of the army after parliament had been stormed. Again, in October, following the election of a socialist government, another attempted *coup* was prevented by the King, acting on intelligence information.[2]

The case of Spain is convenient for showing the reality behind the liberty myth. First, the case of Spain only goes to show that the price of peace is the maintenance of a grossly inequitable social system, with the Monarchy at the apex. Significantly Colonel Antonio Tejero, who led the storming of the Spanish parliament, did so in the name of the King. It is true that it is better to have a liberal monarch than a reactionary one; but it is better still to have no monarch at all. The basic argument behind the liberty myth is a derivation of an ancient logical fallacy, the *ad baculum* fallacy – the appeal to force. The typical form of this argument is to impress upon one's opponent the main force commanded by those who support one's view. This, of course, is irrelevant to the argument, as such. This was the nature of Stalin's response at Yalta to an argument put by the Pope, that a course of action was immoral. 'How many divisions did you say the Pope had for combat duty?', Stalin is reported to have asked.[3] The liberty myth depends upon the argument that it is best that we have a monarchy because there are big battalions waiting to coerce us if we don't. The 'liberty' preserved by monarchy is, therefore, the liberty that goes with a hierarchical caste system. The point is made fully explicit by the Conservative Maurice Cowling. 'The conservative conception of social structure not only assumes that marked inequalities are inevitable, but declines to justify them because their inevitability makes justification unnecessary. To decline justification of the

84

principle is not to say that there cannot be discussion of the content. It is not the principle or the discussion, however, but *the balance of operative power that determines the outcome*, and it is difficult to see how it could be otherwise.'[4] The Monarchy is a bulwark against right-wing tyranny, only so long as potential right-wing tyrants are satisfied that the *status quo* is safe in the hands of the monarch. It is most likely that Britain has retained its monarchy because democracy is tolerated so long as it is a sham or a travesty.

History gives no assurance either that monarchy is a guarantee of liberty. Against the recent ambiguous example of Spain must be set such counter-examples as Italy in 1922, and Greece in 1967. King Victor Emmanuel III proved to be anything but a bulwark of liberty against Mussolini's Fascists. When decisive action would probably have extinguished Mussolini's uncertain usurpation of power, the King refused to sign the necessary proclamation of martial law.[5] Significantly, fear of a palace revolution led by his younger brother, for the throne, played a major part in the King's compromises with the dictator.

King Constantine of Greece similarly lent legitimacy to a right-wing military *junta* after a *coup* in 1967. No doubt too much should not be read into the particularly close family connections between the British royal family and the now ex-king Constantine. Nonetheless, the British royal family attended the Greek royal family's wedding as 'an intimate family affair', and the Duke of Edinburgh, who was born a prince of Greece, was closely related to both bridegroom and bride.[6] There is, however, no doubt at all that the British royal family are deeply conservative in their social caste, their beliefs and their values: the opposite of radicals.

The possibility of a right-wing *coup* in Britain is, unfortunately, not sheer fantasy. In 1967, Cecil King and others decided that the Labour government's policies were unacceptable and approached Lord Mountbatten about the possibility of having an alternative (but unelected) government.[7] Thoughts of such things are no doubt common among a lunatic fringe of M.I.5 officers and military men with no taste for the indiscipline and uncertainties that go with popular democratic liberties.[8] It may be sensible to overlook such people. But the same views also find open expression in the pages of the *Sunday Telegraph*. There, Peregrine Worsthorne has, he believes, shown 'When treason can be right'.[9] That is: '. . . when a Labour government['s] programme of collectivization, expropriation, and enforced egalitarianism, particularly if combined with unilateral disarmament, become[s] so shocking that it becomes quite natural to start looking to the United States [C.I.A.] for succour ...'. This would be permissible even if a far left government 'came to power by due process of election *etc.*' provided 'one' had come to the conclusion that, although the letter of the constitution had been adhered to, the *spirit* had been defied. That is, when 'the far left comes to power using the parliamentary system'. (Each person decides for themselves, presumably, what is shocking within the spirit of the constitution.) John Grigg no doubt has this sort of effusion in mind when he says that 'Now, as before the first world war, some Tories are showing themselves rather shaky in their allegiance to Parliamentary government.'[10]

Where would the Monarchy stand, faced with Worsthorne's brand of treason? The Duke of Edinburgh has said that those with privilege would fight back against legal egalitarianism. A justification is the view already mentioned of Petrie: that the monarch should collude in the by-passing of the process of parliamentary democracy. To do so would display 'an element irrational, merely asserted and upheld, in Kingship', a case of the importance of sovereigns being precisely and simply in that they exist.[11] There is no cause for confidence in the impartiality of the Crown in such circumstances. Nor could a radical government in an elected parliament be confident of the support of the armed forces in such an emergency, since the monarch is constitutionally head of the armed forces. This seemingly archaic function would become very real in a crisis of the sort envisaged by Worsthorne, and there is every reason to believe that the leaders of the armed forces take very seriously the loyalty they supposedly owe to the Crown. The constitutional niceties of the Revolution Settlement of 1689 would almost certainly be lost on soldiers. During the Ulster crisis of 1914, for example, soldiers mutinied at the Curragh barracks in defiance of the government, and they were supported by right-wing politicians who appealed to the Crown.[12] It is frequently reported that regular officers openly profess that their primary allegiance is to the monarch, not the government.[13]

The Monarchy can be expected to preserve democratic 'liberties' only so long as people do not freely and democratically decide radically to transform the system of established hereditary privilege either by opening up the closed social class structure, or by dismantling entirely the inequitable hereditary social caste hierarchy. Monarchy as the preserver of liberty and democracy is just another myth.

It is evident that the beliefs about the Monarchy which commonly prevail in Britain, and which are most commonly cited in its support and defence, are largely groundless. By the ordinary standards of evidence and argument there is little or no reason to hold them. They are myths. Continued belief in them must therefore be explained with reference to their cause, in acculturation and as the effect of incessant propaganda, unless there is some other basis. Such a basis, it is commonly said, lies in the needs of the non-rational nature of people that monarchy satisfies.

PART III: PROFOUND MYTHS AND RATIONALITY

CHAPTER *15* NON-RATIONAL VIEWS OF MONARCHY

As well as the petty myths of monarchy, there are *profound myths*. These are beliefs and feelings supposed by those who have and hold them to provide a more or less profound and not necessarily obvious or widely understood basis for the Monarchy. This basis is typically and above all non-rational. Those who subscribe to the profound myths usually take the view that the importance of monarchy does not lie in any rational considerations that can be tested and found wanting by calaculation, argument and evidence. They will be unimpressed by the dissipation of petty myths, because petty myths are not the real stuff of monarchy. Monarchy, in the profound view, transcends petty considerations which are open to calculation and test. Instead it is more the stuff that ineffable hopes and dreams are made of. Monarchy is rooted deep in the profound complexity of human nature; in emotional needs; in primitive depths of tribal affinities; and in transcendental heights of sublime intuition and aspirations. The character of the profound myths can be understood from some typical pronouncments on the subject.

'What is the most natural government to man?', de Maistre asks, and replies: 'History will reply, "It is Monarchy".'[1] What is 'natural' does not require great thought. 'It is well worthy of the supreme wisdom, which has created and regulated all things to have excused man from deep learning in everything that really matters to him.'[2] Reason is not merely superfluous, it is counterproductive and dangerous. 'The more human reason trusts in itself and tries to rely on its own resources, the more absurd it is and the more it reveals its lack of power. That is why the world's greatest scourge has always been, in every age, what is called philosophy, for philosophy is nothing but the human reason acting alone, and human reason reduced to its own resources is nothing but a brute whose power is restricted to destroying.'[3] In similar vein, Gretton refers to 'the vigorous life of Kingship unsapped by too much thought.'[4] Morrah invokes the complexity of the phenomenon of monarchy: 'Monarchy has come into existence and has been preserved through the ages in response to some innate need of the human heart – and Man, whatever Aristotle may say, is something more than a political animal. The thing we have to study is nothing less than human nature itself.'[5] But complexity is precisely what cannot be faced according to de Jouvenel, who refers to 'some compulsion on the mind which makes us unwilling to submit to reality in the political sphere – the mind longs for the simple and is forever confronted by the complex.'[6] This explains the power of monarchy because, as Nicolson explains, 'The masses, not being really interested in abstract political theories, prefer to personify authority and to be more impressed by individuals.'[7] Whether or not monarchy is the subject of theories, theories will never capture what is essential and important in it. As Enoch Powell has said, 'Nobody made [the Monarchy] so how could anybody know what its function is? The Kingdom is not a deliberate creation. It is not like the motor car, perhaps more like intestines. Analytically it can be viewed as having functions, but they are not the reasons for its existing. The Monarchy is emotional, symbolical, totemistic and mystical.'[8] Henry Luce suggests that 'The illogical, the arbitrary, and the sacred in the Monarchy all contribute to its mysticism, and indeed it may one day take its stand on its mystical significance as the living nation.'[9] Walter Bagehot located the significance of the Monarchy in the same place when he wrote 'So long as the human heart is strong, and human reason weak, royalty will be strong because it appeals to diffuse feelings, and republics weak because they appeal to the understanding.'[10]

It is clear from this collection of expressions of some of the more 'profound' views of monarchy that its true significance is in general supposed to lie outside the scope of rational scrutiny. The general point is frequently sharpened into the proud boast that 'The British are an illogical race and seldom wish to press their theories to extreme conclusions.'[11] In order adequately to appraise the profound myths of monarchy it is necessary here first to consider the non-rational basis on which they are supposed to rest: to see whether rationality is as irrelevant to the emotional, symbolic, totemistic and mystical basis of monarchy as is commonly supposed. Only after that can the profound myths be properly appraised.

There are two sorts of prevalent view which, from different positions, lead to the same conclusion: that there is no useful purpose served by a critical rational analysis of the profound myths of monarchy. First there is what can baldly be called *irrationalism*. This is the set of views based on the assumption that human reason both in its scope and its nature is inadequate to comprehend the full complexity of the relevant phenomena. Typical expressions of irrationalism have just been quoted. Secondly there is *materialism*, derived from Marx's view about people's consciously held beliefs, attitudes and values: that they are only superficial manifestations of more basic material phenomena. As such they are to be explained by the social and economic structures which *cause* people to hold them, not understood and appraised on the *grounds* that people themselves have for holding them.

There is among some people who are hopelessly infected with philosophy, doubt and debate about rationality.[1] According to one view, rationality is nothing more than a cultural prejudice, and there are no absolute, eternal, principles of reason. I do not propose to pursue these issues far here, because arguments against rationality are self-defeating and need not detain us. But something needs to be said. The most extreme claim is that natural science itself not only has been but needs to be irrational.[2] This view is based on an excessively narrow conception of rationality, that equates it with merely mechanical inference-procedures.[3] The force of relativistic arguments derives mainly from the evidence from anthropology, to show that radically different forms of life are based on different and mutually uncomprehending beliefs and ways of thinking. This force is lost when the issue is between different viewpoints in the same culture and society. Most of all, the irrationalist views of monarchy in question are not based on distinct interests, sets of beliefs and styles of reasoning, but on an altogether different set of distinctions.

Irrationalism is most often based on four grounds: complexity, feeling, intuition and will. First, it is said that reality is immensely complex, and attempts by people to be purely rational will inevitably lead to over-simplification. The clearest statement of this view is de Maistre's: 'The human reason is manifestly incapable of guiding men; for few can reason well and no-one can reason well in every subject, so that it is generally wise to start from authority whatever people say.'[4] On this view, authority incorporates desirable prejudice. 'Good citizens need beliefs not problems. The word "prejudice" has been misused. It does not necessarily signify false ideas but only ... any opinions adopted without examination.'[5] Burke also extols the virtues of prejudice:

> We *in England* are afraid to put men to live and trade each on his own private stock of reason; because we suspect that this stock in each man is small, and that individuals would do better to avail themselves of the general bank and capital of nations and ages. Many of our men of speculation, instead of exploding general prejudices, employ their sa-

gacity to discover the latent wisdom which prevails in them. If they find what they seek, they think it more wise to continue the prejudice, with the reason involved, than to cast away the coat of prejudice, and to leave nothing but the naked reason. [6]

Secondly, it is said that 'naked reason' is deficient in natural feeling or sentiment. Edmund Burke is, again, a most eloquent exponent of this view. 'The worst of these politics of revolution is this, they temper and harden the breast ... This sort of people are so taken up with their theories about the rights of man, that they have totally forgotten his nature. Without opening one new avenue to the understanding, they have succeeded in stopping up those that lead into the heart. They have prevented in themselves and in those that attend to them all the well placed sympathies of the human breast.'[7] 'Liberty, equality, fraternity' was for Burke a 'barbarous philosophy ... the offspring of cold hearts'.[8]

Thirdly, against systematic analysis and calculation, is opposed intuition. National qualities, according to de Maistre, are discerned not through abstract thought but through the unconscious grasp of circumstances. He was confident that 'The secret instinct will very often guess correctly even in the natural sciences, but ... it is well nigh infallible in questions of theoretical philosophy, morality, metaphysics, and natural theology.'[9]

Finally, wilful assertion and action are opposed to rational justification. De Maistre, again, is the outstanding exponent of irrationalist views. In anticipation of twentieth century fascism, he advocates that full play should be given to intuitive and irrational impulses as the only paths to the moral truths which hold society together. 'How many arguments there are for showing that sovereignty derives from the people! Yet it is nothing of the sort. Sovereignty is always taken never given.'[10] 'There are very few Sovereignties able to justify the legitimacy of their origin ... The people will always accept masters and will never choose them.'[11] Burke vindicates violent action when, as he sees it, it is aimed at the rule, not the destruction of a country. 'These disturbers are not so much like men usurping power, as asserting their natural place in society.'[12] Similarly de Jouvenel explains how 'The prestige of triumphant Power has graven in men's hearts the feeling for [absolute] Sovereignty; ratiocination, inspired by this feeling follows later.'[13]

CHAPTER *17*   MATERIALISM

Many commentators influenced by Karl Marx take the view that it is futile to examine the reasons people have for their beliefs, because the real reasons are not merely different, but different even in *kind* from what is consciously believed. Ostensibly, beliefs are held and defended as ideas, with more or less rational justification. Really, they are ideological *epiphenomena* of economic and social facts which therefore provide the real basis for explaining them. Passages in Marx's writings such as the following suggest this view.

> Whilst in ordinary life, every shopkeeper is very well able to distinguish between what somebody professes to be and what he really is, our historians have not yet won even this trivial insight. They take every epoch at its word and believe that everything it says and imagines about itself is true.[1]

> The ideas of the ruling class are in every epoch the ruling ideas, ie the class which is the ruling *material* force of society is at the same time its ruling *intellectual* force. The class which has the means of material production at its disposal has control at the same time over the means of mental production, so that thereby, generally speaking, the ideas of those who lack the means of mental production are subject to it. The ruling ideas are nothing more than the ideal expression of the dominant material relationships, the dominant material relationships grasped as ideas.[2]

> In the social production of their life, men enter into definite relations that are indispensable and independent of their will, relations of production which correspond to a definite stage of development of their material productive forces. The sum total of those relations of production constitutes the economic structure of society, the real foundation on which arises a legal and political structure and to which correspond definite forms of social consciousness. The mode of production of material life conditions the social, political and intellectual life process in general. It is not the consciousness of men that determines their being, but, on the contrary, their social being determines their consciousness.[3]

Thus, according to one version of Marx's views – *economism* – people's beliefs in social and political matters are really just expressions of material relationships which are independent of their will, and even their consciousness. On this view, people may, for example, believe themselves to be free and equal members of one nation, with shared interests, but in reality they are subject to coercive persuasion. The ideas which embody and promote the interests of the dominant class or caste, collectively the dominant ideology, are promoted by education, propaganda, and diffuse cultural transmission so that they are accepted, but unthinkingly, by the subservient classes or castes. The reality is manifest in other forms of coercion. First there is the insidious coercion of 'dull economic necessity'. People who own no means of producing their own livelihood must comply with whatever conditions are imposed by those who do in order to survive. If people are entirely dependent for their livelihood upon the cooperation of others whose interests are in opposition to their own, then again cooperation is the only means of material survival. Secondly, if coercive persuasion and insidious economic coercion fail, there is main force: by coercive laws, the police, the courts and the penal system.[4]

The materialist view with reference to monarchy is set out in Marx's discussion of *The Eighteenth Brumaire of Louis Bonaparte*.[5] According to Marx, in the events of 1848-1851, the rival royalist factions — the Bourbons and the Orleanists — were not divided by articles of faith of royalism, as they would profess. Under the Bourbons, big landed property had governed, whereas under the Orleans capital had governed. The former was the political expression of the hereditary rule of landowners and its attendant priests and lackeys. The latter was the political expression of the usurped rule of *bourgeois parvenus*, and their lawyers, professors and smooth-tongued orators. 'What kept the two factions apart, therefore, was not any so-called principles, it was their material conditions of existence, two different kinds of property; it was the old contrast between town and country, the rivalry between capital and landed property.' In the same way, Marx argued that 'for a long time the Tories of England imagined that they were enthusiastic about monarchy, the church, and the beauties of the old English Constitution, until the day of reckoning wrung the confession from them that they are enthusiastic only about *ground rent*.'[6]

CHAPTER *18* RATIONALITY

Both irrationalist and materialist views are based upon fundamental misconceptions about the nature and relevance of rationality. Rationality is not a very precise concept, but it means at least conformity to reason; being judicious and ordering thought systematically according to normative standards. It implies deliberation, not capriciousness. It also implies sanity and sensibility as opposed, for example, to insanity, fanaticism, misguidedness and obstinacy. It goes with effective relating of means and ends. More precisely, it means logical consistency, veracity and pertinence.

The logical aspect of rationality is most simply expressed in the law of non-contradiction. This says, without prejudice to any particular fact, that no statement of fact (or proposition) can be both true and false, in the same sense uttered at the same time by the same speaker. It is perfectly obvious, at least, that contradictory statements of belief can not *both* be true, and scepticism is the only warranted position for anyone who is not in a position to decide. Further, to say that a statement of fact is true, is to say that other statements incompatible with it must be false. For instance, if I say that the Monarchy is indispensable, this means that, necessarily I deny that monarchy can be dispensed with. Unless something is denied, then I cannot affirm anything either. Moreover, if I allow that the same statement may be *both* true *and* false, (that is, if I allow self-contradiction) then, in so far as I deny *nothing*, anything may be true. That is, *anything* may be true if I allow self-contradiction. Now, nobody who takes the trouble to express a view, let alone argue for it, can avoid affirming something. So *all* seriously expressed views are *ipso facto* subject to the 'law' of non-contradiction, that is to logic, or the logical aspect of rationality. None of this is changed by the commonplace occurrence of contradictory opinions and critical dialogues. It would, however, be helpful in banishing obscurantism from such matters, if we consistently referred to conflicting opinions, rather than contradictions, because some people think that the prevalence of *conflicting* opinion demonstrates what is really logically impossible: the equal veracity of mutually *contradictory* opinions. Rationality entails non-contradiction, but without prejudice to any particular matter of fact, belief system or style of reasoning. Therefore, anyone who asserts some view is being rational so long as they are denying whatever is incompatible with what they assert. That is, seriously to assert at all is to be rational.

Secondly, assertions of fact are supposed or intended to be true. Quite simply, the truth of any statement of fact is logically related to the balance of evidence in favour of it. Thus, the evidential aspect of rationality is most simply stated in the maxim that conclusions should not be drawn or held with a conviction beyond what the relevant and available evidence will support. Although, according to Bertrand Russell, this precept, if adopted, would in practice completely revolutionise human life,[1] it must be believed by anyone who seriously entertains and asserts any matter of fact. Thus, without prejudice to any particular matter of fact, rationality relates the truth of a knowledge-claim to the evidence in favour of it. Therefore anyone who maintains, or asserts, any matter of fact whatsoever is committed to rationality, otherwise they can make no genuine assertions at all.

Thirdly, rationality, properly understood is simply sober, judicious and sound thinking. In practice this means, at an absolute minimum, that with respect to any given matter at issue, none of the obviously pertinent factors are disregarded. (Pertinence is determined by the subject matter in question.) Pure logic and rationality are not the same thing and should not be confused. For practical purposes, pure logic may be regarded as the systematic avoidance of invalid reasoning, whatever the argument is about. Rationality has a much wider scope than this, and includes the need sensibly to deliberate and judge the relevance of different factors, and their relative importance. Rationality therefore requires that sound judgement be exercised as to the real nature of matters in question. Anyone who is concerned judiciously to appraise matters in their full complexity is thereby being rational.

In some cases irrationality is avoidable, but it may be that it is desirable. Some of the best examples of such cases are amusements, particularly jests. Since the essence of much amusement and humour is its very irrationality, it would simply be irrational to insist on rationality in such cases. In other cases irrationality is both avoidable and undesirable. This is obviously so in such cases as ignorance, pernicious prejudice, dubitable convictions, and neuroses. In another set of cases irrationality may be unavoidable, but harmless, or even positively beneficial. Cases of this sort are indispensable presuppositions (such as of 'natural order' in scientific inquiry), and indispensable or benevolent 'myths' which form the basis of human groups (such as the 'crack regiment', or moral maxims such as 'honesty pays'). In other cases again irrationality is both unavoidable and undesirable, as in chronic psychological disorders. From this we can see that rationality, by its very nature, both sets limits to the application of pure logic alone, and judiciously recognises the pertinence and weight of factors which are not logical.

If rationality is understood as encompassing self-consistency, veracity and pertinence, and when it is understood that rationality has its own built-in limits, then most objections to rationality prove groundless. The boast that Britons are especially irrational is either a mistake (about rationality, or Britons, or both), or else it is a baseless slander.

CHAPTER *19* RATIONALITY AND IRRATIONALISM

Consider first the view that events are immensely complex, and human reason finite. Burke discusses at length a prime example of the supposed limits of reason, on this basis. According to Burke's caricature, after the Revolution in France, attempts were made to organise the political structure on the basis of geometry, for geographical zoning; simple arithmetic, for population divisions; and elementary book-keeping, for parliamentary representation. The complexities of established natural geography, social and cultural groupings, and the economics and finance of existing wealth-distribution were all ignored.[1] Predictably, the impeccable simplicity of the arrangements as drafted led in practice to chaotic disorder. Burke comments that 'the legislators who framed the ancient republics knew that their business was too arduous to be accomplished with no better apparatus than the metaphysics of an undergraduate, and the mathematics and arithmetic of an exciseman. They had to do with men and they were obliged to study human nature.'[2] But none of this undermines rationality, properly understood. Even if Burke's account were true, it was simply irrational to expect to be able to order a vast political state comprising more than thirty million people as if it were a formal, ornamental garden. It 'stood to reason' that if the methods used were as described by Burke, they were hopelessly simple-minded.

Faced with the immense complexity of the real world, rational people when confronted with a pressing problem will avail themselves of as much of the relevant available experience as they are able to, before they decide what, if anything, can be done. The experience will almost certainly be widely distributed among others, but some individuals who have made it their business to study particular sorts of things and events will have correspondingly greater knowledge of the relevant experience. Such experts, in so far as they are competent, deploy the resources of rational inquiry. It is assurance of the rationality of their inquiries, and their knowledge of the relevant experience, which is the indispensable basis of any authority they have which is worthy of respect.

Prejudice, construed simply as 'opinions adopted without examin-

101

ation', may not be a bad thing. It may even be a good thing, if it is merely a convenient way to use sound knowledge. But the opinions adopted must be rationally defensible, even when they are not defended. It is one thing to say that it is impracticable for each individual to be their own expert on everything; this is a perfectly rational view to take, given obvious facts about human capacities. But it is something else entirely to suggest that unexamined opinions, as such, and in virtue of nothing else, are desirable, even when the opinions will not stand rational scrutiny. This is a recipe for perpetual darkness and frustration in human affairs.

The fact is that the argument against rationality from the complexity of the real world turns out to be a complaint that people are not rational enough. The objection may be that the accumulated rational wisdom of generations is ignored, as when Burke says that it is 'more wise to continue the prejudice *with the reason involved*'. Or the objection may be that there are other things than reason to consider, as when de Maistre says that 'Reason is no doubt good; but it is very far from the case that everything agrees to be settled by reason.'[3] But it is simply irrational to suppose that reason − that is, logic − alone is relevant to human affairs, or is always the most important thing.

Feeling is a fundamental feature of human nature which it would be totally irrational to ignore. Indeed, philosophers have, since Plato, been preoccupied with the relation between reason and passion. Plato argued for the supremacy of reason by referring to the exemplary case of someone who feels an overwhelming need for drink but refuses water because there is reason to believe that it is poisoned. All passions are likely to be misleading in this way, and to be all too liable to inflict damage both on the people who feel them and on others. So, while it is only rational to acknowledge feelings, it is necessary to control them by judicious reason. One way of putting the matter is to say that the development of reason is a process of learning to say 'no' to oneself, not in a merely negative and neurotic way, but out of enlightened interest for self and others.[4] In this way feelings may be more effectively gratified by being redirected. A similar result may be to achieve gratification of feelings deemed by the individual to be more important than others which might otherwise be immediately gratified on whim. Philosophers have also identified 'rational passions', of a special kind to do with truth and reason themselves: that is a passionate concern for the truth, integrity, and honest inquiry. Far from being opposed to reason, such passions naturally go with and are necessary to it.

Most of these points about reason and feeling are well illustrated in a classic dispute between Edmund Burke and Tom Paine over the rights and wrongs of the French Revolution. Burke plausibly claimed that 'our passions instruct our reason',[5] but he was mistaken in supposing that the passions or sentiments we feel are independent of everything else; unaffected by our reason, beliefs, and attitudes. Burke himself was moved by the suffering of royalists during the French Revolution, and this reinforced his conservatism. He was profoundly and eloquently moved by what he supposed was the plight of Marie Antoinette.

Tom Paine, the most notorious apostle of the modern philosophy of reason and revolution was just as instructed by his passions as was Burke, the conservative. Significantly, he had better, first hand, knowledge than Burke of the events referred to, and shared Burke's revulsion at the later persecutions. At considerable personal risk Paine even argued for the life of Louis XIV on the floor of the Revolutionary National Assembly. But his sympathies were wider and extended especially to those who had suffered most and were blameless. Typically he wrote:

> When I contemplate the natural dignity of man; when I feel (for Nature has not been kind enough to me to blunt my feelings) for the honour and happiness of its character, I become irritated at the attempt to govern mankind by force and fraud, as if they were all knaves and fools, and can scarcely avoid disgust at those who are thus imposed upon.[6]

> What is the history of all monarchical government, but a disgustful picture of human wretchedness, and the accidental respite of a few years' repose? Wearied with war, and tired with human butchery, they sat down to rest and called it peace. This certainly was not the condition that heaven intended for men; and *if this be monarchy*, well might monarchy be reckoned among the sins of the Jews.[7]

In the matter of feeling, usually it is not so much a question of whether or not there are feelings. It is more often than not a question of what the feelings are, and to what they are attached. Paine expressed this very clearly in his criticism of Burke.

> From his violence and his grief, his silence on some points, and his excess on others, it is difficult not to believe that Mr Burke is sorry, extremely sorry, that arbitrary power, the power of the Pope, and the Bastille, are pulled down. Not one glance of compassion, not one without hope, in the most miserable of prisons. It is painful to behold bestowed on those who lingered out the most wretched lives, a life without hope, in the most miserable of prisons.   It is painful to behold a man employing his talents to corrupt himself. Nature has been kinder

to Mr Burke than he has been to her. He is not affected by the reality of distress touching his heart, but by the showy resemblance of it striking his imagination. He pities the plumage, but forgets the dying bird.[8]

The view that rationality precludes feeling is based on a mis-understanding of rationality. It would be irrational to deny feelings. But feelings do not occur in a vacuum. They attach to beliefs and attitudes, which may or may not be rationally justifiable. Reason itself can be pursued with a passion for honesty, integrity, and truth.

Intuition may be understood in two relevant ways (although one writer has identified no less than thirty-one distinct definitions and descriptions[9]). It may mean nothing more than the essential act of any knowing. In this sense it is hardly incompatible with rationality, and may amount to no more than informed guesswork. Intuition is more likely to be supposed, by those who deny rationality in human affairs, to be a power or capacity beyond reason, an abnormal method of knowing based neither on the senses nor on deduction, and inexplicable as to its working. The difficulty with intuition understood in this way is that there is no way of drawing the simple but vital distinction between 'intuitions' which are merely unshakeable convictions, and intuitions which are true. Bertrand Russell recounts the report of a man who achieved a perfect 'vision of truth' under the influence of laughing gas, but when he came to he had always forgotten it. Then on one occasion he managed, with effort, to record his intuition whilst in the state of heightened awareness. What he wrote was: 'A smell of petroleum pervades throughout.'[10] As Russell remarks, what seems like insight may be misleading, and must be tested soberly. Since there is no way in which the truth of intuitions can be checked, so long as they are based neither in the senses, nor in reason, and remain inexplicable, then there is no way of deciding between mutually exclusive intuitions. Intuition provides no right to be sure, and no means of resolving conflict between intuitions. Any intuition can be matched by an equal and opposite intuition. Intuition is a rich source of arrogance, error and interminable conflict, which it would, there-fore, be rational, not to say sane, to avoid.

Finally, will can no more be detached from beliefs and attitudes than feelings can be, because we do not will in a vacuum any more than we feel in a vacuum. It is not the case, as de Jouvenel suggests, that 'The solution reached by activity will be very different from that conceived by mind.'[11] Normal human activity involves the wilful pursuit of goals related to beliefs and attitudes, that is mind. Activity divorced from a rational consideration of related means and ends is merely random behaviour. Rational men may be as wilful as they are emotional, as the case of Paine shows. On the subject of the French Revolution he wrote: 'When it becomes necessary to do a thing, the whole heart and soul should go into the measure, or not attempt it. The crisis was then arrived at and there remained no choice but to act with determined vigour or not to act at all.'[12] The view that rationality is opposed to wilful action is based on a misunderstanding of rationality. It would be irrational to desire ends believed to be good, and not to will them and to pursue them by all available necessary and permissible means. What de Maistre advocates is not wilful action in opposition to reason, but mere mindless aggression which is not strictly speaking action at all. In such cases it is rightly argued that men have abandoned specifically human nature altogether, and become mere predatory animals.

Irrationalists themselves are unable to avoid recognising the central place that reason has in the great affairs of public life and politics. The remarks of de Maistre and Burke to this effect have already been cited. Similarly Bolingbroke, whose idea of the patriot king is of a 'standing miracle', argued that human affairs must be regulated by the reason given by God to all men, the same to all, and obligatory on all alike to use. He argued that 'obligation of submission to [reason] is discernible by so clear and so simple a use of our intellectual faculties, that it may be said properly enough to be revealed by God.'[13] Recently Elizabeth Longford has abandoned reason for frivolity, saying: 'Don't say the monarchy is fair; it's fun.'[14] But reason is quickly invoked when irrationality threatens to undermine rather than preserve the cherished myths of monarchy. The coronations of George V on 22nd June 1911, and Elizabeth II on 2nd June 1953, were both marked by rain and very bad weather. An obvious irrationalist interpretation of these events would be that the weather provided bad omens. An impartial view of England's history since 1911 might even persuade us of the veracity of weather omens. Two world wars; the collapse of an empire; a highly controversial abdication; and the catastrophic decline of Britain's industrial supremacy: these events are just about as bad as omens could foretell. But admirers of monarchy are very selective in their wish to be irrational. For Longford points out that: 'No one was crass enough to see an ill-omen in the rain. Public superstition was channelled in the opposite direction, joyously awaiting as if in pure euphoria.'[15]

Irrationalism cannot be systematically sustained even where pure reason is out of place. It is self-defeating to argue for it. It proves to be impossible effectively to practice it. Therefore, even in matters of great complexity, intuition, feeling, and will, rationality has a crucial place to establish properly coherence, veracity and pertinence.

20

The materialist view of the rational justification of beliefs has a very basic defect. It does not distinguish between two totally different objects of explanation. A distinction of the sort in question is brought out in the following droll example. A bank-robber was asked why he robbed banks. He replied: 'Because that's where the money is.'. The reason why the answer is a joke is that the intended object of the question is to establish 'why rob?'. The answer given was to the altogether different question 'why banks?'[1] Something of the same sort of confusion is involved in the Marxist view that philosophy and morality are mere 'Kantian-Quaker chatter', and political beliefs are to be explained by their social, economic and material genealogy, as if the agents were irrational, or their rationality irrelevant. But the explanation required is to be found elsewhere, in the considerations which lead people to hold beliefs, in the terms which they themselves intrinsically understand the matter. As Weber puts it: 'Sociology is the science concerning itself with the interpretative understanding of social action ... we understand what a person is doing when he tries to achieve certain ends by choosing appropriate means on the basis of the facts of the situation as experience has accustomed us to interpret them.'[2] The question 'why believe or act so?' seeks to establish the reasons, grounds and purposes people have. What the materialist provides is an answer to the question 'how come belief and action so?'.

Engels himself elucidated Marx's views to show that the purely materialist interpretation of Marx ('economism') did not reflect his appreciation of the reciprocal influence of ideas on the economic order. 'Political, juridical, philosophical, religious, literary, artistic etc development ... all these react upon one another and upon the economic basis. Men make their history themselves, only they do so in a given environment, which conditions them ...'[3] These ideas of Marx's have been developed most notably by Gramsci who emphasised particularly the influence that traditional beliefs themselves may have on political and economic events. 'Mass ideological factors always lag behind mass economic phenomena and ... therefore at certain moments the automatic thrust due to economic factors is slowed down, obstructed or even momentarily broken by traditional ideological elements.'[4] The influence of 'traditional ideological elements' depends crucially on how events are understood by agents; by people themselves as they have been accustomed by experience to interpret them. Most certainly, the influence of ideas depends very largely on whether they are believed to be true, just or beneficial. And questions of truth, justice, and utility can only be decided after appropriate rational scrutiny of the issues involved.

It is appropriate now briefly to summarise this discussion of rationality and its supposed limits. Two sorts of view suggest that the use of reason should be limited in or altogether excluded from human affairs. On one view, human nature has essential but irrational elements, of feeling, intuition, and will. This goes with a view that life and society are so profoundly and irreducibly complicated, that reason is helpless at best; misleading, at worst. This view has been shown to be mistaken because the comlexity of events requires the extension of rational inquiry, not its termination; and feeling, intuition, and will cannot be detached from reason, or beliefs and attitudes which are rationally accountable. On the other view rational enquiry is superfluous, because there are global factors of economic and social organisation which determine beliefs and events by the exercise of power, not reason at all. It is evident that such a view greatly underestimates the importance of ideas and beliefs themselves in determining events, including social conditions and power. Rational scrutiny of ideas is a crucial factor in deciding whether they are accepted, and so whether they may be influential. Neither of the a-rationalist views in question succeeds in showing that rational inquiry is inappropriate in complex human affairs to do with feeling, intuition, and will, or where there are structural factors in society which influence belief. It is quite appropriate and necessary, therefore, rationally to examine views of the British Monarchy which are supposedly based on considerations said to be non-rational; that is the profound myths of monarchy.

PART IV: THREE PROFOUND MYTHS

CHAPTER *21* MYTH

The first profound myth of monarchy is the view that monarchy is an indispensable expression of something very deep in human nature, which supposedly nothing else can replace (at least in the lives of Britons, or at the very least the English). This is the monarchical-myth myth.

Minimally, myths are fictional pictures or stories which describe and explain things in some way, and at the same time express some moral option. It is perhaps true that no human society worth the name could exist without some sort of myth. Myths, as symbolically expressed, form the necessary background to culture, and provide the *raison d'être* for social institutions and common projects. All effective myths relate the experience and actions of individuals to some significant order beyond their own lives. The order or scheme will, in some way, relate to a profound source of values that is timeless. In this way individuals' lives acquire meaning, value, and purpose, which otherwise they would not have. Shared myths and shared symbols are the basis of shared lives. In practice the myths, and all they entail, are effectively sustained through rituals. Ritual objects, persons, actions, and ceremonies, provide a means whereby individuals are initiated and reaffirmed in their mutual commitment to their communal life in accordance with the myth. It is important to understand that myths do not merely *express* a conception of the world: they *establish* a view of the world. Profound myths are to be contemplated. They are not the objects of analysis, so much as the necessary basis for a life in which analysis is possible. The transcendental and timeless nature of myths goes with an element of mystery associated with things unworldly and other-worldly.

The best known living examples of profound myths are religious. The Christian myths of the creation and the fall have provided a rich basis for 'understanding' and guiding human life, and a source of emotional security for individuals by linking them to the creator. Other myths may have no specially religious significance at all. It may be that a society as a whole, formulated as history, itself provides the source of mythic significance. The myth of military invincibility in Prussia, and the myth of the limitless frontier in America, are examples.

Societies subsist on ordered activities. Societal myths, according to one theory, find expression in four basic kinds of ritual community drama, which reflect the primary importance of social order and consensus: these are the ritual dramas of guilt, victimage, redemption, and hierarchy.[1] Guilt dramas deal with cases which threaten internal social order, by denouncing culprits. Victimage dramas follow from guilt dramas, by reviling or punishing scapegoats. Redemption dramas demonstrate, typically in political rhetoric and literature, the triumph of good over evil. Hierarchy dramas affirm the social order. According to Duncan:

> The study of differential status is necessary to any kind of hierarchy, as well as to the satisfaction of our own moral needs as citizens ... For among kings as among common people, status is won by successful appeals to others who, like the audience of a great drama, determine our success and failure as we play our many roles in society. Status enactment is always a *plea*, a petition; for status is *given*, never taken.[2]

It is said that the British Monarchy is indispensable because it has mythic significance of the sort described here. It symbolises the endless continuity of the nation's history, and personifies organic unity. As the apex of a long established order, it incorporates the moral option of hereditary social hierarchy. The social order and the hierarchical value describe the British nation, and provide the resources for explaining the events of British life. Individuals derive the meaning of their lives from their participation in the social order and by sharing the values which the Monarchy represents. Royal pronouncements are calculated to establish this identity. As Queen Elizabeth II has said: 'Nations need to be reminded of their corporate identity from time to time so that they can plan together for the future life of all of their people.'[3] According to Edward Shils and Michael Young, in Britain these shared values are generosity, charity, loyalty, justice in the distribution of opportunities and rewards, reasonable respect for authority, the dignity of the individual, and his right to freedom.[4] Royal occasions and honours are practical means whereby individuals and groups are recognised and incorporated into the nation.

The mystery surrounding the British Monarchy is one of its most salient features. As one euphoric writer has put it: 'Just as the lover seeks and finds in the beloved, something beyond the limits of the finite and the temporal, so the British people seek in their sovereign something that transcends the common limited experience. And astounding as it may seem, what they look for they find.'[5] Even the advent of television and the walkabout add to rather than detract from this. Television exploits the idea of the remoteness of celebrity from ordinary lives, and walkabouts are choreographed to convey an impression of gods descended among mortals.[6] No innovation in royal protocol has ignored Bagehot's warning that mystery is the Monarchy's life, and daylight must not be let in upon magic.[7] All of this may be regarded as mumbo jumbo, but it is said that we have in Britain the *best* mumbo jumbo.[8]

The Status of Myths

Even if myth is not dismissed out of hand as pure fantasy, it may not be as indispensable as is often supposed or in the form supposed. Karl Marx took the extreme view that the need for myths disappears with real knowledge of the world. 'All mythology subdues, controls and fashions the forces of nature in the imagination and through the imagination; it disappears therefore when real control over these forces is established.'[9] This was certainly true of myths applied to the natural world. As Marx said: 'What is Vulcan compared with Roberts and Co.; Jupiter compared with the lightning conductor; and Hermes compared with the *Crédit Mobilier*?'[10] The queston is whether the same demythologising process goes on in the social world. There is no reason to suppose that it does not.

One serious difficulty with the view that large modern industrial societies depend upon indispensable myths, is that there is insufficient evidence to support it. Most of the hard evidence for the role of myths in establishing and promoting common values and social order comes from anthropological field studies of relatively small unindustrialised and isolated societies. There is far less evidence that vast plural societies comprised of widely varied caste, class, ethnic, religious, and cultural groups, subsist on universally shared myths. There are alternative ways of explaining social order, such as the division of labour, economic necessity, various forms of compulsion, and plain old ignorance, resignation and apathy. It is too easily assumed that, in the absence of overt social conflict, the mere existence of social order is in itself sufficient proof that there are shared beliefs and values (myths). For social order may be the result of mere compliance, fear, indifference or necessity, rather than consensus.[11]

The mystifying function of myths may be far more dangerous and harmful than is supposed. All myths distort reality. The proponents of mythologies invariably presume that the distortions are beneficial, not harmful. Pethick-Lawrence, for example, typically writes about myths as romantic make-believe, to be counted along with the song of the nightingale, the rapture of spring, the lovers' first kiss, and the smile of the babe on its mother's breast. He says that without such things life would be devoid of colour and the poets would cease to sing.[12] How true; but how much else are we allowed to know? Is the distortion produced by myths always as harmless or as beneficial as love and poetry?

Myths and symbols may 'work' perfectly well, and precisely according to the way they are supposed to do, by providing groups and societies with a *raison d'être*, and a working set of beliefs and values. But that is no guarantee that the interests of the people concerned are best served in this way. Myths may be dysfunctional because the distortions they produce are more pernicious than beneficial. De Laguna points out that:

> elaborate and monstrous systems of belief cannot possibly be accounted for by any simple theory that beliefs are determined by their successful "working" in practice ... The truth is ... that some more or less organised system of beliefs and sentiments is an absolute necessity for the carrying on of social life. So long as group solidarity is secured by some such system *the particular beliefs which enter into it may to an indefinite degree lead to behaviour ill-adapted to the objective order of nature.*[13]

Securing the solidarity of particular groups may not be the highest value in life, however. Two examples show that it is not; that people may be pointlessly destroyed by mythological delusions. The Ghost Dance religion, which exploded among the North American Indian tribes in 1890, contained all the ingredients of effective myth. According to the inspired vision of the Paiute prophet Wodziwob, a cataclysm would destroy the hated whites, but leave their possessions to Indians who joined the cult, and heaven would be created on earth. The teachings were promulgated by the shaman Wovoka, who fell into a trance during a solar eclipse, and awoke to report that God had shown him dead Indians resurrected, young, and happy again, and how to dance in order to achieve this miracle. The Sioux version of Wovoka's teaching included the belief that the Ghost Dance had the power to render Indians invulnerable to the firepower of white men's guns, because their dance shirts were bullet proof in virtue of the symbolic designs on them, of arrows, birds, stars, and suchlike.

The Ghost Dance religion revived the dignity and hope of people whose lives, societies, and culture were destroyed by whites. What happened then was that the Sioux rebelled. Their chief, Sitting Bull, was killed and the Indians were massacred at Wounded Knee, where predictably their ghost shirts provided no protection at all against bullets. The Ghost Dance cult was extinguished, and the Indians died, because their myths failed adequately to connect with the objective order of things.[14]

Another object lesson was provided by the Japanese, who entered the Second World War under the leadership of a war party whose outlook reflected the mythic mediaeval *Samurai* warrior codes. As one Japanese commentator has explained: 'We believed with a blind fervour that we could triumph over scientific weapons and tactics, by means of our mystic will ...'[15] The war was started as a result of a mistaken intuitive 'calculation' which transcended mathematics. The characteristic reliance on intuition by the Japanese blocked the objective cognition of the modern world. The requirement in post-war Japan was seen to be to reverse the culture of Japan away from the intuitive and towards a propensity for the intellectual.[16]

It may be that effective myths are natural, or spontaneously generated, not manufactured. But not all natural myths are tolerable just because they are natural, and for no other reason. Group solidarity may depend on *some* myths, but this tells us nothing about *which* myths are necessary or about whether the group's solidarity is desirable anyway. The racial myth of Aryan supremacy may have been necessary for the group solidarity of the *Waffen S.S.*, but that is to say nothing about whether the racial myths or the *Waffen S.S.* were desirable or necessary.

The case of Hitler's Germany demonstrates another vital feature of national myths: the difference between overt, rhetorical values, and the values otherwise tacitly incorporated in the social order sustained by the myth. The values proclaimed for the Third *Reich* by the National Socialist German Workers' Party were nationalist, anti-capitalist, and socialist. The values that were promoted in reality were ambition, prejudice, resentment, envy, and avidity for power and wealth.[17] It is not sufficient to take the profound myths at their advertised face-value. It is necessary to examine the real consequences of a myth in order to establish its real value and influence.

Roland Barthes has identified a number of ways in which myths systematically distort reality.[18] The main function of societal myths is to render 'normal', 'natural', and therefore 'inevitable', social orders which in reality are the products of human history. Human aggression, exploitation, and mythification may have produced the social order by all too intentional and arbitrary means. But the result is incorporated and promoted in myth as 'the natural order of things'. Myth transforms arbitrary history into inevitable nature. Another feature of myths is that they rename or redescribe real features of society. Typically a ruling class interest, such as a *bourgeois*-capitalist interest, is called 'the national interest', and everyone is called upon to promote and defend it, whether or not they have any real interest at stake at all. Tom Paine alluded unintentionally to this phenomenon when he scoffed at Burke's claim that people had no right to change the constitution: 'that men should take up arms, and spend their lives and fortunes *not* to maintain their rights; but to maintain that they have *no* rights is an entirely new species of discovery, and suited to the paradoxical genius of Mr Burke.'[19]

Paine was mistaken, however, in thinking that people do not fight to maintain what in reality are their own relative social disadvantages, for this is commonly achieved by mythic delusion. Again, typically, social, political, and economic strength is mythified by giving it the form of duty. Rulers who make servile their subjects, pose as servants themselves, and in this way mystify the real relations between rulers and the ruled.

CHAPTER *22* THE MONARCHY MYTH

The claim that monarchy is *the* natural form of government for human societies simply beggars belief. It may have been convincing to chauvinistic and uneducated people at Queen Victoria's funeral in 1901, when it might have seemed that the entire civilized world was composed of hereditary monarchies. Only the first great modern republics, the United States and France, were excepted. But since the First World War, republicanism has prevailed virtually universally. There is no substance whatsoever in the claim that nations need monarchs for social order and prosperity. The more specific claim, that monarchy is the natural form of government for Britain, is no more plausible than it is for anywhere else. The best explanation on offer by enthusiasts such as Dermot Morrah is that 'the British peoples have made their brief experiment with the republican way of life, and discovered that it was not for them.'[1] But this argument is extremely weak and unpersuasive. Ten years of *interregnum*, three hundred and thirty years ago, do not prove conclusively and for all time that the British are incorrigible royalists.

The history of the United States of America should be proof positive that English-speaking peoples, with the same British traditions of parliamentary democracy, are as capable as any other of surviving and thriving without a monarchy. The supposedly paramount and indispensable role of monarchy, of providing a unifying symbol of nationhood, is not discharged in other nations either. Switzerland is a perfect example. The Swiss have sustained a polyglot society of mixed cultures, religions, national origins, histories, and even languages, perfectly well for seven hundred years without ever having even considered monarchy. The Swiss have not suffered conspicuously as a consequence; quite the opposite.

As for the supposed need for a personified symbol of nationhood and national unity, that too is groundless. Unless the mass of British people are infinitely more stupid than their counterparts elsewhere, there is no reason to suppose that they are incapable of comprehending principles. But they are not the clods Bagehot described, unable to comprehend an idea unless it looks like a king or a policeman. From the start, the people of the United States have, as Abraham

Lincoln said, been devoted to a *proposition* ('. . . that all men are
created equal, that they are endowed by their Creator with certain
unalienable rights, that among these are life, liberty, and the pursuit
of happiness.'), and the chief symbols of nationhood in the United
States are a flag and an anthem. Chief reverence is reserved for an
office, not a person at all. Even in England, the nation has been
naturally symbolised by something other than a monarch. Gretton has
pointed out how the Puritan army became the embodiment of the
people.[2] Curiously, but unsurprisingly, Adolf Hitler recognised this.
He said he would have called his storm troopers 'Ironsides' if he had
been starting a party in England, because that name was typically
English.[3]

So far the monarchy myth has been considered against bald facts. A
more systematic examination of the myth is called for. First, consider
the coherence of the idea of monarchy. It is supposed to be the most
natural and therefore indispensable form of human government, but
the historical and political facts do not support this claim. One attempt to vindicate it is Gretton's. He says that it is a mistake to
assume that where the *title* of 'king' has disappeared, the place in the
national life which kingship fills has disappeared.[4] What is this but to
resolve to call *any* working form of government 'monarchy' − a mere
resolve to redefine words out of their plain ordinary meanings? By this
means, Adolf Hitler, Joseph Stalin, and Fidel Castro become kings.
This is ingenious, but totally unedifying as to the facts of human
nature, myths, and government.

It is inappropriate entirely to regard myths rationally. This much
has been established. But there is no basis either for abandoning
reason altogether. The internal consistency of the British monarchical
myth certainly bears examination. Consider four important aspects.
First the basic picture that the myth presents, as a model of the proper
social order. Various writers offer quite different and sometimes
diametrically opposed pictures. The main models of monarchic
society are: The Family[5]; The Body[6]; The Organism[7]; The Estate[8];
The Personality[9]; The Beehive[10]; The Machine[11]; and The Arch[12]
There are two fundamentally incompatible types of picture: the
organic or natural pictures; and the artefactual ones. Where natural
pictures are involved, the implication is that human intention has
little or nothing to do with the social order. Constructed systems, on
the other hand, depend almost entirely upon human intention. Both
cannot be accommodated in the same mythology without inherent
contradiction about such important matters as deliberate change for

the better. One other problem must be mentioned, out of countless others too numerous to mention. The myth is represented in an amazing variety of iconic images – that is, interpretable pictures – but none of them makes the hazardous leap from far-fetched and strained metaphor, to the radical but simple view that society is, or may be, a more or less voluntary association of competent, rationally self interested, conscious agents with a certain amount of fellow feeling, and with basically social inclinations.

Another question of internal consistency is raised by the principle of social order promoted by monarchy. According to one view, for example: monarchy is an egalitarian institution, and as such fully compatible with a democratic society. The reason for this is that, compared to the monarch, all other ranks, classes and persons are reduced to the same level: that is, equal insignificance.[13] Bagehot, the fount of so much monarchical wisdom, took the opposite view that: 'Our court is the head of an unequal, competing, aristocratic society.'[14] This suggests that monarchy is totally incompatible with democratic society.

A third issue is that values promoted by the Monarchy are in fundamental ways mutually incompatible. One set of values is conventional and restrictive. These include loyalty, justice, respect for authority and the dignity of the individual, 'official' values typically associated with the intellectual or Appollonian impulses, striving after measure, order and harmony. Another set of values is fantastic and unrestrained, to do with the eternal source of colour, poetry, rapture, and, more sinisterly, wilful assertiveness. These tacit values permit restraints to go on holiday; they are associated with the passionate and dynamic or Dionysian aspects of the will to life and power. According to certain mythic conventions, the life source is symbolised by the 'trickster' who is exempted from social rules, conventions, and *mores*. Curiously the Winnebago trickster Wakdjunkaga has a very long penis which has to be wrapped around him and put over his shoulder in a box. Bits broken from the penis are transformed into flowers and plants for people.[15] The British Monarchy clearly functions as trickster, to the Inland Revenue at least. The parallel to Wakdjunkaga is a matter only for idle speculation.

Another question of internal consistency concerns the power of the monarch. One popular view is that the Monarchy has no real power left to act at all. This is reinforced by the view that its continuing survival requires that it should remain completely outside of and above the political arena, where the exercise of powers might be required, even if they existed. On this view, the usefulness of the Monarchy depends on its powerlessness. There is another view, quite incompatible with the first, that the Monarchy has both considerable influence and very real powers, even if dormant ones. On this view the usefulness of the Monarchy depends on its powerfulness.

Clearly, whatever view one adopts of myth in general, the myth of the British Monarchy is hopelessly riddled with basic internal contradictions. These are potentially as hazardous for a nation which believes the myth, as other flawed myths have proved to be for other nations.

It is appropriate also to examine the burden of evidence for the monarchy myth. The main concern is not to establish its truth or falsity, for that would be to misunderstand the nature of myth. What is required, is to establish whether the claims made about the prevalence and effectiveness of the myth can be borne out.

The most obvious question is whether the myth, as described by the enthusiasts of monarchy, is even understood, let alone accepted as such by the mass of British people. Recognition of, and due regard for the head of state, can perhaps be taken for granted, but there is no very convincing evidence that the supposedly more mythic aspects of monarchy are understood by the great mass of people. Elaborate accounts of the symbolic significance of the royal offices and the great ceremonial acts, of coronations, openings of parliament, jubilees, *etc.*, are offered by royal heralds extra-ordinary, belted earls, Oxbridge readers in history and anthropology and conservative sociologists ransacking the archives of cultural anthropology for a vocabulary. These all have an air of fantasy about them that matches the content of their explanations. In so far as the British people participate in the public expressions of monarchy, it is much more plausible that they do so because they enjoy spectacles and a good time. They have far fewer festivals and holidays than most other peoples, when all is said and done. Those who read mythic significance into the presence of those royal, should listen again to the raucous chanting of soccer-tribal allegiances that drown out royal plaints at pre-match Wembley. The more heady delights of myths and mysticism are almost certainly a matter of cultivated and decadent taste, not at all shared by plain folk.

A much more serious issue is whether the values expressed by the Monarchy are the subject of universal consensus. Even the 'official' values of family, hierarchical order, duty, respect for authority, individual liberty, and conservatism, are by no means universally accepted. There is a powerful tradition based on different and often opposing values of community, equality, autonomy, and radicalism. There is no good reason to support the view that there is national consensus around the official values of monarchy. The real values promoted by monarchy, based on arbitrary caste hierarchy and privilege, could not possibly be the basis for consensus among intelligent and self conscious people. Norman Birnbaum has commented on the difference between the ritual and the real values of monarchy. Writing about the coronation in 1953 he points out that ritual may satisfy the outward demands for conformity and allow transgression of the rules to go unimpeded. 'In the ceremonial throng at Westminster Abbey, there may have been one or two accomplished evaders of income tax. Yet we have no evidence that ritual enthusiasm moved any such person to make remissions to the Chancellor of the Exchequer.'[16] All the available evidence suggests that the very opposite is true.

The unifying function claimed for the myth is at least very misleading. Far from uniting the nation, the institution of monarchy probably has in the past contributed, more than any other single factor, to division and conflict. Throughout history, disputes over the hereditary succession have been a more potent source of strife than political faction has ever been. Not only the institution, but the persons of monarchy are potentially, and in practice, deeply divisive. Even in living memory, the nation was torn between royalism, and the prospect of a 'King's party', on one hand, and the primacy of parliament, on the other. The problem was not made easier because Edward VIII was regarded as potentially a radical monarch who wanted to do something about the condition of the deprived mass of his subjects. The fact seems to be that the Monarchy must uphold the social *status quo*, that is caste and class divisions. The myth of monarchy distorts the truth, so that the real history of caste and class distinctions, and the conflict arising from them, is suppressed, and the myth of unity perpetrated instead. According to this myth, class war is alien to the British tradition.[17] But the real tradition is one of conquest, expropriation, exploitation, and repression; of rebellion, uprising, revolt, revolution, and industrial class conflict. The force that has been deployed to suppress this is the sword, wielded by the real powers. These have been transposed by the myth into the symbol of the mitre and the 'duty' of the sovereign.

In the present, the Monarchy does promote the mere idea of unity. However, as a study of modern British society shows, there is no real unity of interest between the castes and classes. There are two British nations, the haves and the have-nots. By persuading people that there is only one, the Monarchy is an instrument of mystification and delusion of the nation's have-nots.

There is an interesting parallel between the case of Louis Bonaparte in France, in the mid-nineteenth century, and the British Monarchy in the late twentieth century. Louis Bonaparte was widely popular among the French lower orders, even though he represented an authoritarianism that was both unconstitutional, and opposed to the people's real interests. Marx explains the emperor's popularty in two ways. First, the people were not conscious of their real interests. Second, they looked to the emperor as a source of miraculous solutions to their problems, because they associated him with the myth of Napoleon Bonaparte's glories. In this, they were, as Marx says, 'hankering for a return from the perils of the revolution to the flesh-pots of Egypt'.[18] Similarly in the 1980s, the British Monarchy enjoys a level of popular regard that is inexplicable in terms of its real social and economic status and influence. Like the French peasants in the mid-nineteenth century, most British people are systematically deluded about the real nature of their social condition. Again, likewise, monarchy is a symbol of former imperial glories, which can be looked back on with characteristic pride, where there is nothing much to look on now with comparable satisfaction, and not much to look forward to with hope. If anything, the British Monarchy works to defuse and suppress long delayed social conflicts, which, like festering sores and deep psychological disorders, it may be better to call by their real names and to confront openly.

The monarchy myth works as a deluding fantasy to prevent healthy realism of this sort. When Pethick-Lawrence wrote, at the time of the Queen's coronation in 1953, that 'The sovereign must be the fairy queen out of the story book.'[19], he was saying more than he intended. Numerous commentators have seen how the greatest danger of monarchy lies in its magic, in the tendency to substitute fantasy for rational acceptance of justifiable authority and institutions.[20] Antony Sampson has pointed to the ultimate consequence: that the suspension of disbelief towards royalty spills over into a suspension of realism towards everything else.[21] Among other things the Monarchy preserved dangerous illusions of grandeur and inhibits real national revival.[22] It is as if the prevalent British propensity to dwell in the past is based on the hope that Hegel was right when he observed that all events and personalities of great importance occur twice; but as Marx points out, 'he forgot to add: the first time as tragedy, the second as farce'.[23]

It is simply a mistake to suppose that because *some* myth may be indispensable to a society, then *any* myth will do. It may be that effective myths can not be manufactured to order. Nevertheless the success of Britain's prevailing monarchy myth only goes to show how far reality can be distorted, and in what unlikely directions, without straining credulity. It is unlikely in the extreme that a clan of German mercenaries, far removed from even the slender thread of legitimate succession, should be imposed upon the British people as their very personification. It is downright incredible that a totally undisting-uished and avaricious (not to mention venal) dynasty should come to be accepted by the nation. And yet all of this has happened. Are people so perverse, even in their mythological moments, that they will revere an itinerant tribe of Hanoverians, but simply refuse to accept the most worthy and dignified strands of British nationhood? There is myth enough in the rich tapestry of the nation's history to reassure anyone that they live in a society with a *raison d'être* totally other than the *charades* of third generation Windsors. As Colin McInnes has pointed out: 'The real English myth we should cherish and which can sustain us, is not enshrined in an archaic monarchical survival. It exists in what is essential to us, and which kings have never formed; our blend of races, our created language; our scientific, commercial and artistic skills; our faith. "God save the king" is a splendid motto; "God save ourselves" is a real one.'[24]

CHAPTER 23 RELIGION

An influential variant on the mythic view of monarchy is the religious myth, according to which there is something essential to human nature or psychology, which is religious in the sense that it seeks to transcend all mundane worldly matters and connect with something sublime. This cannot be explained in terms of a mere ritualisation of real life concerns. Instead, real life is informed by values which transcend it, especially moral values, derived from some extra-mundane source. Those who exercise authority based in these values are endowed with a special legitimacy not attainable by worldly means. According to one view, authority is always rooted in the sacred.[1] The aura of religiosity that surrounds authority so based, its *charisma*, is the most powerful means of commanding respect and commitment.

Monarchy in the grand and sanctified form of the British Monarchy is said to satisfy this basic human yearning for the sublime. The divine right of kings is often supposed to be a dead letter, but *Filmer's syllogism* still explains the basic rationale behind the religious myth. 'What is natural to man exists by divine right. Kingship is natural to man. Therefore kingship exists by divine right.'[2] The precise formula for the religious significance of monarchy varies. The strongest claim is that monarchs are themselves gods, as James I believed. A less megalomanic version is that monarchs are God's lieutenants or representatives on earth.[3] Another version is that monarchy is a special supernatural element in the nation.[4] At the very least, it is said that the monarch needs (and has) an aura of official religiosity.[5] This religious significance of monarchy is expressed most clearly in ritual, above all in the coronation ceremonial. Dermot Morrah wrote: 'As the great old solemn rites took their stately course ... the whole nation felt itself to be dedicated to the person of the Queen ... [though] there were probably few to reflect that they were repeating the experience of their earliest Christian ancestors.'[6] Edward Shils and Michael Young were not so sceptical about the significance people would be able to read into the ceremony. According to them, behind the archaic *facade* of the ceremony was a vital sense of permanent contemporaneity. For example: when the Archbishop of Canterbury anointed the Queen, saying: 'and as Solomon was anointed king by Zadock the priest, and Nathan the prophet, so be thou anointed, blessed, and consecrated over the peoples', this was not merely an analogy: it was a symbolisation of reality, in conformity to sacred precedent. She showed her submission before the archbishop as God's agent, kneeling before him while he implores God to bless her.[7] It is in such ways that authority is linked to religion, and in the process legitimised and strengthened.[8] That is why the constitution, by the Act of Settlement 1701, requires that 'whosoever shall hereafter come into the possession of the Crown shall joyn in communion with the Church of England as by law established'.[9] That, in brief, is the substance and profound importance of the religious myth. The present queen, Elizabeth II, we are told, takes her religion seriously, and without qualification, and so fulfils the requirements of the myth to perfection.[10]

The religious myth is already largely dissipated even within the established monarchic tradition. The divine right of kings was rebutted in the seventeenth century by John Locke, on the basis of both scriptural authority and simple arguments. The simplest and most telling is that there is no conceivable way that the lineal ancestry of the British monarch can be traced to Adam, and so to the legitimacy of God's ultimate sanction.[11] Bolingbroke, writing as a practical politician, argued that 'Divine Right to govern ill is an absurdity; to assert it is Blasphemy.'[12] Even more destructive of the idea of divine right is an obvious interpretation put on it in practice, which shows it to be empty of any significant content at all. According to Canon XXVIII of Bishop Overall's *Convocation Book*, 'after all rebels have organised a government, its authority is from God'.[13] This is to say no more nor less than that anyone who succeeds in establishing a government, has a right to govern, which excludes nobody, not even usurpers and revolutionaries, so long as they are successful. Henry IV, for example, took the crown by force, and parliament duly recognised the right God had given 'by conquest'.[14] Henry VII, metaphorically, found his crown in a bush. The divine right of kings has long been superceded by the divine right of peoples in the history of the world's constitutions, including Britain's. The religious myth of monarchy can be seen from this viewpoint as a religious vestige. It does persist, however, in influential circles at least, and calls for further examination.

First there are questions to do with the very idea that the queen is head, not only of the established church of England, but of the nation's entire religious life. The Church of England is the official Christian church, but there are numerous other Christian denominations and sects which differ in important matters of doctrine. In addition to other episcopal churches (protestant churches with bishops) there are Presbyterians, Baptists, and Methodists, and other trinitarian churches. Other churches and religions close to Christianity include Mormons, Jehovah's Witnesses, Spiritualists and Rastafarians. Most conspicuous are the Roman Catholics, who in 1985 numbered more (2.3 million) than Anglicans (1.9 million). The constitution expressly excludes Roman Catholics from the highest position in the land.

The Bill of Rights 1689 explains that experience shows that 'it is inconsistent with the safety and welfare of this Protestant Kingdom to be governed by a Popish Prince or by any King or Queen marrying a Papist ... all and every person and persons that is are or shall be reconciled to or hold communion with the See or Church of Rome ... or shall marry a Papist shall be excluded and be for ever incapable to inherit possess or enjoy the Crowne.'[15]

It is difficult to understand how papists can readily regard the Monarch as the natural head of the religious life of the nation, even if religion is construed absurdly narrowly as just Christianity. Ulster Catholics, for example, can hardly welcome the symbolic religious supremacy of a protestant queen to whom their 'loyalist' compatriots claim supreme allegiance. And, of course, in Ulster such things are not a laughing matter. How the Queen is to establish precedence over Haile Selassie, ganja weed, and reggae, remains to be seen.

Even more than the sectarian divisions of Christianity, the growing diversity of religions that flourish in Britain makes nonsense of the claim that the Monarchy is the head of all religious life. Judaism, Hinduism, Buddhism, Islam, and Sikhism are just a few of the main alternative religions it would be preposterous to suggest look to the monarch in religious matters. Some of them have no church; some have no god. Atheists and agnostics form another very substantial group, for whom it is vacuous to speak of religious life at all, let alone of the Monarchy symbolising its religious life. As with so much else, the pathetic lameness of the explanations as to how the Monarchy is supposed practically to realise the claims made on its behalf, only go to show how preposterous the claims are. On the subject of the royal function as head of all the nation's religious life, Dorothy Laird typically says only that after six years' reign, the Queen had shown in conversation on many occasions her concern for the welfare of the free churches; that she invited Dr Billy Graham to preach before her and to luncheon afterwards; that the Queen and other members of the royal family made private donations to the fund for rebuilding St

George's Roman Catholic Cathedral at Southwark (gratefully received); and received a large party of Australian pilgrims, and then 'graciously waved goodbye as she entered the castle'. Although after six years' reign the Queen had not attended a Jewish religious service, the Duke of Edinburgh was present at a special service in the Spanish and Portuguese Synagogue in the City of London, in December 1951, to mark the 250th anniversary of the synagogue.[16] Obviously, none of this has to do with religious leadership and ecumenism.

Agnosticism and atheism raise the whole question of the status of religious belief. Unless there is believed to be at least some substance to religions, most people would find the religious myth pointless. However, it is notoriously difficult, if not impossible, to establish the veracity of religious beliefs by intellectually sound arguments which are acceptable to those who are not disposed to believe anyway, regardless of whether there are good reasons. Faith is the last resort of believers, but there is a very high price to pay. As Donald McKinnon has argued, faith encourages dishonesty; it tends to obscure the honesty of the judgment concerning untestable beliefs, and affects adversely intellectual honesty and integrity in general. This, as McKinnon points out, is a *moral* objection, because it argues that faith, as the Christian understands it, is incompatible with a proper intellectual objectivity.[17] Another kind of moral objection to Christianity is that it frequently promotes conformity and acquiescence in intolerable wrongs, and a cultivation of obedience for obedience's sake, when revolt rather than acceptance is a plain human duty.[18] This has typically been the effect of the conservative influence of monarchy. For example, in 1975, Prince Charles addressed the inhabitants of Papua New Guinea, who had been in dispute with an American mining company, with a homily from the epistle of St Paul to the Romans, as follows:

> Everyone must obey the State authorities, for no authority exists without God's permission, and the existing authorities have been put there by God. Whoever opposes the existing authority, opposes what God has ordered, and anyone who does so will bring judgment upon himself.[19]

The practical consequences of religion raise a whole other set of questions that cannot be deal with here. Bertrand Russell has conveniently enumerated among the contributions of religion to civilization: dogmatism and intolerance; repression of healthy natural impulses, such as sex; anti-social egoistic individualism; and cruelty and sadism, masked as righteousness.[20] Intellectually Russell was a hard man, but fair. It is far from obvious, to say the least, that religion provides a proper or desirable basis for political society.

Leaving aside the arguments for the merits and demerits of religion in its own terms, what of the balance of evidence for the efficacy of the religious myth of monarchy? First, let us note something fundamental about religious objects in general: people can find religious significance in virtually anything, regardless of any practical significance. Certain Australian tribes worship vomit.[21] The fact that some people attach great religious significance to the Monarchy should not impress us unduly. But let us not prejudge the issue. The most striking thing is just how flimsy the evidence is that religion, in any shape or form, has anything to do with social and political life in Britain, or with anything very much at all, really, in the 1980s. A simple and unbiased look at the official statistics quickly shows that religion has diminished almost to vanishing point as a significant factor in the lives of most people.[22] According to *Social Trends* published by the Central Statistical Office, in 1985 only 16 per cent of people in Britain belonged to any Christian church at all. About another 3 per cent, or 1.5 million, belong to non-Christian churches and religions. Membership of the established Church of England is at an all-time low of much less than 5 per cent of the adult population (1.9 million). The general trend is an accelerating decline in religious belief. Between 1970 and 1985 the number of Anglican churches alone fell by over one thousand, and between 1970 and 1980 the number of full-time Christian ministers by 2,500. Nor is it the case that those who give up church membership continue to hold their religious beliefs. According to opinion polls, the great majority of defectors from Anglicanism, at any rate, say that they have ceased to have any religion.[23] In the face of such evidence, it is perverse to persist with the idea that the normal condition of humanity is religious. It is equally perverse to suggest that there is an overwhelming sense in Britain of the religious significance of monarchy, which explains its persistence. It would be very strange indeed if this were true. No other nation on earth has the same supposed need for a sanctified monarch. It is improbable in the extreme that, left to their own devices, that is without incessant royal propaganda, British people would feel such a need either. Even with all the propaganda, the established church is disappearing. As John Weightman observed with some foresight in 1953: 'as far as the body of popular emotion is concerned, the monarch could dispense with the archbishop, but the archbishop could hardly dispense with the monarch.'[24]

There is hardly any reason at all to suppose that there is a specifically religious basis for monarchy. There is some evidence, however, that the residual effects of religion may have a bad effect on people's attitudes. According to one view, the religious myth satisfies a British love of processions, of uniforms and ceremonial, which is 'the love of proximity to greatness and power, to the charismatic person and institution which partakes of the sacred'.[25] Not everyone would agree that this sort of sycophantic tendency is healthy and desirable; not after the Nuremberg rallies, certainly. A curious result of social surveys reflects another disturbing tendency. Notwithstanding low church membership, apparently more than half the British people (53 per cent) suppose that 'God guides this country in times of trouble.' This belief is held by far more people who are royalists, than are not. The researchers, Rose and Kavanagh, drew the conclusion that 'support for the monarchy thus appears to encourage irrational and mystical confidence in political authority.'[26] Fortunately, as they point out, British government has, in practice, been based not on royalist faith but on Cromwell's maxim 'trust in God, and keep your powder dry'.[27] If anything, the connection between religion and the full panoply of British state ceremonial has a detrimental effect, even on true religion. True religious insight, if it is to be had at all, is unlikely to come in the shape of elaborate public mime and show, but rather in the quiet and personal commitment of serious persons. The claims for the hold of the religious myth on the popular consciousness of the nation should be tested against live popular culture. High-minded exponents of the myth should leave their studies and cloisters, and listen to the response of a 1980s Wembley cup final crowd to the playing of 'Abide with Me' before the sovereign. Raucous partisan tribal chanting and ribald singing drown out the strains of the Guards band. In the city of Glasgow, Celtic fans ritually jeer at the national anthem 'God save the Queen'. As Hugh McLachlan says: 'Let anyone who believes the myth that the Crown promotes political stability and unity pay a visit to a Rangers-Celtic football match.'[28]

There are, finally, certain prosaic but telling difficulties with the religious myth, even for the Monarchy itself, in an ecumenical age.[29] The British constitution both requires the monarch to be a member of the Church of England, *and* excludes the monarch from membership of the Roman Catholic Church. If the two churches were ecumenically united, then either the British Monarchy would effectively be abolished, or the constitution would have to be changed, to separate church and state. The political consequences of the ecumenical movement are, therefore, obvious, and devastating for either the Monarchy, the myth, or both. There are, therefore, three main considerations which together undermine the religious myth. Above all it is patently pretentious and implausible in a religiously plural and really largely agnostic or atheist society. It creates constitutional problems which cannot be solved except by abolishing the Monarchy or separating the state from religion. Finally, it infringes the personal liberties of monarchs themselves immediately as to the kind of religion they may subscribe to. More generally it prevents them from rejecting religion altogether.

CHAPTER 24 PSYCHOLOGY

Modern psychology of the unconscious furnishes the third profound myth of monarchy – the psychology myth. According to the view advanced originally by Freud's biographer, Ernest Jones, human nature is inevitably fraught with two incompatible but equally basic tendencies.[1] One is the expressive tendency, which is thwarted by restraints. The other is a restricting tendency, which is reflected in a desire to be ruled. These tendencies are obvious in early stages of human psychological development. In maturity they may persist, but are largely unconscious.

In childhood, people relate to their parents in both ways: they tend to express affection for parents, but also to resist and resent parental restraint, especially fathers'. Growing up involves replacing childish resentment of, but dependence on, the constraints of parents, with self reliance and a voluntary relationship of autonomy and equality with parents. These facts of development are said to have relevance to political life, because parental authority in childhood and governmental authority in adulthood are analogous. This is apparent in two ways: first, it is common for adults irrationally to attribute to governments exaggerated powers for good or evil, just as children exaggerate the power and influence of parents. Second, political experience has shown that the development of independence of persons from their parents needs to be parallelled by a similar process of development of the governed from government.

According to this view, constitutional monarchy has profound psychological importance, because it is an institutional device which meets the need of the governed to develop independence from government in a way that reconciles the need for restraint and security with the need for expression of resentment at restraint. Security is achieved by attaching allegiance to the unpolitical figure of the constitutional monarch as head of state. The expression of resentment against restraint is achieved by attributing the restraints of authority to the head of government, the prime minister, who can be disposed of appropriately through the ballot box. Disposal of the head of government can be given a more precise psycho-analytic intepretation by the theory of the Oedipus complex, according to which authority is identified with the fathers people wish to destroy. The Monarchy is an indispensable component in the constitution, therefore, because it satisfies a deep, unconscious, psychological need in people to have the security of established authority, while at the same time enjoying the liberty to reject its restraints when they become intolerable. That is the psychology myth.

Consider first its internal coherence. Jones writes: 'No psycho-analyst would hesitate, on coming across the person of a ruler in a dream, to translate "ruler" as "father", and he would at once be interested in the way in which the subject's conscious attitude towards the ruler was being influenced by his underlying attitudes to his father.'[2] Not only feminists will object to this inference, although the first thing to notice is that the gender of the monarch is of paramount importance. This is doubly true for Freudian interpretations, which attach so much importance to sexual aspects of symbolism. Even if kings take on a paternal role for some people, there is no reason to suppose that queens do as well, or in the same way, or for the same people, or for the same reasons. Apart from gender and sex, there is also the age of the head of state to be considered. A very young monarch cannot plausibly be regarded as a father figure for most of the population. Queen Elizabeth II was aged twenty-three at her accession in 1952, when the prime minister Winston Churchill was seventy-eight years old. It is just absurd to suggest that, if anyone, it was the Queen who was regarded by the nation as a 'father figure'.

Again, it is not the case for everyone that heads of government can be removed as a means of satisfying an unconscious need to express resentment at restraints. Tens of millions of people are frequently in a position where they cannot remove an undesired government, because the ballot box accounts only for the aggregate of the nation's wishes in the matter. This is only one crucial defect in the suggested analogy between individual personal psychology and supposed 'group psychology'. There is no reason to suppose a group psychology in such matters at all.

The main disanalogy between individuals and groups is that there is no relevant parallel between the development of self sufficiency of individuals in relation to parents, and of peoples to governments. Self sufficiency is self sufficiency, and is presupposed by the democratic process. In a democracy the relation between government and governed is like the relation between mature, grown up people and their peers, because it is, in fact, a reflection and extension of that relationship. It is merely to pervert analogies to suppose that mature individuals revert to infantile and puerile dependence in their relationship to government.

The Oedipal complex is badly named by Freud, because in the original myth Oedipus copulated with his mother and killed his father without knowing who they were. Freudian theory inverts the classic relation. People know who their parents are, but the desires for copulation and murder are unconscious. The Oedipus complex so-called is, therefore, not a good model for authority relations anyway, but it is especially inappropriate for the relations between female subjects and their king, and male subjects and their queen. No doubt it is *decorum* which prevents apologists for monarchy, who are influenced by Freud, from drawing sexual inferences from the Queen's apparently wide popularity among her male subjects.

We might well ask more generally why people who provide a psychological, and especially a Freudian psycho-analytical basis for monarchy, are so selective about the aspects of theory they deploy. Why, for example, isn't more use made of the supposed relevance of dreams? Even 'positive' dreams about monarchy can be given negative interpretations. By Freud's theory, dreams are a mode of wish fulfilment. Many dreams about royalty may merely satisfy an unhealthy wish for power and celebrity. Other dreams may express a wish that monarchy be diminished or humiliated. One reported dream showed the Monarchy to be in a bad way, reduced to a modest hotel in Kensington. Another had parliament turn Buckingham Palace into a rooming house, with the queen serving *espresso* coffee from a machine, and wearing stained and tattered coronation robes. In a third, the Queen Mother lost her passport, and was obliged to stay in quarantine in a kennel along with dogs.[3] Are we to accept Freud's theory of dreams as wish fulfilment, and to take such dreams as evidence for subliminal republicanism? If not, why not? Perhaps we do not, because people agree with William Archer, who complained that: 'Freud allows himself such licence of interpretation, that he could extract a more or less objectionable meaning from the Lord's Prayer, or "Twinkle, twinkle, little star".'[4]

Freudian theory is only one among numerous competing theories of the unconscious. It is, therefore, even more arbitrary to appeal to Freud, than it is, having chosen him, to select his Oedipus complex, in order to vindicate the Monarchy. Alfred Adler, for example, disagreed with Freud fundamentally, and their differences were precisely relevant to understanding people's attitudes to authority. Heinz Ansbacher has suggested that Freud's theories reflect the fact that he himself was a first-born; that he was his mother's favourite; and that he was conscious of his social status. He had a deep sense of the unworthiness of human beings (even of analysts). According to Ansbacher, these attitudes explain why Freud assumed that people were in need of constant control by some higher authority. In contrast, Adler's theories reflect the fact that he was a later-born. Adler rejected the 'firstborn' notion of the Oedipus complex because of its excessive emphasis of parent-child relations. He investigated instead sibling-sibling interaction, and thought of his patients as victims of their struggle for greater power. Unlike Freud, he believed that people are basically worthy, and he supposed that neurosis could be cured by the promotion of egalitarian attitudes and social awareness.[5] Adlerian psycho-analytic theory thus suggests that monarchy is a constant source of frustration to people who are not firstborn: that is, most of the population. That would explain why republicanism has eventually prevailed in most political societies. Britain, by this account, suffers uniquely from a form of corporate first born retarded adolescence; manifested in its apparently obsessive attachment to monarchy. The fact is that attempts to support monarchy by appeal to psycho-analytic theory are problematical, to say the least. No serious store can be placed in them.

The most basic problem with the psychology myth is that it presumes that psycho-analytic theories of unconscious motivation are sound enough to provide reliable explanations, whereas notoriously it has proved to be difficult, not to say impossible, to establish an adequate *rationale* and justification for classic psycho-analysis, even as it applies to individuals. First of all, the extension of abnormal individual psychology to normal individuals is problematic.

Richard Peters has forcefully argued that Freud himself proposed only that his theories explained behaviour so abnormal that no ordinary explanation was available, or anyway plausible.[6] In the case of the Monarchy, there are so many plausible explanations for its existence and apparent popularity, that it is totally unnecessary to resort to precarious speculation about the unconscious to account for it. Conquest, coercion, cultivated ignorance, and relentless propaganda, for example, are powerful forces that Freud does not concern himself with at all. None are to do with the unconscious processes of individuals' minds. If the extension of abnormal individual psychology to normal individuals is problematic, then the further extension to entire populations has no basis in logic whatsoever.

Not only the scope of psycho-analysis is questionable. Many

authorities on scientific method, such as Karl Popper and Peter Medawar, deny that it can provide legitimate explanations at all.[7] The reason for this is not that the processes supposed to explain things are unconscious, and so unobservable (it is commonplace for scientists to deal with unobservables). The fatal flaw in psycho-analysis is that the actual processes supposed to explain things are speculative constructions by analysts which cannot be tested, and so potentially falsified and eliminated. There is no way of choosing between different, even opposed, but equally coherent and equally plausible explanations of the same phenomena, because no evidence could count against them. Such explanations can explain nothing, because they rule out nothing. As Karl Popper says: 'the criterion for the scientific status of a theory is its falsifiability or refutability or testability ... [no substantially stronger claim to scientific status can be made for] Freud's epic of the *Ego*, the *Superego*, and the *Id* ... than for Homer's collected stories from Olympus. These theories describe some facts, but in the manner of myths. They contain most interesting psychological suggestions, but not in any testable form.'[8] The basic credentials of psycho-analysis are suspect.

When all is said and done, the psychology myth is simply preposterous, because it requires us to believe that, in political matters, British grown-ups are not really grown up at all. They supposedly suffer from deep Freudian psycho-pathological disturbance. However, British people are at least as grown up and uncomplicated as people of any other nationality. If they are not, then the Monarchy is the most likely cause of such a highly abnormal state of affairs. Most other nations manage perfectly well without a monarchy, and there is no evidence whatsoever that the political psychology of British people is inherently different from others, except perhaps as a result of insidious propaganda, which can be changed or stopped.

CHAPTER 25 SUMMARY AND CONCLUSIONS: MYTHS

At the outset the 'official' picture of the British Monarchy was out-lined. Its main components are the beliefs that: it is a symbol of national unity; it sets exemplary standards of morality; it is impartial and unpolitical; and it is a safeguard against despotism.

The belief in one nation is a myth, because Britain is an acutely divided caste-hierarchical society. There are two nations, the haves and the have-nots. Perniciously, the Monarchy serves to delude the have-nots about the real nature of their position, and is a potent factor in promoting acceptance of it.

The belief that the Monarchy exemplifies high moral standards is a myth because, in general, the arbitrary caste-privilege it exemplifies and sustains is inherently inequitable, unjust, and severely detrimental to the interests of most people. In avariciousness, in particular, the Monarchy sets a very bad example which is all too easily followed by members of the privileged castes.

The belief that the Monarchy is impartial, and above political faction, is a myth, because it is perpetually, and by heredity, wedded to the interest of high caste privilege. It is absurd to suppose that hereditary millionaires with direct access to influence and power, will not resist political measures to promote social equity which is against their personal and private interests. As the Prince Consort has said, such measures would not receive the full support of the privileged, who might even 'fight back'.

The belief that the Monarchy is a safeguard against despotism is a myth, because its natural allegiance is to the privileged and powerful castes. Despots of the Right more than likely look to the Crown, as head of the Armed Services and agent of emergency powers, as the focus of a government of 'national unity'. This myth is pernicious because it deludes people about the real possibility of despotism of the Right, with no corresponding possibility on the Left.

The official view of the Monarchy is thus really a myth, or rather a cluster of myths. The effect is pernicious to the life of the nation, and demonstrates a profound lack of an appropriate sense of moral priorities.

The myth is sustained by a number of popular beliefs about the Monarchy, which are either irrelevant, or more or less untrue. These are the petty myths of monarchy: belief in its popularity, hard work, utility, tradition, morality, internationalism, wisdom, impartiality, powerlessness, and guardianship. The myth is thought to be justified also by a number of supposedly weighty beliefs which are quite groundless, or at any rate indecisive. These are the profound myths of monarchy: its mythic function; its religious significance; and its psychological function. The few plausible reasons for maintaining the Monarchy turn out to provide no good reason for it that would not apply as well to other constitutional alternatives.

There is neither rhyme nor reason to the British Monarchy. But it does have definite and detrimental effects. It deludes people about the real nature of society, and their real position in it. It sets bad moral examples. It encourages fantastic and dangerous delusions about Britain and its place in the world. It sustains an archaic cultural climate in which caste, deference, and humbug prevail over equity, self respect, and honesty in public life. Belief in the value of the British Monarchy, therefore, may be classified along with those irrational beliefs that are harmful but avoidable.

Popular and 'profound' beliefs about the Monarchy prove to be both groundless and pernicious. The question therefore naturally arises as to whether there is any justification for it at the level of principle.

PART V: THE MONARCHY AND DEMOCRACY

It will be instructive at this point to recall some of the main ideas and events in the evolution of the British constitution. Before the Norman conquest, kingship was elective, and had a mundane basis in local communities, utility and the common law. William the Conqueror and his successors attempted to impose an absolute monarchic authority that was rejected once and for all by *Magna Carta* (1215). *Magna Carta* puts English political society on a legal, not a regal basis, and secures the rights of property owners against the Monarchy. The concept of absolute monarchical authority was re-invented by James I and developed by Filmer, this time on the religious basis of divine right. As James I put it in an address to parliament: 'Kings are justly called gods, because they exercise a manner of resemblance to divine power on earth ... They have power to exalt low things, and abase high things, and to make of their subjects like men at chess.' [1]

The civil war, which established the first republic of the modern era in England, was therefore a reassertion of the principles of *Magna Carta* against divine right absolutism. Its leading philosopher (or apologist), John Locke, argued that all men with powers of reason and self direction have equal rights to determine their own destinies. But Locke notably excluded the mass of property-less individuals, because he believed that poverty amounted to the same thing as ignorance, indolence, and possibly moral turpitude. In this he was merely following the doctrines set out in *Ecclesiasticus*, where it is asked:

> How can he get wisdom that holdeth the plough, that driveth oxen, and is occupied in their labours, and whose talk is of bullocks?. [2]

Burke's *Reflections on the Revolution in France* gained great favour with George III, by reiterating similar views:

> The occupation of a hair dresser, or of a working tallow chandler, cannot be a matter of honour to any person, and if such description of men are permitted to rule, the state suffers oppression. [3]

The progress from feudalism to modern political democracy and universal adult franchise can thus be seen as the progressive rejection of the idea that social status, occupation, and wealth, are necessary requisites for full personal recognition, for participation in political society, and for entitlement to the various rights that that entails.

Students of philosophy will recognise here the essence of morality as defined by Kant: that is, to treat human individuals as ends in themselves. Every advance in human liberty and welfare in Britain, as elsewhere, has gone with a practical recognition that human individuals are people, and that people, as such, have a right to respect, and to determine their own affairs. It is almost universally accepted now that the interests of people are best served by democratic societies; that is, societies governed by the members themselves, for their own benefit, as they themselves conceive it.

Even in Britain, most conservatives who value social hierarchy pay public obeisance to democracy, which they suppose to be compatible with hierarchy. If not ideally good, democracy is accepted as anyway the least bad political system. Democratic principles thus provide appropriate criteria for a more systematic examination of the British Monarchy, which can be assessed by the ideal standards of liberty, equality and justice, and fraternity.

CHAPTER 27   LIBERTY: THE IDEAL

Liberty is the first, and, many people believe, the most important democratic ideal. Britons pride themselves in their liberties. Many people think that the Monarchy is the best guarantee against despotism, of the political Right or Left. The reality falls far short of the mythology in this, as in so much else. We are surely concerned here with real freedom, not abstract, or merely formal freedom. We are not, for example, concerned with the metaphysical freedom of the Stoics. Stoicism is the view that you can be free from the need for shoes by cutting off your feet. Conservatives advocate this view of freedom. It is the counsel of accepting one's lot, stoically.[1] This is advocated even when the institutions and practices in question may be rationally and morally unjustifiable, heinous even. As Lord Hailsham put it: 'Conservatives ... believe, in the main, in the acceptance of established authority *wherever* it is found, without enquiring too closely into its documents of title. They cannot profess to justify this principle by any abstract argument of reason, but every practical advantage is on their side.'[2] We do well to ask whose advantage is served by this autocratic practice. We need not speculate idly about where the Monarchy stands. The Prince of Wales unburdened himself of the following (politically neutral) views in 1975:

> Everyone must obey the state authorities, for no authority exists without God's permission, and the existing authorities have been put there by God. Whoever opposes the existing authority, opposes what God has ordered, and anyone who does so, will bring judgment upon himself.[3]

The King is out to polo, the poor man stands stoically at the gate. This picture is, of course, the *epitome* of moral turpitude and a denial of democratic freedom. Real freedom is the positive exercise of human autonomy, not the *lumpen* acceptance of whatever arbitrary authority claims.

But we have come too far too fast; we must consider what 'liberty' means. 'Liberty' must signify the liberty of some individual(s) to do something, without constraint. So we have three things to consider. First is the question of who is free: of how freedom is distributed. Freedom for the pike is death for the minnow. And just as a nation is

143

not religious because it has a few devout citizens, so a nation is not free because a few persons enjoy liberty in it. The question of whether Britain is a free country, and how far the Monarchy is consistent with or permits freedom can only be answered in the light of the other conditions for freedom.

The power to *do* something means having the capacity and re-sources to do it. A notional freedom to employ a personal physician is not real freedom, if you can't pay. Prince Henri, Count of Paris, and pretender to the French throne, grasped this point firmly. He said that:

> one is free when one can act; and as power in the real world comes from money, one is not free when one has none.[4]

Of course, some differences in real power are natural, warranted, or unavoidable; but not all. Lack of power may be, and frequently is, a consequence of arbitrary and unjustifiable social factors that can and should be changed. This is the sort of power and powerlessness pertinent to the question at issue here. The distribution of freedom in Britain will accordingly correspond roughly with the distribution of powers to do as one wishes, notably economic power. But now it is perfectly clear that there is a staggering maldistribution of freedom in Britain, because of the arbitrary distribution of wealth. One figure alone is edifying. The Royal Commission of Inquiry into the Distribution of Wealth and Income reported in 1976, that in Scotland in 1974, the richest 5 per cent of the population owned 65 per cent of the wealth, and the poorest 80 per cent just 4.5 per cent. If freedom is the power to act, the the Duke of Buccleuch enjoys at least forty times more freedom than most of his countrymen, and two hundred and fifty times more freedom than the poorest. To the extent that the Monarchy symbolises, exemplifies, and perpetuates the social and economic divisions that exist in Britain, then it is an obstacle to greater freedom for most people.

Finally, there is the question of what we must be free of or from if we are to be really free. This, in truth, is the most interesting question with regard to the Monarchy. There are those who believe that the Monarchy best secures us freedom from coercive military tyranny of the sort that Spain, for example, has suffered. There may be an element of truth in this; although (as we have seen) there is no reason to be confident that the British Monarchy is especially unsympathetic to the Right, or is sympathetic to the Left. But military tyranny is only one sort of constraint. There are other, covert, forms of repression.

As Isaiah Berlin has pointed out: 'The triumph of despotism is to force the slaves to declare themselves to be free. It may need no force: the slaves may proclaim their freedom quite sincerely: but they are none the less slaves.'[5] Mill tells how the British Monarchy is the chief instrument of the repression of the British people when he explains how individuals may be crushed by the weight of custom.[6] The British Monarchy is the central symbol of a social system which is in reality coercive, notwithstanding the popular mythology. This is coercion by the mass hypnosis of custom and organised propaganda: in education[7]; in the media, especially television[8]; by the church and by all major political parties[9].

Some people may be outraged by this suggestion. But those who know the history of the British Monarchy will find that this is not only true, but has long been proclaimed to be an indispensable, if not positively desirable, feature of British social and political life. The definitive statement of it is in Bagehot's classic work on the English constitution, which therefore deserves our close attention. Bagehot writes:

> ... Cabinet government ... is only possible in deferential nations ... [that is] nations in which the numerous unwiser part wishes to be ruled by [an] *élite*. England is the type of deferential countries, and the manner in which it is so ... is extremely curious ... [for] when you see the select few, you perceive that ... they are ... the last people to whom, if they were drawn up in a row, an immense nation would ever give an exclusive preference ...

> In fact, the mass of the English people yield a deference rather to something else than to their rulers. They defer to what we may call the theatrical show of society. A certain state passes before them; a certain pomp of great men; a certain spectacle of beautiful women; a wonderful scene of wealth and enjoyment is displayed, and they are coerced by it ... The climax of the play is the Queen ... Philosophers may deride this superstition, but its results are estimable. By the spectacle of this august society, countless ignorant men and women are induced to obey the few nominal electors ... What impresses men is not mind, but the result of mind. And the greatest of these results is the wonderful spectacle of society.

> The apparent rulers of the English nation are like the most imposing personages of a splendid procession: it is by them the mob are influenced; it is they whom the spectators cheer. The real rulers are secreted in second rate carriages; no one cares for them, or asks about them, but they are obeyed implicitly and unconsciously by reason of the splendour of those who eclipsed and preceded them ...

It cannot be said that the mass of the English people are well off. There are whole classes who have not a conception of what the higher orders call comfort ... who cannot lead the life that becomes a man. But the most miserable of those classes do not impute their misery to politics ... these miserable creatures would say that ... for all they have heard, "the Queen is very good". And rebelling against the structure of society is, to their minds, rebelling against the Queen.[10]

Kingsley Martin thought that organised deception of this sort was a thing of the past,[11] but who can read Bagehot today, and contemplate the incessant preoccupation of the media with the royal family and its doings, without realising that nothing has changed at all, except the names and the potency of the media through which the propaganda is orchestrated?

Every conceivable opportunity is seized to mount the royal *charades*: anniversaries, birthdays, official birthdays, jubilees, official openings, weddings, christenings, funerals, sporting events, theatrical occasions, garden parties, banquets, holidays, illnesses, recoveries, strolls, and on and on. Every commonplace royal virtue is glorified, and every mundane action is magnified. On the other hand, royal shortcomings, vices, and misdeeds are censored by the self imposed ordinance of the media themselves (especially the press) in the name of good taste and patriotism. Popular criticism, where it is allowed at all, is merely cosmetic. Serious republican dissent hardly exists. Willie Hamilton is unique, but he is suffered only as a licensed jester, and even then at the cost of his political career.

Only a full and systematic sociological inquiry would reveal the extent and influence of monarchist propaganda and censorship; but there is strong enough evidence already, both *prima facie* and from research, to demonstrate that attitudes to the Monarchy, and thereby to the legitimacy of the present social structure in Britain, are substantially influenced by organised propaganda that saturates our national life,[12] and as Bagehot recognised, coerces British people into accepting social, economic, and political constraints on their personal freedoms. The Monarchy is, therefore, a substantial obstacle to more real freedom for most Britons, both because it exemplifies and sustains gross maldistribution of social status and economic power, and because it is the main instrument of coercive constraint by organised propaganda.

CHAPTER 28 EQUALITY

The second great democratic ideal is equality, and closely related to it is justice. It is futile to dispute whether men are equal; as a plain matter of fact, they are not. There are other issues worth discussing at another time. But the central issue is very simple: whether men are due equal respect and consideration. Colonel Rainborough, the Leveller, put it with stark simplicity, as follows: 'the poorest he that is in England hath a life to live as the greatest he.'[1] The appropriate relation of persons one to another is in this important sense egalitarian, and this relation determines practical institutional relations necessary for people to flourish.

Egalitarian practice depends on a distinction between basic personal needs (such as life, health, and personal development), and personal indulgences (such as expensive recreations, like polo) and dispensable protocol privilege (like executive toilets). An egalitarian community, therefore, will be one in which, first, the members will have an appropriate attitude of respect for one another by virtue of their status as persons, and second, institutional arrangements ensure that the basic needs of each and every member are prior to the personal indulgences of any member. So, what of the Monarchy and equality?

First, the question of attitude. There are some people (such as Simon Raven) who positively want to look down on others, and to have others look down on them:[2] for moral defectives such as these, the Monarchy is the ideal institution. But a (democratic) nation's constitution should not be designed to reflect and satisfy the perverse yearnings of moral defectives. Monarchy on the grand and sanctified scale that exists in Britain is utterly inegalitarian. Such pseudo-respect as exists between British monarchs and British people is comprised of highness and condescension on one side, and lowliness and deference on the other. If we were in doubt, Peregrine Worsthorne reminds us that 'The essential function of royalty involves being set apart from and above the rest of mankind.'[3] The British Monarchy, therefore, is an institution, less egalitarian than which, none is conceivable.

There is nothing so inconceivable, however, that someone cannot be found who will testify to being able to conceive it. Worsthorne himself achieves the very considerable feat of convincing himself that

the British Monarchy is, and always was, a most egalitarian institution. The reason is that 'The democracy ... approaches the monarchy from a posture of subjection.'[4] This perverse looking-glass view
presupposes that, in a democracy, legitimate democratic authority is
in need of subjection. It is not. It also overlooks the plain fact that
hereditary monarchs are only human too, and have no rational or
moral sanction for their inherited status. There is no reason to believe
that monarchy promotes egalitarian attitudes.

There is even less reason to believe that, as an institution, it
promotes the satisfaction of the basic needs of all people, before the
personal indulgences of a minority. The Monarchy itself epitomises
conspicuous consumption and personal indulgence on a grand scale,
while millions of compatriots lack the wherewithal to meet basic
needs. Cynical shows of piety and cosmetic charity do not alter the
simple and sometimes terrible truth. Gross inequality in the distribution of personal welfare among compatriots, such as has been (repeatedly) referred to, has only to be stated to be seen to be unjust as
well as inegalitarian.

Egalitarians are often accused of envy, and something needs to be
said about this. Envy is indeed evil, if it means begrudging others
what is unavoidably or rightfully theirs. But language and reason are
abused when everything begrudged is thought to be a matter of envy.
There is such a thing as righteous indignation that goes with begrudging others what they have because their having it is unjustifiable and
avoidable. Righteous indignation is a proper rational and moral response to the unjustifiable privilege of personal indulgence enjoyed by
a minority, when the basic needs of others are not satisfied. Egalitarian criticism of the Monarchy and, more important, the social system
it represents is not based on envy, but on righteous indignation.

This elementary truth has been doubted. One of the most implausible arguments ever committed to print is that capricious social inequalities are more bearable to those who suffer by them, than inequalities
based on merit and desert.[5] If this were true, then the Monarchy is all
the more bearable because the Windsor family is unmeritorious and
undeserving. But it is not true.

People just do not commonly envy and resent others whose advantages are natural or merited. Most people are not so mean spirited. It
is transparently obvious, on the other hand, that unmerited and
unjustifiable privilege is deeply resented. H.G. Wells expressed such
profound indignation, as follows:

For my own part, I heard too much of the dear Queen altogether. I conceived a jealous hatred for the magnificent housing, and all the freedom, of her children and, still more intensely, of my contemporaries, her grandchildren ... various desperate and fatiguing expeditions ... deepened my hostility and wove a stout, ineradicable thread of republicanism into my resentful nature. [6]

Nothing less than an orchestrated programme of propaganda and indoctrination, could subvert natural and healthy indignation of the sort expressed here. That is why it is both fatuous and wrong to dismiss righteous indignation as mere envy. The moral onus is upon those who give cause for indignation, to eradicate the inequity, not upon those who suffer by it. Moreover, people cannot be expected to be committed wholeheartedly to community with others, when they feel relations between them are inequitable, unjust, and unfair.

CHAPTER 29 JUSTICE

We may now turn to the question of justice. Justice is a concept that has proven notoriously difficult to define. This is because there are at least three different ideal standards of justice: rights, deserts, and needs.[1] Whichever of these standards of justice we choose, however, the Monarchy fails the test.

First consider rights. The Monarchy can claim some sort of 'right by conquest'. This provides no rational or moral justification at all, however. Or it might be said that the Monarchy has a contractual right, derived from parliament, and the Revolution Settlement of 1689. This is true, but again entirely begs the question of rational or moral justification. (Was the Revolution Settlement a reasonable and good thing?) We find that there is no justice in right in the Monarchy, and therefore slim hope of it promoting justice.

Next consider deserts. Nobody seriously believes that hereditary royal families are inherently deserving of great privilege. Conceivably some freak of genetics might have produced a royal superspecies, but there is no evidence at all for this. The circumstantial evidence on the Hanover-Windsor family supports the opposite conclusion. Far from deserving its position, monarchy tends naturally to promote the opposite: that is, provides a disincentive to the proper recognition of just desert.

David Hume is an unlikely source of argument against traditional institutions, but against monarchy he argued that 'valuable and deserving activities are likely to decay because they are less honourable. In a monarchy, birth, titles, and place must be honoured above industry, and while these notions prevail, people will be tempted to pursue employments to which privileges and honours are annexed.'[2] Hume thus diagnoses and explains 'the British disease'.[3] These things are attributed to the cultural ethos surrounding and generated by the Monarchy. So there is no justice in desert in the Monarchy either.

It goes without saying that there is no justice in the Monarchy based on the needs of royalty. But there may be justice based on the needs of others. John Rawls' theory of justice as fairness, would show us whether there is.[4] Now it seems unlikely that monarchy could be a fair institution. But Rawls' theory provides interesting reasons for looking further into this. He suggests that we can best reach a clear

150

idea of justice, if we consider what all men might agree was the best (fairest) basis for organising society, if they were free of personal bias. His procedure is to suppose that everyone is put in an 'original position', where everyone has full knowledge of human nature and society, but no knowledge of their own position in it. This is hidden behind a 'veil of ignorance' to be removed only after the general principles of social organisation have been agreed. And in this original position, rational and reasonably prudent people presumably would not agree to social arrangements which might be unfair, and seriously disadvantage themselves in reality, once this is revealed.

Rawls plausibly argues that from this position, two principles of justice would emerge. The first concerns maximum individual liberty; the second is that inequalities in the distribution of various social and material goods are permissible provided 'that the inequalities result in compensating benefits for everyone, and in particular the worst-off members of society'. Taking this view, monarchy, even on the grand and sanctified scale of the British Monarchy, could be a just institution. Thus it might be argued (i) that the Monarchy is the only guarantee against tyranny, or (ii) that it provides an indispensable focus for feelings of belonging to a community for many people whose lives would be meaningless deserts without it. And if the institution can be justified in this way, then other things follow. The extravagant grandeur of the Monarchy may be necessary for maintaining its special status in the eyes of the masses, as Bagehot argued. The inequalities of hereditary royal privilege may be the minimum price necessary to persuade mere pecuniary mortals to accept a life as living icons. And so on ... Well, do arguments of this sort, from need, carry any weight?

The mere fact that Britain is the last monarchy on the planet, on the grand imperial scale, ought to persuade everyone but the most irredeemable chauvinists that monarchy isn't the only safeguard against tyranny. In particular, the once revolutionary republican states of France and the United States have at least as much claim to stability as the United Kingdom. In fact most other nations manage very well without the supposedly indispensable need for monarchy. There is in Britain a certain precious, and impertinent condescension towards 'municipal' societies without royal pomp and majesty, and the heady but opaque vapours of mystical and religious pretensions.[5] But these are no more than cosmetic matters of personal taste and style, with no serious bearing on the rational and moral justification of political constitutions.

The Monarchy, it seems, is not indispensable to the general welfare, and so there is no special justice or fairness in it. We thus have no need to consider further any secondary questions about the justice or fairness of specific practices. Rawls' analysis does show the fundamental *un*-fairness of the Monarchy. It was argued earlier that the Monarchy legitimises an inequitable social system, and that it deludes people about the real nature of their society. Now consider these things as options in Rawls' original position. Would rational and reasonably prudent people knowingly opt for a system which systematically denies them equity and the satisfaction of basic needs; and which, moreover, deludes them about this very fact by means of organised deception — even goes so far as to persuade them to proclaim that they are free and devoted to the system which does all this? Surely not. So there is no justice as fairness in the Monarchy.

CHAPTER *30* FRATERNITY

Fraternity is the third, last, and least discussed of the great democratic ideals. And yet it is the most important of all. We may not go so far as William Morris, who believed that 'Fellowship is life: lack of fellowship is death',[1] but it is difficult to secure the moral (as opposed to prudential) foundations of liberty and equality anywhere else but in the fellowship or fraternity between people. Equality and fraternity have common roots in Christian teaching. We are told in *Galatians*, for example, that 'we are all children of God by faith in Jesus Christ.'[2] Similar roots may be located in biology and social anthropology, where Kropotkin found them; and in moral psychology, where Butler and Hume found them. Butler thought that love of one's neighbour includes all that is good and worthy.[3] Certainly it follows as a matter of logic as well as sentiment from 'fellow-feeling' that we acknowledge the autonomy of others, as equal to ourselves, when we see ourselves in others. It is for this reason that fraternity is the proper foundation of democracy, and of liberty and equality, not their goal. For, without fraternity, such freedom and equality as might be legislated for will be crabbed and insecure things. As Halsey says: 'The priority of fraternity is that it is the principle that defines the group within which certain social values are to be applied. These values are essentially those of recognising a common humanity; quintessentially they consist for each individual in recognising the value of life for the other, and the common fate of death for all.'[4] The subjective feeling of fraternity is brotherhood; the objective behaviour is altruism. Exemplary fraternal practice is voluntary blood donorship, through which fraternal relations are literally and symbolically affirmed.[5]

So, what of the Monarchy and fraternity? To be clearer it will help to draw some distinctions. First, we can identify the feelings and attitudes of fraternity, and also the behaviour and institutions that follow from them. Second, we should distinguish between fraternity and pseudo-fraternity. Thirdly, we should distinguish between personal and institutional fraternity.

So far as attitudes are concerned, monarchy is inimical to fraternity, because nobility is having someone to look down upon; because the very essence of monarchy is majesty or highness,[6], which necessarily entails the opposite for others: baseness and lowness, and because the essence and function of royalty involve being set apart from and above the rest of mankind.[7] Being set apart from and above mankind is the opposite of fraternity. It is wholly unsurprising that in reality the British royal family is breathtakingly ignorant about the lives of most British people, because they are intent on preserving the necessary illusion that 'divinity doth hedge a king'.[8] Reference has already been made to examples of this in practice.

In this travesty of fellowship the Monarchy may well be as much victim of the social structure as its subjects. Nevertheless the fact remains that a society constituted to propagate notions of royal majesty, will almost inevitably be rigidly hierarchical. Its institutions will be chronically class ridden and obsessively status conscious. Citizens, if they are content, will be deferential, not fraternal. This is what we have in Britain.

There is, of course, amongst the propaganda, a great deal of rhetoric about fraternity.[9] Talk is cheap, and creates the right impression. Royal manifestations such as pious speeches about caring and common interests, public appearances, and charitable 'patronage' are the stuff of pseudo-fraternity in an unjust and inequitable society, even if royal persons deceive themselves and believe in it all implicitly. There is, in particular, a great deal of talk about 'the national interest', but there is really no such thing. We assume that the country is the joint possession of all the people, whereas actually the mass of people own no part of it. Organised deception through the orchestrated rhetoric of fraternity succeeds in producing only pseudo-fraternity. The havenots are deluded into thinking that they enjoy fellowship with the haves. The Monarchy is the chief instrument of this disastrous deception.

This is an appropriate point at which to return briefly to the question of justice. It was mentioned earlier that there are three ideal standards of justice: namely, rights, deserts, and needs. These standards may conflict in practice. Thus it may be harmful and wrong to deny someone their legitimate rights. It may also be harmful and wrong to deny someone their just deserts. Again, it may be harmful and wrong to deny someone their basic needs. Given limited resources, a just distribution may differ crucially according to the standard of justice applied. Someone may have a legal right or entitlement to scarce resources. Someone else may deserve the resources, by virtue of worth and effort. Again, someone else may need the resource. In a fraternal society the conflict would be resolved by the criterion of need. Legal rights and just deserts would be waived to meet the basic needs of fellows. In Britain, we find that basic needs of our compatriots are *not* met, because limited goods and resources are distributed without due regard to need. The Monarchy exemplifies, sustains and legitimises this unfraternal system. The pseudo-fraternity, focussed on the Monarchy, that surrounds us on all sides, merely serves to hide this fact.

Many people, of course, reject fraternity. There is a special sort of English frostiness about fraternity. James Stephen typically expressed the view that 'It is not love that one wants from the great mass of mankind, but respect and justice.'[10] Fraternity as a social ideal he rejects because he thinks it is unrealistic; because it fails to account for the ordinary worldly man who doesn't give a tinker's curse for fraternity. This is the sort of ordinary man who prefers to spend his money on holidays and his children's bicycles, rather than on relieving poverty or on medical treatment for needy compatriots. Here are fascinating and important issues that cannot be dealt with fully, but something should be said. Stephen made a very revealing remark to his brother at the astonishing age of four, on the subject of caring for others. He said 'You should keep your love locked up as I do.'[11] What emotional pathology is revealed here in the unfraternal mind, and what pathology of early experience and education? Psychologists tell us how vitally important such things are. One wonders what might be achieved for the nurture of fraternal attitudes, and the promotion of fraternal institutions based on them, if the *same* orchestrated efforts and influences were brought to bear in that worthy direction as are now dissipated on the monarchic fantasies which sustain coercive traditional hierarchies of caste, class, status, and privilege.

Another way with supposedly realistic criticism of fraternity is to be *really* realistic. Some ordinary worldly men do indeed neglect their fellows with practical indifference to their deprivations and suffering. In the real world there are other ordinary worldly men, notably those whose basic needs and interests are being neglected, who respond to injustice, inequality, and indifference with feelings of resentment and violent action. It is natural that they do so. The evidence of Northern Ireland, Palestine, Poland, Toxteth, and all the rest, is utterly conclusive. Margaret Simey was absolutely right, also, when she opined that there was nothing wrong with the people of Toxteth who rioted in the summer of 1981, but that there would have been something wrong if, in the circumstances, they had not rioted.[12]

Thus, apart from fatalistic resignation, there are, in general, two real, practical, alternatives to unfraternal attitudes and institutions, of which the Monarchy is the chief one. People can acquire fraternal attitudes through upbringing, education, and other social and cultural influences. There would be no place for monarchy if this happened. Alternatively, the true nature of unjust, inequitable, and unfraternal institutions may be just cause for righteous indignation, and rejection of those institutions.[13]

It may be that the Monarchy could be justified if it contributed to the general welfare by being more efficient than other alternatives. There are three main ways in which this has been thought to be so: by the effective division of authority; by conservation; and by convenience.

Dignified and Efficient Branches of Government

Walter Bagehot distinguished two different sorts of political institution, or parts of a constitution. There are *efficient* parts which do the work, and rule. There are also *dignified* parts which preserve and promote the allegiance of all classes of society to the established authority.[1] The same distinction is drawn by de Jouvenel who refers to the authority that fosters cooperation and stability as '*Rex*' and the authority that promotes and leads activity as '*Dux*'.[2] The distinction between political functions goes with the supposed psychological function performed by constitutional monarchy. That is to say, public feeling and resentment, which will inevitably be stirred by the active or efficient part of government, needs to be contained without irreparably damaging or altogether destroying the social fabric. The domain of the *Dux* is precisely the domain of party faction, conflict, and resentment caused in reaction to political activity. The efficient part of government is, therefore, incapable of containing the divisions it inevitably creates and exacerbates. The *Rex* functions institutionally to provide a (metaphorical) 'lightning conductor' for strife and to promote the mutual commitment of political antagonists to the social commonweal. The Monarchy serves the *Rex* function by being above politics, and by representing the people as a whole.

The need for a division of authority into *Rex* and *Dux* is most plausible when there is a large politically unsophisticated population, incapable of comprehending and effectively participating in political society. Bagehot recognised the way in which the Monarchy served deceptively to impress upon the 'masses of Englishmen not fit for an elective government' the authority of government by an 'efficient' *élite*. Where there is an educated and politically aware society, the need for such a division of authority is less obvious. Bagehot himself knew that it was unnecessary in the United States, even in the nineteenth century.[3] Richard Crossman has drawn the natural inference that the mass deception of the Monarchy is not indispensable.[4] It is certainly dispensable for an educated society.

There may however be a more worthy or edifying function for the *Rex*, than the wholesale and systematic deception of the populace. It may serve the purpose claimed for it by theorists, such as de Jouvenel, for whom the primary political concern is the maintenance and enrichment of social co-operation;[5] and for whom the function of *Rex* is essentially to preserve and consolidate the social order in being.[6] So far as this function is concerned, there is no reason to suppose that it must be fulfilled by an hereditary monarchy that perpetuates a caste system. It is conceivable that other constitutional arrangements could embody the virtues of distinguishing between efficient and dignified institutions. As it is, the British Monarchy has both dignified and efficient functions. Some apologists, such as Robert Blake, believe that they can not be completely separated without undermining the 'Dignity' of the Monarch. There is, therefore, no reason to suppose that the British Monarchy exemplifies perfectly the ideal separation of efficient and dignified functions. Moreover, there may well be alternatives to the Monarchy which would serve the *Rex* function at least as well, but without the socially pernicious effects. De Jouvenel's concern to preserve the social order *in being* raises further questions to do with the conservation of society.

The Conservation of Society and Culture

There is, of course, no reason at all to suppose that all 'social orders in being' deserve conservation. But even the most beneficial social change is liable to create potentially harmful stresses, for individuals and in society. Tolerable and enduring change is unlikely to be achieved unless it is brought about within established frameworks which provide, throughout change, a continuity of life and institutions which mitigate stress, and enhance the durability of desirable changes. 'Dignified' authority as exemplified by the Monarchy may be supposed to serve this conservationist function. At the very least, by preserving the *appearance* of tradition and continuity, monarchy may make palatable even the most radical social changes. In short, social conservation, or the appearance of it, is facilitated by the Monarchy.

A related consideration is the need to preserve culture. Aesthetes such as Clive Bell[7] and T.S. Eliot[8] have argued that the highest achievements of human culture are only possible if there is a leisured *élite* whose primary function is to preserve and develop culture, to be disseminated downwards through lower cultural orders. Eliot expressly links the *élite* to high social class (really caste) because culture can not develop adequately without the extensive relationships that caste provides, particularly families.[9] On this view the preservation of culture depends upon a caste hierarchy to sustain the necessary *élite*. The caste hierarchy is in Britain closely identified with the Monarchy which is at once its apex, its central pillar, and its symbol. On this view, therefore, the conservation and dissemination of culture depends upon the Monarchy, at least indirectly.

'Dignified' authority may well serve to facilitate progressive, beneficial, social change on a *laissez faire* basis, but de Jouvenel himself recognised 'the danger inherent when sovereign authority does not make its presence felt', in the facilitative way necessary.

> If a retiring spirit on its part is accompanied by the feeling that the authorities to favour are the old authorities, *laissez faire* of this kind will be conservative in character, not progressive ... Then the thwarted ambitions will bring the whole edifice down, except in the event, unlikely in such cases, of the sovereign authority disposing of repressive strength on a considerable scale. [10]

All evidence suggests that the British Monarchy is conservative and socially reactionary, rather than supportive of progressive change. Conservation may be promoted through a whole fabric of perennial institutions such as education, the professions, voluntary associations, and the like, which do not, as the hereditary monarchy does, *intrinsically* embody arbitrary caste values.

There is no reason why cultural *élites* should be linked to a ruling political *élite*. Scientific, artistic, and inventive *élites* can flourish independently of political *élites*. Eliot's view that *élites* cannot flourish merely on the basis of shared interest without a common high caste social background is to say the least tendentious. Nor is a ruling caste essential to the transmission of culture. Other social groups based on religion and scholarship, for example, have been at least as important as high caste families for cultural transmission.[11] In any case the whole argument presupposes that only high caste *élites* could have the leisure and wherewithal to develop culturally. But in an egalitarian society, especially a highly technological one, the conditions for the development of culture may be very widely distributed.

Eliot himself recognised that the conditions of leisure and resources associated with high caste status are merely necessary for, but not sufficient to ensure the development of culture.[12] This is abundantly demonstrated in practice by the British Monarchy. The idea that the Hanover-Windsor family is the bulwark of British high culture is merely a joke. The dynasty's philistinism is legendary. Mr Max Bygraves leading a Royal Command Performance singalong of the ditty 'Oh! you beautiful doll' in loyal tribute to Her Royal Highness Queen Elizabeth, the Queen Mother, is all the more accurate a cultural measure for being unintentional. It can hardly be what Mr Bell and Mr Eliot had in mind, however. Nor are hunting, riding, shooting, and fishing.

Social order needs to be conserved throughout even the most beneficial change. So too is it necessary to secure the conditions for the conservation and development of culture. Neither of these worthy ends is necessarily connected to the existence of an hereditary monarchy, and certainly not to the Hanover-Windsor family.

Convenience

It is desirable that the transfer of authority between successive heads of state is as swift and uncontroversial as possible. Constitutions with elected heads of state suffer from difficulties on both counts: monarchists say elections are protracted, and leave the state headless for the duration. Even worse, the process of election is political and potentially fraught with partisan strife, whatever the outcome. It is said that monarchy with hereditary succession solves both of these problems of practical administration very conveniently. At the death of a head of state, the next in line automatically, and without need of ceremony, literally inherits the role. 'The King is dead. Long live the King!' is the cry. Since the Monarchy is above politics altogether, there can be no aftermath of bitterness among losing factions or debts incurred to partisan supporters. An hereditary monarch who is a true patriot king has neither embittered and resentful opponents, nor embarrassing or dangerous allies. There is an additional convenience in that heirs to hereditary thrones can serve an apprenticeship, custom made for the job, in a way that no other sort of incumbent could. In Bolingbroke's view: 'On these and upon most occasions the multitude do at least as well to trust to chance as choice and to their fortune as judgement ... elections are attended by such national calamities that even the best reigns cannot make amends for them ... whereas in an hereditary monarchy, whether a good or bad prince succeed, these calamities are avoided.'[13]

The first thing to notice about this view is that it is irrational. Trusting to chance rather than judgement denies the simple effectiveness of rational appraisal of the competence of individuals. Significantly it is difficult, even for exponents of the view, consistently to sustain it. Bolingbroke is typical. Abandoning the selection of head of state to chance is inconsistent with his view that it is in general necessary to use reason, which is god-given. Even more precisely he argues effectively against his own view of succession as follows, in connection with successors to the founders of royal dynasties: 'Merit had given rank, but rank was soon kept and which is more preposterous, obtained without merit. Men were then made kings for reasons as little relative to good government as the neighing of the horse of the son of Hysaspes.'[14] Hereditary succession cannot guarantee a good prince and it encumbers nations with bad ones whom they cannot easily be rid of. Bad heirs are only as educable as nature permits. Argument aside, history shows that often 'allegiance to the throne [has been] lost in the waste of hereditary claims.'[15]

On the most mundane practical level of constitutional provision for succession, it is simply false to suppose that hereditary monarchy is the only way to secure convenience and to avoid political strife. Other systems permit the principle of automatic transfer of authority on the death or incapacity of a head of state. The United States provides a conspicuous example. The problem of political faction might be solved by other sorts of constitutional arrangement. These possibilities are discussed later. It is surely evident, however, that it is not beyond the wit of man to conceive of a workable alternative to an hereditary centi-millionaire. Only benighted and besotted Englishmen would suppose that it is.

CHAPTER *32* SUMMARY AND CONCLUSIONS: DEMOCRACY

Most popular ideas about the Monarchy are either inane, disingenuous, or insupportable, and there is no rational or moral justification for it. It is an obstacle to freedom, it is incompatible with equality, and it is inimical to fraternity. In short, it is inconsistent with morality and democracy. In keeping with this fact, there are a number of scenarios for the future. The Hanover-Windsor family could reach the same conclusion reached here, and abdicate as a matter of moral integrity, renouncing all claim to privileges, prerogative powers, Crown lands, wealth, and income. Perhaps they could be persuaded to continue as hereditary ceremonial heads of state at Equity rates, plus expenses: that would be a real example to us all, but is a remote possibility.

Secondly, the British people themselves could come to recognise the organised deception, and through their representatives in parliament peacefully foreclose on the Hanover-Windsors' contract under the terms of the Revolution Settlement. This scenario seems to be the most desirable, as it would constitute the emergence into political maturity of the British people. This also seems a remote possibility.

A third scenario, which only recently was thought to be quite likely, is that in the not too distant future, Britain will enter a period of unprecedented political instability. With no clear majority in parliament for any political party, the residual constitutional powers of the monarch would then be decisive. Although wholly unaccountable to anybody, the monarch has the power in such a situation to decide who will form a government, and on which policies and conditions; also, the power to refuse to dissolve parliament if there is no clear leadership in the country. In this situation, the Hanover-Windsors might just conceivably endorse policies that would bring about major social change to benefit most people, but there is no precedent for such a thing in Britain, and the Hanover-Windsors are notoriously conservative. In this scenario, the interests of the have-nots would not be realisable by legitimate means any more than they were in 1931.

A fourth scenario is suggested by developments during three terms of Thatcher-Conservative government in the 1980s. Three trends are significant: Britain's continuing industrial decline (measured by industrial production and balance of trade); the multiplication and widening of social divisions (in employment; by wealth and income; by region; between urban and suburban-rural areas; and ethnically); and the increasingly centralist, authoritarian, and repressive state. In a foreseeable future, these trends could converge, perhaps when North Sea oil revenues dry up, to create a situation of uncontainable political unrest.

In either of these last two scenarios, the stage is set for the unfinished business of a people's revolution (peaceful or otherwise) against the forces of conservatism and reaction mobilised around the Crown, as the symbol of traditional state authority. It is high time that the British people stopped being complacent and fawning, and started to think seriously again about the Monarchy.

On the best reckoning, there is a need for a massive programme of moral and political education to be undertaken, to exchange the naivety, cant and downright cynical deception that prevails now, for a fraternal society in Britain. On the worst reckoning, we are faced with unthinkable, but all too real, political possibilities, which are at present hidden from us by manufactured ignorance and complacency. The Monarchy and our attitudes towards it are both symptoms and causes of the state of British society. The time is long overdue when we should examine them again, openly and seriously, at the level of principle. It is impossible to foretell the consequences, but the time is surely right for a resurgence of Republican vitality in the best traditions of Tom Paine and Lafayette who, during the American War of Independence, said that in order for Man to be free of monarchy, it is sufficient that he wills it.

PART VI: ALTERNATIVES TO MONARCHY

CHAPTER *33* CONSTITUTIONAL CHANGE

In view of the highly problematic nature of the Monarchy, it is remarkable that there is virtually no open public debate about it. A significant indicator of how the problems of monarchy are studiously avoided in Britain is the standard text on *The British Constitution* by Harvey and Bather.[1] Although the text is written for students in universities, and for those studying for professional examinations, it does not mention a single problem of serious principle or practice in a discussion of the Monarchy running to twenty-three pages. The absence of public debate on the Monarchy is all the more remarkable because there has in recent years been a substantial increase in interest in a wide variety of other constitutional issues, some of which are much less significant in their ramifications than the Monarchy. A written constitution, a Bill of Rights, constitutional premiership, devolution, electoral reform, referenda, the judiciary, and the reform of the Commons, have all been thought in recent times to be in need of urgent action.[2] The abolition of hereditary representation in the Lords was proposed in the Queen's speech to parliament in November 1967, and only lack of time has prevented such a change from being enacted. The way that the Monarchy has been left warily alone in discussion of the constitution has been remarked on by more than one commentator.[3] Those who have been aware of the problematic status of the Monarchy in recent politics have been concerned not to challenge it, but to preserve it from harm to which it may be exposed through overt involvement.[4]

Further evidence of evasion is provided by the selective influence of the greatest source of conventional wisdom on the English constitution, Walter Bagehot's book on the subject published in 1867. It is interesting to notice how those who commonly revere Bagehot remain silent on his critical views of the constitutional role of hereditary monarchy in a democratically constituted state. Nothing is heard nowadays of Bagehot's view that 'As far as experience goes, there is no reason to expect an hereditary series of useful limited monarchs.' Although there has been recurrent and growing concern expressed about a possible end to two-party politics, and the spectre of hung parliaments, there is no mention of Bagehot's belief that 'The characteristic use of an hereditary constitutional monarch, at the outset of an administration, has greatly surpassed the ordinary competence of hereditary faculties.', or his belief that the same holds true during the continuance of an administration.[5] Furthermore, Bagehot was in no doubt that a good administration could be started without a sovereign monarch.[6] A wide discussion of these and other constitutional issues is now overdue. The two main questions are: first, whether change to the Monarchy is desirable; and second, if so, what form that change could take.

There can be no doubt that there are many neglected facts and arguments to show that the Monarchy is a bad thing for Britain, both morally and constitutionally. The moral case against monarchy has already been made out here. Monarchy is incompatible with the democratic ideals of liberty, equality, and fraternity, in principle. In practice it raises other problems of deception and repression. As Gladstone perceptively pointed out, government must be conducted by 'force, fraud or good-will'.[7] Force and good-will are both deployed in the governance of Britain. The Monarchy is the main instrument of fraud. Precisely how this works is a subject for another book on the cultural influence of the Monarchy in Britain through socialisation in the family, schools, the churches, and by propaganda, especially in the mass media. That the Monarchy functions so as to delude people cannot seriously be doubted by anyone who devotes time to the study.[8] At their least objectionable, the national royal delusions are merely harmless, if inane, fantasies of fairytale princesses. However, the same processes contribute in a far more insidious and harmful way to the development of a 'mumbo jumbo, medicine man frame of mind' as Leonard Woolf put it. They lead to the worst kind of chauvinism and a lack of realism about political life. Most of all the royal fantasies defraud masses of British people of a true picture of British society, and exercise a 'hegemonic' social control.

The political and constitutional problems of the Monarchy have also been enumerated. The monarch is unelected, unrepresentative and unaccountable, and has considerable influence and prerogative powers. The nature of the prerogative powers is very imprecise without a written constitution. There is no reason to expect the existing powers to be always exercised judiciously. The circumstances in which the powers may be exercised are, in the late twentieth century, becoming increasingly likely to arise. The Monarchy fails adequately to represent and defend the national interest, especially that of the worst off, against misgovernment. Finally, attempts to reform society are hampered by outmoded political institutions, the Monarchy included.

For all the reasons given here, it is both desirable and necessary to consider the place of the Monarchy in the British constitution in the late 1980s. Conservatives and radicals can agree that the role of the monarch in the British constitution requires substantial review and revision. Conservatives are concerned to remove the Monarchy from the sphere of possible direct political controversy in order to preserve it. Radicals will abolish the Monarchy altogether. It will be useful therefore to consider ways in which the Monarchy might be reformed to remedy the moral, social, and constitutional problems it presents. Two broad possibilities are open. The institution might be reformed, as it has been throughout history, according to changed circumstances. It might also be abolished, in which case there is a need to consider what might replace it in the constitution.

CHAPTER 34 REFORM

It is commonly said that the British Monarchy has survived by effectively adapting to changed circumstances. Criticism of the Monarchy at the outset of the present Queen's reign was directed to that purpose, by such people as Lord Altrincham and Malcolm Muggeridge, who were mainly concerned to eliminate sources of complaint in order to make the Monarchy more acceptable and secure.[1] There was nothing new in this. Disraeli had retrieved Victoria from fifteen years as a recluse in response to public complaints and a rising tide of republicanism. It is even possible that his radical change of mind about the value of a British empire, was motivated by a wish to preserve the Monarchy by finding it an acceptable role. (Before the growing public outcry against the absent queen, he had regarded the colonies as a 'millstone'.[2]) So, it has typically been the case in recent times that criticism on either moral or constitutional grounds has been intended constructively by those who favour the Monarchy – and even take its existence for granted. Unfortunately the effects of such criticism have not yielded very great change. The British Monarchy survives on the grand imperial scale as an anachronism in a world in which really Britain is neither imperial nor very grand. The Monarchy has been remarkably resistant to change in a time of unprecedented changes in Britain itself, and to Britain's position in the world. Changes there have been, to be sure. The practice of having '*débutantes*' presented at court was discontinued. Royalty now goes 'walkabout'. And members of the royal family occasionally appear as human beings on television screens, sometimes even to talk. Royal princes now venture public examinations and enrol at Oxbridge colleges.

None of the changes over the last thirty-five years has been substantial or structural, and none has made any signifcant difference to the institution of monarchy or its role. They are scarcely worth discussing. *Débuts* were only one especially inane, blatant and offensive sort of privileged flummery that could easily be dispensed with, without loss. Walkabouts are choreographed to magnify rather than diminish the real distance between royalty and their subjects. Similarly, the extreme deference and unction with which royal persons are addressed on television does nothing to diminish the myth of natural

170

hierarchic status that monarchy represents. The comparatively poor performances of royal princes in public examinations does nothing to diminish their prospects for admission to Oxbridge. This merely displays their hereditary privilege all the more openly. The privilege is not diminished at all.

Moral reforms

In 1952 Michael Stewart outlined a modestly Fabian set of proposals for adapting the Monarchy to the needs of the time.[3] None of these was particularly radical. A consideration of them now, nearly thirty-seven years later, is very instructive. It shows how little has been done in the 'New Elizabethan Age' to reform the Monarchy in desirable ways.

First: the circle of royal acquaintances should be widened. All that has been done is to arrange one or two more garden parties and a few informal lunches each year with guests such as university vice-chancellors, sporting and show-business personalities, company directors, and suchlike 'commoners'. This does not even begin to meet the need for a democratic head of state to know about the real lives of most British people.

Second: honours associated with class and privilege should fall into desuetude. In fact, the whole range of honours including hereditary peerages remains still largely intact under the Queen's patronage. The Queen even intervened, though unnecessarily as it turned out, to stop Emrys Hughes' bill to abolish the present honours system.[4]

Third: the Queen should use her social influence to the full to discourage racial discrimination. In fact, the royal entourage is still conspicuous for its lack of 'new Commonwealth' people, despite the fact that Britain has long been a multi-cultural society with large minority populations from the Caribbean and the Indian subcontinent. Prince Philip conspicuously avoided answering a pointed question on this put to him by Willie Hamilton, saying it hadn't much to do with 'modernising' the Monarchy.[5] In this matter more than most, actions speak louder than words.

Fourth: reasonable discussion of questions affecting the Monarchy should be encouraged. In fact, serious criticism of the Monarchy is almost unheard of. The press especially imposes its own self-denying ordinance against all but the most trivial discussion of the mundane affairs of royalty. Serious dissenters like Willie Hamilton are suffered only as court jesters, and even then at heavy cost to their political careers. Even in parliament itself, serious debate about the affairs of the Monarchy, such as the Civil List, is considered to be in very bad taste, if not treachery.

Fifth: royal advisers should be openly recruited to have a wide knowledge of people. In fact the class and working background of royal advisers continues to be as limited as their racial type.

Sixth: the education of the royal family should be in touch with the age. Cheam School, Gordonstoun, Cambridge, and the Armed Forces, are not the best places for a British hereditary head of state to learn about the economic and social lives of the people. State schools, civic institutions, are where most people are educated. This is especially true of pupils with no great academic distinction, such as the Windsor children. As ever, industry and commerce are known to royalty only by hearsay and contrived official 'visits'.

Seventh: the cost of the Monarchy should be reasonably related to the duties of a head of state. This has been done, though it must be said that great difficulty has been created in the process for serious auditors. The real financial problem with the British Monarchy however is not its cost, but its great secret untaxed wealth.

Here, then, are numerous ways in which the Monarchy can be reformed; ways that were pointed out before the Queen's accession, but which have, to all practical intents and purposes, been ignored. There are other ways also suggested by an unbiased scrutiny of prevailing practice.

Eighth: media reportage of royal persons and events should be diminished, and made more 'balanced' and less blatantly propagandistic. Only in this way can a climate of informed consent be established and tested. This goes with a need for political education in schools, adequately to instruct citizens in the advantages of the republican alternatives to monarchy. Without these changes the apparent popularity does nothing to justify it.

Ninth: the royal family, including the Queen, should work harder; mainly working more days in the year. A typical working year of 166 days of official engagements is not hard work by any standards. And engagements include picnics, horse racing and suchlike non-Stakhanovite labours. One way in which royalty could usefully spend more time would be to live in ordinary communities for extended periods, especially deprived and disadvantaged ones. Another would be to spend time really meeting ordinary people in something like ordinary circumstances.

Tenth: income from the private wealth of the monarch should be taxed at the appropriate rate. The Queen is supposed to set a fine moral example. The conspicuous example set by royal tax avoidance is all too easily followed, but it is not moral at all. It is precisely because she is special that she should pay taxes, not the other way about. It is simply morally wrong that someone with an estimated private fortune of £4.5 thousand million pays no income tax. It is doubly offensive that the same person is lauded as a paragon.

Eleventh: the royal lands and private estates should be nationalised. Ownership of the Duchies of Lancaster and Cornwall, and private estates such as Sandringham which have been purchased with revenues from these estates, should belong to the nation.

Reforms along these lines would substantially transform the British Monarchy into an institution more in keeping with the principles of morality and democracy. None of them materially affects tradition, ceremonial, the unique role of the *Rex*, or the cost of maintaining such a 'dignified' head of state. What we would be left with, however, would certainly be more in keeping with the times, like a Scandinavian-style monarchy. But such a monarch with a private fortune and a civil list would nevertheless not be needing a bicycle.

Constitutional reforms

Bagehot saw the constitutional difficulties with hereditary monarchs very clearly; particularly with respect to their exercise of prerogative powers, such as the appointment of a prime minister in a 'hung' parliament. He saw that 'There is a great danger ... that the judgement of the sovereign can be prejudiced.'. He further argued that 'If constitutional monarchs be ordinary men of restricted experience and common capacity (and we have no right to suppose that by miracle they may be more), the judgement of the sovereign will often be worse than the judgement of the party, and he will be very subject to the chronic danger of preferring a respectful commonplace man ... to an independent first-rate man.'[6]

The problems presented by the limitations of hereditary monarchs, and their congenital inabilities to make unprejudiced and informed decisions on important constitutional matters can be ameliorated in one of two radical, if now improbable, ways: either by introducing a form of elective monarchy, or by changing the dynasty to one that is congenitally more able, and perhaps incidentally, more truly British.

First: the monarch could be elected from the members of the established Hanover-Windsor dynasty. This would widen the field of choice and ameliorate the ever-present problem threatened by strict hereditary succession; that the inheritor may be a more than usually selfish, ineffectual, reactionary, or insane head of state. In the Saxon kingdom of England the Crown was hereditary in a particular family, and choice was frequently exercised outside the line of strict succession. There is therefore impeccable precedent for such a sensible reform to the present system.[7] In practice something of the sort operates tacitly. The abdication of Edward VIII in 1936, for example, was not unconnected with the establishment's view that he was emotionally and morally inadequate, and therefore unacceptable.

Second: a new dynasty could be established which was more capable and more British than the incumbent Hanover-Windsors. The limitations of the Hanoverians and their predominantly pecuniary interests are well known. Less well known is the fact that their claim to legitimacy is quite tenuous. Even so conservative a commentator as Sir Ivor Jennings has pointed out that there are far more direct descendants of James I than Elizabeth II.[8] In fact the founder of her dynasty, George I, was fifty-eighth in line of succession to the throne at his accession.[9] Thackeray said of George I that 'His aim was to leave England to itself, as much as possible, and to live out of it as much as he could. "Loyalty", he must think, "as applied to me, is absurd." '[10] It should not be beyond the powers of British genealogy to unearth a worthy British family fit to provide elective heads of state, deserving of the name and capable.

Whatever dynasty reigns, or whatever the means of determining succession, there remain problems of the prerogative powers exercised by the monarch. This suggests:

Third: the prerogative powers of the monarch should be clearly set out in a written constitution, and unconstitutional legal powers removed. It is unacceptable in a democracy that an unrepresentative, unaccountable, hereditary billionaire should be allowed to exercise personal discretion, in matters of the greatest political importance. And yet, as

Vernon Bogdanor has said, 'The sovereign's discretion comes to be enlarged, while the rules which guide her use of this discretion cease to provide authoritative landmarks.'[11]

It is unacceptable also that the head of state should be permitted to operate *without limits being set to what can legitimately be done, and in secret*. Bogdanor shows that this secrecy is, at present, part of the essence of constitutional monarchy in Britain.[12] The need for new constitutional laws and conventions to define and limit prerogative powers is clear and pressing.

Fourth: the main prerogative powers vested in the monarch should be transferred to other offices and institutions. Several commentators have remarked on how the prime minister may, and has, spoken for the whole nation in certain circumstances. Also, experience in other countries shows that politicians can negotiate under their own auspices, without the need for royal mediation.[13] Here again Bagehot's judgement is sound. He argued that parliament itself positively should be made to feel responsibility for the formation and maintenance of governments. In his view, so long as parliament thinks it is the sovereign's business to find a government, it will be sure not to find a government itself.[14] Specific powers, notably the appointment of a prime minister; the decision to dissolve parliament; and the power in certain constitutionally vital cases to refuse to endorse legislation could alternatively be transferred the speaker of the House of Commons.[15] This sort of arrangement has been established in other countries, notably Sweden. In other countries, including Denmark and Belgium, *informateurs* are appointed to mediate between contending factions for the appointment of heads of governments and other purposes. *Informateurs* are elder statesmen or worthies generally considered to be above political faction, but who have the capacity to facilitate the necessary constitutional arrangements. In practice they function in other countries in much the same way that royal private secretaries have functioned in Britain.

Conclusive proof that such things are possible lies with the fact that since 1974, the Swedish monarch has no prerogative powers at all. By Article I of that country's Instrument of Government, 'All public power in Sweden emanates from the people.'[16] The radical transformation of the Swedish constitutional monarchy in this way stops short of complete abolition. The Swedish king is purely an ornamental head of state. There is no good reason why the British Monarchy should not go the same way. Against that possibility, it is argued by some monarchists that real prerogative powers, however dormant, are essential to any useful role the institution may take.[17] Bagehot compared the purely 'dignified' parts of a constitution to the solely ornamental wheels of clocks that serve no useful purpose, but only cause friction and error.[18]

This then raises the final general possibiity for constitutional reform: the abolition of the Monarchy, and the question of what might replace it. What has been shown clearly so far is that there is considerable room for reforming the Monarchy both morally and constitutionally. Reforms which stop short only at complete abolition, to leave only a vestigial or ornamental headship of state, probably create more problems than they solve, and for that reason, complete abolition may be preferable. To that large issue, we may now finally turn.

CHAPTER 35   ABOLITION OF THE MONARCHY

In the late 1980s the Monarchy seems to be so entrenched in British life, and apparently so popular, that its abolition will seem unthinkable to many British people. But reasons for considering this are clear, numerous, and decisive, as has been shown.

Before going on to consider this further, it will be helpful, because of the entrenchment, to be reminded of the position of the British Monarchy in wider perspectives. It is the only monarchy on the grand imperial scale left in a world full of republics. Only a few bicycle-monarchies remain elsewhere. Consequently although Englishmen (supposedly) cannot conceive of constitutional alternatives to monarchy, this is no more than comic parochial prejudice. The great modern republican movement started in English colonial America, and was inspired above all by 'the greatest Englishman', Tom Paine. In recent history, and to mention only a British case, Southern Ireland made the transition to republican status in 1949 without noticeable effect on its political 'nature'. It is well to recall also that the king was not accepted as the natural lord of all Englishmen until Norman times.[1] The parliamentarian *interregnum* of 1649-1659, far from being 'England's failed experiment with Republicanism', as royalists wish to believe, was only one important manifestation of perennial English republicanism. The first four Hanoverian Georges made any alternative to monarchy seem attractive to most Englishmen.[2] Republicanism was received wisdom among educated middle-class Englishmen in the nineteenth century.[3] Jeremy Bentham and John Stuart Mill, typically, believed that the Monarchy was immoral, obsolete, and would soon disappear. Edward VII himself was convinced that his heir George V would be the last king of England.[4] In 1936, during the abdication crisis, there was very strong feeling among half the population that the Monarchy should be abolished.[5] The Monarchy's wide popularity in the 1980s is a local, synthetic, and shallow phenomenon. Enough has been said here to show that it is far from warranted. It is very far from unthinkable, therefore, that the Monarchy should be abolished. In what follows, all that is attempted is a brief outline of the principles that should guide abolition, and some speculation about the form that change might take.

Requirements of a headship of state

The constitutional case for abolishing the Monarchy is based mainly on the facts that it is arbitrary, unrepresentative, unaccountable, partial, socially divisive, and exercises a pernicious influence and privileged prerogative powers. Despite these fatal disadvantages, the Monarchy has served various functions which would continue to be served by any practicable alternatives. Two sorts of use correspond to the dignified and efficient functions of the head of state. Most states must have a formal head of state who serves as a focus of national unity, performs ceremonial rituals, and promotes voluntary participation in the life of the nation. Also, there is arguably a need for constitutional safeguards against the possible excesses of an elected majority, in some circumstances. In eliminating arbitrary hereditary and vested interests, there is a need to secure impartiality, and the constitutional safeguards supposedly provided by prerogative powers. In order to achieve these ends, therefore, whoever replaces a constitutional monarch as head of state must, in brief, be demonstrably able, representative, accountable, impartial, and capable of legitimate action in the national interest when necessary. The practical forms that such changes might take are innumerable. I will mention just two: elective presidency, and a bicameral option.

An elective presidency

The obvious alternative to hereditary monarchy, which would satisfy so far as possible the requirement for a democratic head of state, is an elective presidency of some form. Direct elections, or indirect election through delegate conferences, are the most obvious ways of doing this. There is so much experience of elective presidency in politically stable democracies, that it is unnecessary to spend time describing the variety of constitutions, in order to show how similar arrangements might work in Britain.[6] Instead I will consider some general objections.

Elective presidencies are commonly said to suffer from two main drawbacks, compared to constitutional monarchies. The main objection is that an elected president would inevitably be a politician, and so would owe allegiances to political parties and other politicians. This raises difficulties of political partiality. These may become so acute, as to render government almost impossible. This happens in the United States and France, when a president of one political persuasion mayhaps must govern with an elected assembly of an opposing political persuasion. Against this objection it may be said that it may in certain circumstances be no bad thing in a democracy if an executive is a balance of opposing forces, if these forces reflect real differences of opinion in the nation. The British prejudice in favour of uncompromising government, even if it is also disastrously misguided government, is not easily justifiable. However, the presumption that an elected president would inevitably have a political pedigree with its accompanying bias need not in practice be justified. Already the role of speaker is fulfilled in the House of Commons by a respected career politician who is usually acceptable to all parties. It is commonly the case that election to that office is in itself a way of elevating the incumbent above mundane political factions. Should such a person prove to be unacceptably partisan, then constitutional means of legally removing them could be arranged. It is possible, however, to devise arrangements whereby the office of head of state is debarred to career party-politicians, and open only to mature persons of proven capacity. These possibilities will be discussed presently.

The other main drawback to an elected presidency, it is said, is that there is no adequate substitute for an hereditary monarch so far as the dignified function of the head of state is concerned. The *aura* and prestige attached to hereditary monarchs – their *charisma* – cannot be attached to any elected official; nor is there that special, sanctified sort of legitimacy derived from ancient genealogical succession. These objections to elective presidencies carry little force. It is, to begin with, simply a fact that elective offices can carry the *aura* of great prestige, as the office of President in the U.S.A. shows. As far as ritual and ceremonial are concerned, there is no evidence that this depends for its effectiveness on the selection by heredity of the main participants. There is no hereditary archbishop of Canterbury. There is no hereditary pope. And yet nobody supposes that the effectiveness of the great rituals involving the church, or even the selection of Christ's vicar on Earth, depend upon heredity. Ceremonial rituals are perfectly effective in nations where hereditary offices, and even religion, are positively unconstitutional, as in the U.S.S.R.[7] It might also be said, however, that a diminution in the purely charismatic aspect of monarchic authority, together with a corresponding increase in what Weber calls 'rational legal' authority[8] is highly desirable, in keeping with sound democratic principles. There is, therefore, no reason to suppose that an elected British head of state must necessarily be deficient in dignity or authority.

In short: there is no good reason to believe that an elective presidency would have serious disadvantages, either of efficiency, or of dignity, over an hereditary monarchy. On the other hand, there are numerous moral and practical advantages in an elected head of state who would be as demonstrably able, representative, accountable, impartial and effective in certain circumstances of emergency, as it is possible to be.

A Bicameral Option

Since the main objections to the British Monarchy stem from its unjustifiable hereditary basis and its constitutional prerogative powers and privileges, it is appropriate to consider its abolition in connection with that other great hereditary branch of the legislature: the House of Lords. It may be that the best practical alternative to hereditary monarchy can be provided by arrangements involving a second elected chamber.

As long ago as 1649 it was openly proclaimed that the House of Lords was 'useless, dangerous, and ought to be abolished'.[9] The functions of the House of Lords which might justify its retention are said to be five-fold. It is a forum for debate on general issues of policy; it is a final court of appeal; Commons bills are debated there, amendments suggested, and controversial bills delayed; bills are formulated there; and private members' bills are considered in detail there. As Ivor Jennings has so clearly shown, none of these functions of the present Lords is indispensable.[10] The debates of the Lords are, in practice, usually disregarded, and, given its composition, that is neither surprising nor to be regretted. Only a few select Law Lords in sub-committee decide cases of appeal, and this does not depend on the existence of the chamber of peers. Peers can only delay government legislation, and this may be either too long, or altogether undesirable. Few bills originate in the Lords, and none are of over-riding importance. There are other ways of considering private members' bills, such as Commons select committees.

None of the arguments for retaining the House of Lords in its present form has force. There is, on the other hand, a decisive reason for abolishing or reconstituting it, and that is that it is for all practical purposes an outpost of the Conservative Party by heredity. It has been truly said that nothing passes the House of Lords except by permission of the Conservative Party whether the party is in office or in opposition.[11] This is because, by the heredity principle, the number of Conservative peers who inherit seats in the Lords is so great that a permanent over-all Conservative majority is assured. In 1986 the distribution of peers by declared party allegiance was as follows: Conservative – 418; Labour – 123; Liberal – 40; SDP – 42. Crossbench peers who had declared no party affiliation numbered 236.[12] Clearly, only an alliance of all non-Conservative peers could possibly overcome the Conservatives. The possibility of this is only hypothetical. In practice, most cross-benchers are conservative, if not Conservative.

So blatantly unjustifiable is this state of affairs that numerous proposals, including Conservative ones, have been made to change it, notably in 1918, 1967, 1969, 1977, and 1978.[13] In the Queen's Speech of November 1967, it was announced that 'legislation will be introduced to reduce the powers of the Lords and eliminate its hereditary basis, thereby enabling it to develop within a framework of a modern parliamentary system'. A large measure of inter-party agreement was reached on ideas incorporated into a Parliament (No. 2) Bill 1968. The bill was never passed, however, because final agreement could not be reached about the precise composition or functions of an upper chamber.[14] The main reasons for disagreement are important, and suggest ways in which a second chamber might be reconstituted. First, the proposed composition of the second chamber proved controversial, because it was thought that the prime minister would have too much power of political patronage in the appointment of members. Also, it was believed that there would be too few suitable politicians to fill the proposed preponderance of cross-bench seats. Second, the proposed powers of the second chamber were controversial, because Labour politicians wanted minimal debate and delay, whereas Conservative politicians wanted real powers of amendment and delay.

There are very strong and perhaps decisive arguments for the existence of a second chamber of parliament. As Ronald Butt has pointed out, Britain is the only important Western country lacking a constitutional check on an elected majority.[15] The only points at issue are to do with the precise composition of a second chamber and its powers. The solution to these problems might be part of the solution to the problems of establishing an acceptable alernative to the Monarchy. One way forward is to recall the origin of the second chamber of parliament. That is the use early sovereigns made of the advice of powerful and influential individuals. This was related to a practical need to recruit and maintain the support of those who otherwise had the power effectively to oppose lawful government. This was the basis of the Anglo-Saxon *Witangemot* and the Norman *Curia Regis*. Recent commentators have supposed that the principle of recruiting the support of powerful interest groups either continues conservatively to justify the existing preponderance of ancient landed interests in the House of Lords.[16], or else to warrant the extension of representation, more accurately to reflect real powerful interests at the present time, mainly party-political ones, and some individuals of great personal distinction.[17]

The principle is open to interpretation and modification in other ways, however. In the first place, the concept of interest embraces more than just powerful groups and individuals. Many of these may have no morally respectable claim to special representation. Some of them need to be controlled by governments, not recruited to them. There are other interests represented by established social formations, which have at least equal claim to recognition and representation in the process of a non-party-political government. Some theorists, such as Ernest Barker[18], G.D.H. Cole[19], and Harold Laski[20], have argued along these lines for wide representation of whatever interest groups may legitimately establish themselves. Barker has argued, for example, that 'associations which are living and acting like persons under social recognition, should be accorded both legal and political recognition'.[21] Cole argued that it was desirable to find an association and method of representation for each function of society. He even suggested the maxim: 'One man as many votes as interests, but only one vote in relation to each interest.'[22] What is central to all such theories is the need to incorporate in the process of government, real interests which may not be co-extensive with those of established political parties. Such interests need not rival or challenge popularly elected parliaments, but could provide the informed audit of the work of the Commons and some of the constitutional safeguards supposedly now provided by the House of Lords and the Monarchy.

Precisely how such representation should be established, and its form, is not a matter central to the present discussion. Some variant of previous proposals would be suitable; continuing established institutional interests such as the judiciary and the churches, with regionally elected representatives, and representatives of the kind mentioned, for example by occupation and professions; and substantial voluntary associations, which draw support from across political-party lines (such as voluntary services and the arts). The main principle of candidature for the second house should be proven ability in non-party-political spheres. It would be doubly advantageous to set a lower age limit for candidature – say 50. This would both secure the necessary maturity of judgement, and also tend strongly to deter those with merely personal ambition, since gratification so long deferred and uncertain, is unlikely to attract opportunists. One possible objection to such a proposal is worth rebutting here. Harold Laski argued that the view of representatives of unpolitical interest groups would be totally devoid of relevance to the majority of the decisions they would have to make.[23] This objection misses the point of distinguished representation of interest groups: that the views of such able people on matters outside their sphere of greatest expertise is of very great importance in auditing the general acceptability of policies pursued by party politicians.

Ways can be devised of composing along such lines a second chamber (or Senate) which removes it from the direct influence of party-governments; which is elective, able and accountable to the public; but which also represents non-arbitrary real national interests. Hereditary representation, being arbitrary, would, of course, have no place.

The functions of such a second chamber could in some ways be similar to the present House of Lords. With a reformed composition, the debates of such a body would be informed, relevantly representative, and authoritative; and so would command wide respect. Similarly, bills and amendments originated by it would be authoritative. The powers of a second chamber should never rival the authority of the popularly elected legislative assembly in the Commons. Powers of the second chamber, apart from advisory ones, should be restricted to the power to require that tendentious general issues be put to the electorate, in the form of referenda. (David Hume, in his *Idea of a Perfect Commonwealth*, proposed something similar to this for a second chamber of 'competitors', whose only powers would be the power of accusing, and appealing to the people.[24]) By confining the powers of the second chamber to major issues of general policy, it would be practicable to invoke referenda. Referenda on important issues of general concern need not take a long time to organise; weeks only. The powers of sheer delay exercised by a second house would therefore be very limited.

One great advantage of such a proposal is that it would solve the problem of the 'bogus mandate' that governments nowadays claim they have for all their policies, even though the electorate is obliged to vote only indiscriminately for a party 'ticket'.

As Ivor Jennings has said, at present 'Every parliament passes laws which would not be acceptable to an electorate, as separate proposals.'[25] Where a government with a parliamentary majority seeks to pass laws that there is good reason to believe would not be acceptable to the great majority of the electorate, then the second chamber would be empowered to require that the electorate be consulted on the matter. In this way, some of the most unjust and disastrous policies of the past could have been avoided. In this way also, the powers of the second chamber, though purely negative and very limited, nevertheless would be practically effective, and would imbue its deliberations with even greater authority.

Appointing the head of state

The *excursus* on the composition, function and powers of a reconstituted second chamber is not divorced from the matter of appointing a head of state. The sort of second chamber proposed would be composed entirely of the sort of individuals who have demonstrated the qualities required of a dignified and efficient head of state. It is indeed very much like an electoral college: a secular equivalent to the college of cardinals that elects the pope.

A nation such as Britain, which is preoccupied with tradition, should have no difficulties or qualms about adapting the experience of centuries codified in the Roman Catholic *Codex Iuris Canonici*. These procedures for electing a pope are easily adaptable for the election of a head of state by an elected British senate.

The Senate, *Witan*, House of Elders, or whatever, would meet in conclave, and by a process of elimination, elect from among its apolitical number a head of state and a deputy. The deputy would also serve as *pro tempore* depute head of state in the event of the head of state being indisposed; in the case of his demise, the deputy would be *pro tempore* head of state, pending an early conclave. In this way, the problem of succession, which monarchists believe only heredity can solve, is settled.

This speculative flight would not be complete without some recognition of the political realities in Britain in the 1980s. It would be possible to accomodate the currently great popularity of the royal family in such reforms. Let us say that the next heir to the throne be made first (honorary) president of the British senate, and (presumptive) head of state: this would be acceptable to reason and morality with an eye to prevailing political realities, provided it was universally understood that the arrangement was purely temporary; and that the Monarchy would die along with Elizabeth II's successor. By this gradualist approach, the nation could be accustomed and schooled to the idea that it was a republic, and weaned bloodlessly from its monarchic myths in the lifetime of a generation now living. That would be a very old-fashioned, decently British, way to dispose of unwanted things.

Functions and powers of the head of state

The main functions of an elected head of state would of necessity be both dignified and efficient. All of the ceremonial and official functions would be performed, as well as any other democratic presidential head of state. As elected head of the senate, the head of state would give effective expression to the views of the nation where these might clearly depart from the policies of an inadequately representative government. Other functions such as being the focus of public life and the fountain of honours, could also continue to be fulfilled by the head of state where necessary. The armed forces should owe allegiance to the people only, that is to the officers of the elected legislative assembly, not to the titular head of state. The powers of the head of state could usefully be twofold. First, to act where necessary as an arbitrator in cases of irresolvable stalemate in the legislature. Such necessities might include the appointment of a prime minister or the dissolution of parliament. Secondly, the head of state would also have the power to require that controversial legislative measures that would change the nature of the constitution be put to the electorate in referenda. Such powers would be negative only, and strictly limited to constitutional issues. There would, therefore, be no substantive rivalry with the legislature, and all differences would be settled by the people anyway.

It would be necessary to specify in detail appropriate procedures, and the circumstances for the operation of the powers of the head of state, in order to avoid the excess of discretion that now prevails.

What is intended here is not an exercise in speculative armchair constitution building of a ten-a-penny kind. What is intended is precisely to show that the requirements of a serviceable, decently moral, and democratic constitution are not beyond even modest wits, when they are exercised on the matter. Whether or not these particular sketches contain so much as a germ of workable constitutional alternatives to hereditary monarchy is hardly relevant. It will be clear in any case that some workable alternative must be both thinkable and practically attainable.

Leaving aside the possibility of non-political ways of change, it is worth briefly considering the practical possibility of substantial change to the status and role of the British Monarchy in the foreseeable future. Career politicians of any established party are in general unlikely to pursue policies, however worthy, that they perceive to be widely unpopular and so potentially detrimental to their own prospects of achieving power. It is for that quite general reason unsurprising that in the 1980s no British political party treats the status of the Monarchy as a live or pressing issue. None of the principles or arguments or facts advanced in this book is a matter of concern to them. The Labour M.P. Willie Hamilton is virtually unique in being renowned among politicians as a republican and vociferous critic of the Monarchy. Typically he is regarded as a licensed jester, or an eccentric, to be tolerated, even savoured, but not taken seriously.

The case of the British Monarchy demonstrates the truth of the definitions of conservatives, as people who believe that nothing should be done *for the first time*; and of moderates, as people who believe that it should . . . *but not now!!*

If the Church of England is the Tory Party at prayer, then the Monarchy must be the answer to its prayers. As Kingsley Martin has explained, Disraeli, by a stroke of genius, related the Queen to the interests of the nation, as conceived by the Conservative Party.[1] After that it became impossible radically to question a conservative view of the nation and the national interest, without being charged with disloyalty to the Queen. And as Lord Esher candidly observed, the monarch is naturally bound to the Tory party.[2]

Liberals have, *in principle*, been opposed to monarchy, though the practice has been different. In the 1820s, Jeremy Bentham criticised practical reform projects of his time because, he said, 'the Radical as well as the Liberal respects the existence of the monarchy and the House of Lords.'[3] Gladstone was in a position possibly decisively to undermine the Monarchy, but desisted from doing so out of deference to the Queen.[4]

The Labour Party's declared ideals are socialist and egalitarian. In practice, it is entirely committed to working within, and even preserving, established institutions of government.[5] Labour politicians have typically embarked on their political careers as radical social reformers, and then changed their opinions when exposed first-hand to the mystique and prestige of royalty. Ramsay MacDonald and John Weightman are just two would-be republicans who became their majesty's most loyal subjects.[6]

On such a view of political trends, the Monarchy may seem to be safe. This is not the only view, however. Along with the 'Matterhorn' of royal propaganda, and 'guff and gush' hagiography, there are now some signs of a growing tendency to more open expression of public disenchantment with, and criticism of the Monarchy. Often these are based on nothing more than exasperation at the relentless propaganda and media exposure of fashionable royal persons. There is, however, at the same time, a more trenchant tone to some recent criticism, which suggests that far more principled objections are being aired.[7] There is evidence, also, that the supposed popularity among ordinary people is exaggerated by opinion polls.[8] This suggests that the popular social and political climate could easily change – to put the question of the Monarchy back on the agenda for the established parties.

The *Conservatives* are on the face of it the least likely to contemplate change. Under the leadership of the new hard right, however, Tory ideology in the 1980s has been closer to the Victorian values of *laissez faire* 'free market' liberalism and *arriviste* meritocracy, than it is to Victorian establishment royalism. It is not unthinkable, if this were to continue, that the Monarchy could come to be viewed very differently by the new 'On yer bike' Conservatives.[9] In any event, true conservatives conserve whatever the initiative of others proves to be of value. From this point of view, the 'stupid party' represents no permanent obstacle to constitutional change, since it can be relied upon to 'accept established authority, wherever it is found, without enquiring too closely into its documents of title.'[10]

The *'Democrats'* and the *Social Democratic Party* are in some ways inheritors of the nineteenth century republican-radical tradition. (Remarkably, in 1983 85 per cent of S.D.P. activists had higher education, compared to 25 per cent of Labour activists, and 27 per cent of Tory activists.[11]) This might explain Neil Ascherson's claim that the British Alliance parties were in 1985 closest to continental-style republicans, in that they represented the views of self-confident rationalists who are prepared to embark on sweeping reforms, without fearing that they are breaking established conventions and overturning hallowed institutions.[12] By contrast, the Labour Party, it is said, is still the royalist party of the working class.

This is true but remarkable, because the *Labour Party* at its inception was opposed to all hereditary offices of state. Its declared object still is to achieve social justice. Keir Hardie was a life-long republican who scandalised parliament with his anti-monarchist speeches. Indeed, the first three leaders of the party – Hardie, MacDonald and Barnes – were all at some time openly declared republicans. A proposal to abolish the Monarchy was debated at the party conference in 1923. George Lansbury's reply on behalf of the executive set the tone for all later party policy. He said that 'When the workers have won the social revolution, they could then be quite sure what they would be able to do with the King, Queen, President or anyone else.' He concluded that 'One of these days, by law established principles, we will not have a King or Queen, but what is the use of bothering about that just now?'[13] This has continued to be the Labour Party's pragmatic view to the present time.[14] Unfortunately, in the late 1980s, there is little evidence that such pragmatism has substantially influenced the hereditary social hierarchy in Britain.

The Labour Party, nevertheless, remains the most likely source of serious constitutional reform of the Monarchy. Not only is monarchy opposed by the youthful and militant elements.[15], there is also an anti-monarchist tendency among even 'moderate' Labourites.[16]

The Monarchy is the big *taboo* of British politics. It is incompatible with every principle of democracy. In practice, however glaring social inequality and injustice become, the central pillar of unjustifiable privilege remains unchallenged, even by political parties dedicated to promoting social justice. The *taboo* works because pragmatic politicians believe that the Monarchy is very popular. To challenge it would seem to be electoral suicide. But the popularity of the Monarchy is very shallow and unmerited. It depends on myths that are easily dispelled. The first step towards the radical reform or abolition of the Monarchy is to break the *taboo* and set about dispelling the myths that surround it and make it popular. This book is offered as a contribution towards the accomplishment of that very important task.

CHAPTER 37 AFTERWORD

Although I have addressed all of the arguments and grounds I have been able to find that are supposed to justify the Monarchy, it is true that I have reached comprehensively negative conclusions. Some people might think that there must be something to be said in its favour. My first response to this thought is to note that most of the myriad books to do with the Monarchy assiduously avoid any and every kind of serious criticism. There is, therefore, good reason to offer some undiluted criticism as an antidote. Nevertheless, I mention here some of the things that might be said in monarchy's favour.

As a general idea it may have application in small organic communities where the analogy with a certain defensible kind of family life is apposite. Alternatively, it may have had advantages in inchoate and uneducated societies. (Such conditions do not hold in Britain today.) The mixed constitutional form of limited hereditary monarchy established in Britain has advantages in what it is not, rather than intrinsic value of its own. It is not, or not obviously, absolute or tyrannical rule. (But then neither are the systems in innumerable republics.) The Hanover-Windsor dynasty has since 1917 proved to be more public-spirited, and less rapacious and catastrophic, than other royal houses. (Earlier manifestations of the dynasty, however, have been as bad as any other.) Queen Elizabeth II and some members of the current royal family diligently discharge their duties, as they see them. Personally, they have as much charm and humour as most of their subjects, and that is more than history or protocol entitle us to expect. (The diligence and charm of particular people, however, have little or nothing to do with social and political institutions and their justification.)

Historically, monarchy may have been an indispensable means of creating coherent and peaceful societies out of a landscape of warring baronial factions. (If this were true in the past, there is no reason to suppose that it is still true.)

Psychologically, the Monarchy may satisfy a human need for what Percy Black calls 'reciprocal complementarity' – a need to bestow high status on others, and to derive satisfaction from the recognition granted in return. (This may explain the Monarchy's popularity but does not justify it. The same need might be met by more justifiable objects.)

Sociologically and anthropologically, the Monarchy may provide a myth of national identity. (A monarchy myth is not indispensable. Other nations achieve a cohesive identity by means of more admirable and harmless myths.)

Politically, the Monarchy may fulfil the 'dignified' role of *Rex* to complement the 'efficient' head of government, or *Dux*, by acting as a political 'lightning conductor'. (The same function can be performed by more worthy and uncontentious objects.)

It is evident that monarchy might be justifiable in conceivable circumstances, some of which may have prevailed in the past in Britain. At the end of the twentieth century, these conditions no longer prevail. Any useful purpose that the British Monarchy serves can be served as well or better by realistic alternatives which are more worthy and justifiable in a developed, educated, and politically sophisticated society at the turn of the twenty-first century.

At the end of 1988 some desperate Left thinkers are looking (in vain) to the Monarchy as a bulwark against an elected Right wing dictatorship which has neither *noblesse* nor *oblige*. As we have seen, help cannot seriously be expected from Regal quarters. The European Community is more likely to rescue the British people from their unwritten constitution and iniquitous electoral system. The Monarchy itself would not survive for long in a United States of Europe.

Finally, it is worth saying something about the commonly expressed view that criticism of the Monarchy in Britain is inadmissible, or at any rate very unjust, because royal persons are not in a position publicly to respond and to defend themselves. The very prevalence of this idea is in itself indicative of political immaturity and a gross lack of realism about such things in Britain.

It is simply untrue that royal persons cannot respond to criticisms, because they do. Moreover, they are defended by people employed for the purpose. Other prominent persons of distinction can be relied upon when the need arises to purvey defences when bidden or voluntarily. If the Monarchy presumed to be above the need to respond to well-founded criticism, then that would be a *privilege* others do not enjoy, not a *problem* as its defenders suppose. Above all, to suggest that incumbents in public office should in practice never be criticised, for whatever reason, is practically to put them above and beyond criticism altogether. Such a privilege is not claimed even on behalf of God's vicar on Earth himself, and most surely cannot be justified in a democracy.

NOTES AND REFERENCES

INTRODUCTION – No references

CHAPTER 1 – THE MONARCHY AS PERNICIOUS MYTH

1 Morrah (1958, p.41).
2 Worsthorne (1977).
3 Maisky (1962, p.173).
4 Parker (1983, p.262).
5 MacMillan (1972).
6 Martin (1937, p.15).
7 McGirk (1984).
8 Bolingbroke (1926, p.84).
9 Harris (1966) (Mass Observation Surveys); (National Opinion Polls)
   Political Bulletin October 1969 Supp.2, p.2; *NOW* 8th February 1980,
   pp.14-15 (Marplan); *The Times* 10th September 1980, p.4c (Opinion
   Research); *Mail* 23rd March 1986 pp.32-33 (National Opinion Polls).
10 Morrah (1958, p.45).
11 Bolingbroke (1926, p.38).
12 Flew (1967, p.510).
13 Nairn (1988a; 1988b).

CHAPTER 2 – THE MORAL PROBLEM

1 Burke (1969, p.172).
2 Black (1980, p.355).
3 Black (1980, p.356).
4 Black (1980, p.355).
5 Black (1980, p.356).
6 Black (1980, p.358).
7 Black (1980, p.358).
8 Grice (1981).
9 Health Education Council (1987).
10 Townsend and Davidson (1982).
11 Veitch (1987); Rentoul (1987, pp.34-35).
12 Veitch (1986).
13 Halsey *et al.* (1980, pp.163, 172).
14 Halsey *et al.* (1980, p.172).
15 Halsey *et al.* (1980, p.172).
16 Halsey *et al.* (1980, p.209).
17 Halsey *et al.* (1980, p.201).
18 Harris (1966 p.179); *cf.* K. Joseph (1979). 'Is there mobility between
   classes? . . . . . . the blessed answer in this blessed country is that there is
   almost infinite mobility.'
19 Goldthorpe *et al.* (1980, p.252).

20 Goldthorpe *et al.* (1980, p.57).
21 Goldthorpe *et al.* (1980, pp.27, 252); *cf.* Atkinson and Maynard (1983).
22 Goldthorpe *et al.* (1980, p.114).
23 Goldthorpe *et al.* (1980, p.27).
24 Smith (1926, p.14).
25 Rousseau (1954, p.32).
26 Hobbes (1982, p.374).
27 Rentoul (1987, p.26).
28 Rentoul (1987, pp.136-137).
29 de Jouvenel (1957, p.162).
30 Rentoul (1987, p.44); *cf.* Inland Revenue Statistics 1982, Table 48; cited in Atkinson (1983, p.21).
31 Rentoul (1987, p.44).
32 Atkinson (1974, p.23).
33 Inland Revenue Statistics 1983.
34 Rentoul (1987, p.58).
35 *Labour Research*, April 1979; cited in Counter Information Services (1979, p.16).
36 Townsend (1979, pp.272-303).
37 McGlaughlin (1987).
38 Rentoul (1987, p.36).
39 Atkinson (1983). Note that Rentoul estimated in 1987 that Britain had a similar level of wealth inequality to other industrial countries (Rentoul 1987, p.43).
40 Polanyi and Wood (1974).
41 Atkinson (1983, pp.174-177).
42 Glass and Hall (1954); *cf.* Goldthorpe *et al.* (1980 pp.22-23; pp.72-83; p.252).
43 Harbury and Hitchins (1979).
44 Griffith (1977).
45 Levinson (1981a).
46 Levinson (1981a, p.106) and *Legal Action Bulletin* 83, April 1980.
47 Reid (1981); cited in Field (1981, p.171).
48 Levinson (1981b).
49 Griffith (1977, p.213; p.215).

CHAPTER 3 – THE SOCIAL PROBLEM

1 Glass *et al.* (1954); Halsey *et al.* (1980); Goldthorpe *et al.* (1980); Atkinson (1983).
2 Winchester (1982).
3 Simpson and Knightley (1981).
4 Cooke (1977, p.76).
5 Shirer (1960, pp.785-792); *cf.* Cave-Brown (1987, pp.676-683).
6 *Private Eye* (18th November 1983, p.5).
7 Edward VIII and the present Queen's father, George VI, took their leave of one another as masons (Bryan III and Murphy (1979, p.287)). The Duke of Edinburgh's suit to Elizabeth was made by her father conditional on his joining a masonic lodge (Knight (1984, p.211)). Although the masons require secret sworn allegiance to the queen as a condition of membership, it

is reported that the two Queens are unhappy about masonry. Not, however, because it is secret and privileged, but because it excludes women. Prince Charles' refusal to join the society therefore probably reflects his anachronistic chivalrous impulses more than his commitment to an egalitarian, open society (*Guardian*, 12th July 1979, p.6).

8 Rentoul (1987, p.51; p.148).
9 Halsey *et al.* (1980, p.186).
10 *The Dukes*, BBC2 Television 1983; repeated September 1984.
11 Duncan (1970, pp.115-116).
12 Longford (1974, p.49).
13 Longford (1974, p.156).
14 Barnett (1966, p.291).
15 Quoted in Hughes (1956, p.173); Hale (1972, p.42).
16 Hibbert (1964, p.285).
17 Morrah (1958, pp.16-17).
18 Luce III (1969, p.133).
19 Petrie (1933, p.282); Young (1957, pp.72-73).
20 Einzig (1969); Wiener (1981).
21 Hume (1948, p.319).
22 Barber (1986, p.16).
23 Daily Telegraph Editorial, 'Intrusive Body', 14th May 1983, p.14; *Daily Telegraph* Editorial, 'M.P.'s Pay', 9th July 1983, p.12; Julian Critchley, 'Your M.P. − you pay for what you get', *Daily Telegraph*, 3rd May 1986, p.14.
24 *Guardian*, 12th July 1979, p.6.
25 de Jouvenel (1954, p.54); Benn and Peters (1968, p.146f).
26 Hamilton (1975, pp.51-53).
27 Blake (1971).
28 Hamilton (1977, p.153).
29 Stone and Stone (1984).
30 Abercrombie *et al.* (1980).
31 Thomas (1979, p.158); *cf.* Rentoul (1987, p.88).
32 Barthes (1976, p.141).
33 Duchy of Lancaster Revenue Account 1983; Duchy of Cornwall Revenue Account 1985.
34 *Fortune Magazine*, September 1987; cited in *Evening Sentinel*, 21st September 1987 p.1.
35 British Field Sports Society (1981).
36 Grice (1979).
37 British Equestrian Federation (1980).
38 Cameron (1981).
39 Hamilton (1975, p.236).
40 Duke-Wooley (1981).
41 Smith, G. (1981).
42 George (1981, p.40).
43 Downes (1981).
44 *Guardian*, 1st February 1983, p.3.
45 *Question Time*, BBC1 Television, 16th April 1981.
46 Priestley (1962, p.486); Hoggart (1982); Sampson (1982); Bailey (1984).
47 Blake (1971).

48 Mountbatten (1983, p.147).
49 *The Times*, 10th September 1980, p.4).
50 Abercrombie *et al.* (1980). The expression is Marx's − *Capital* vol. 1 p.737.
51 Murray-Brown (1969, p.37); Blake (1971); Hamilton (1975; 1977).
52 Bagehot (1965, p.249).
53 Blumler *et al.* (1971, p.162).
54 Rose and Kavanaugh (1976, pp.563-564).
55 Scott (1982, p.91; p.150; p.157).
56 Duncan (1970, p.40).
57 Petrie (1933, p.76).
58 Petrie (1933, p.17).
59 Petrie (1933, p.270). By 1952 Petrie had, for obvious reasons, suppressed this candid opinion (Petrie (1952)).

CHAPTER 4 − THE POLITICAL PROBLEM

1 Hood-Philips (1970, p.23).
2 Emergency Powers Act 1920, chapter 55; Emergency Powers Act 1964, chapter 38; extracts in Hennessy (1983, pp.270-273).
3 Simon (1982, p.65).
4 Bagehot (1965, p.99).
5 Lord Simon of Glaisdale, McKendrick v Sinclair (1972), SLT HC 110 at 116, 117; cited in de Smith (1981, p.138, n. 80).
6 Heuston (1964, pp.73-74).
7 Routledge (1985a; 1985b). If the Queen did not explicitly say that the mineworkers' union president was to blame for the strike, it is reasonable to suppose that this was an accurate interpretation of her remarks to *Times* reporters. Certainly her husband expressed similar views only a few days earlier in a public address to the Institution of Mining Engineers (Routledge (1985a)).
8 Quoted in Hardie (1979, pp.44-45).
9 Grainger (1977); Worsthorne (1977); Murray-Brown (1969).
10 Prince Charles, in a speech to 'Scottish Business in the Community', 26th November 1985; reported in *Guardian*, 'Prince sees U.K. in fourth division', 27th November 1985, p.1.
11 Ascherson (1985, 1988); Brendon (1986).

CHAPTER 5 − POPULARITY

1 de Jouvenel (1957, p.276).
2 Carlyle (n.d., p.190).
3 Bullock (1962, p.310); Shirer (1959, p.255f; p.229).
4 Reith (1975, p.96).
5 Harris (1966, p.153).
6 Holden (1979, p.41).
7 Rose and Kavanagh (1976, p.556).
8 The Marplan Survey of December 1979 for *NOW*, 8th February 1980, pp.14-15.
9 Harris (1966, p.144).
10 Harris (1966, p.144).

11 Cited in Hamilton (1975, p.55).
12 Mckenzie and Silver (1968, pp.145-152).
13 Heatherington (1981); Roscil (1981).
14 Low and Lean (1981).
15 In a letter to Kugelman, 27th July 1871; epigraph to Curran (1973).
16 Woolf (1935, pp.31-33).
17 Postgate (1951, p.251).

CHAPTER 6 – HARD WORK

1 Young (1957, p.73).
2 Buckingham Palace Press Office (1983).
3 Buckingham Palace Press Office (1983, 1986).
4 Grigg (1969, p.56).
5 Duncan (1970, pp.329-331).
6 Morrah (1958, p.187). (There are conflicting reports from approved sources, *cf.* Laird (1957, p.70).)
7 Laird (1957, p.69).
8 Memorandum of the Queen's Private Secretary to the Select Committee on the Civil List (H.C. 29 (1971-72)), Minutes of Evidence, App.13, Para. 3; cited in de Smith (1981, p.121 n. 10).
9 Duncan (1970, p.103).
10 Morrah (1958, p 110).
11 Secrest (1984).

CHAPTER 7 – BUSINESS

1 St George (1981, p.10).
2 Harris (1966, p.32).
3 Blumler (1971, p.154).
4 Bolingbroke (1926, p.116).
5 Frazer (1970, pp.351-355).
6 Wells (1939, p.35).
7 Duncan (1970, p.17; p.67; p.334; p.342).
8 Buckingham Palace (1983) and Central Statistical Office (1982, pp.318-321; 1986, pp.231-234).
9 World Tourism Organisation (1981; 1986).
10 British Tourism Authority (1971); cited in G. Young (1983, p.42).
11 World Tourism Organisation (1982).
12 Davie (1988).

CHAPTER 8 – TRADITION

1 Whitaker's Almanack 1983, pp.220-224.
2 Fulford (1948, p.107).
3 Bradlaugh (1874).
4 Heuston (1964, p.25).
5 Petrie (1933, p.50).
6 Gretton (1930, p.146).
7 Bocca (1959, p.210).
8 Arthur (1935, p.269).

9 Wells (1944); Nairn (1981); Brendon (1986).
10 Cannadine (1977, 1983).
11 Warwick (1983, pp.128-131).

CHAPTER 9 – MORALITY

1 Bolingbroke (1926, p.124).
2 Duncan (1980, p.14).
3 Petrie (1933, p.67).
4 Cited in Longford (1974, p.200).
5 *Reynolds' News* (1887).
6 Editorial, *Daily Telegraph*, 30th March 1978.
7 Holden (1980, pp.52-53; p.333).
8 Duncan (1970, p.166).
9 Baistow (1977, p.242).
10 Dowd (1984).
11 Holden (1980, p.175).
12 Warwick (1970, p.121).
13 *Reynolds' News* (1887).
14 Dalton (1962, diary, October 19th 1947; cited in Hale (1972, p.155f)).
15 Crossman (1971, pp.721-722).
16 Laird (1959, p.5).
17 Laird (1959, p.341); *cf.* Morrah (1958, p.5; p.172).
18 Central Office of Information (1969).
19 Hamilton (1975, pp.66-69).
20 Whale (1971).
21 Blake (1971).
22 Knightley (1981).
23 Knightley (1980a).
24 Knightley (1980b).
25 Wardroper (1981).
26 Warwick (1980, p.70).
27 Pine (1962, p.25).
28 Woolf (1935, pp.34-35).
29 Martin (1937, pp.102-103).
30 Muggeridge (1981).
31 Sampson (1971, p.220).
32 Cited in Stephenson's Book of Quotations, 9th Edition, 1958, p.1037.
33 Holden (1980, p.334).
34 Herbstein (1981).
35 Hamilton (1975, pp.235-236).
36 Moore (1982); J. Evans and S. Milligan (1982, p.2).
37 Kennedy(1987); Editorial, 'Out of sight out of mind', *Guardian*, 8th April 1987, p.12; R.Bramley, letter to *Guardian*, 9th April 1978, p.14.

CHAPTER 10 – COMMONWEALTH

1 Morrah (1958, p.49).
2 Mann (1939, p.34; pp.50-62; p.94; p.97).
3 Morrah (1958, p.47).
4 Hatch (1977).

5 Adamson (1981).
6 Powell (1986); Editorial, 'The Queen's Alien Circle', *Spectator*, 26th July 1986, p.6; P. Worsthorne, 'God Save the Queen from damaging the Crown', *Sunday Telegraph*, 20th July 1986, p.2; Editorial, 'Who Cares?', *Sun*, 17th July 1986, p.6.
7 Keatley (1984).
8 Longton (1984).
9 Editorial, *Sunday Telegraph*, 22nd January 1984, p.16.
10 Nichols (1973c, p.18).
11 Duncan (1970, p.x).
12 Davie (1982).
13 McClachlan (1977).
14 *Sunday Times*, 14th October 1981, p.6.
15 Smith, A. (1981, p.267).

CHAPTER 11 – CONTINUITY

1 Namier (1955, p.14).
2 Paine (1792); cited in Hamilton (1975, p.192).
3 Gibbon (1960, p.47).

CHAPTER 12 – IMPARTIALITY

1 Bolingbroke (1926, p.98).
2 Home (1981).
3 Morrah (1958, p.45).
4 Laird (1959, p.68).
5 Nichols (1973a).
6 Duncan (1970, p.220).
7 Windsor (1981a, p.21).
8 Longford (1974, p.89).
9 Longford (1974, p.91).
10 Atkinson (1974, p.21).
11 Petrie (1933, p.81).
12 Mountbatten (1980, p.12); edited to '... unlikely to give you their loyal support' (1983, p.25).
13 Spender (1923, p.171).
14 Saxe-Coburg-Gotha, Victoria (1931, p.170).
15 Hardie (1979, p.77).
16 Thompson (1971, p.145).
17 Esher (1934, pp.433-434).
18 Sommer (1960, p.231).
19 Cowling (1971, p.365).
20 Hale (1972, p.110).
21 Montgomery (1957, p.239).
22 *Manchester Guardian*, 23rd October 1935; cited in Hale (1972, p.133).
23 Hale (1972, p.133f).
24 Hale (1972, p.90f).
25 Longford (1974, p.195).
26 Hale (1972, p.88).
27 George (1981, p.48).

28 Crossman (1981, pp.249-250).
29 Profile, *New Statesman* 93 (2411), 3rd June 1977, p.741.
30 Holden (1980, p.330).
31 McInnes (1966).

CHAPTER 13 – POWERLESSNESS

1 Nicolson (1962, pp.290-291).
2 Higgins (1969, p.95).
3 Simon (1982).
4 Phelps (1977, p.26f).
5 Clarke (1974); Simon (1982); Bogdanor (1982).
6 Morrah (1958, p.5).
7 Morrah (1958, p.165).
8 Editorial, *Guardian*, 28th August 1982, p.8; Bogdanor (1982; 1983).
9 Blake (1969, p.22).
10 Kent (1950, pp.51-52).
11 Hale (1972, p.53).
12 Nicolson (1962a, p.292).
13 Petrie (1933, p.292).
14 Emergency Powers Acts 1920, 1964; extracts in Hennessy
     (1983, pp.270-273).
15 Nicolson (1962a, p.294).
16 Worsthorne (1979); Mountbatten (1980).
17 Blake (1984).
18 Simon (1982, p.65).

CHAPTER 14 – LIBERTY

1 Morrah (1958, p.167).
2 McGirk (1984).
3 Copi (1972, p.74).
4 Cowling (1978, p.11).
5 Cassels (1969, p.39; p.32).
6 Morrah (1969, p.112).
7 Walker (1981).
8 Wright (1987, pp.363-372).
9 Worsthorne (1979).
10 Grigg (1978b).
11 Gretton (1930, pp.70-71).
12 Martin (1937, p.102).
13 Middleton (1957, p.35); Laird (1958, p.206); Longford (1974, p.74).

CHAPTER 15 – NON-RATIONAL VIEWS OF MONARCHY

1 de Maistre (1965, p.114).
2 de Maistre (1965, p.187).
3 de Maistre (1965, p.195).
4 Gretton (1930, p.49).
5 Morrah (1958, p.39).
6 de Jouvenel (1957, p.229).
7 Nicolson (1962a, p.302).

8 Powell; cited Luce III (1969, p.129); *cf.* Grainger (1977).
9 Luce III (1969, p.131).
0 Bagehot (1965, p.86).
1 Nicolson (1962a, p.280).

CHAPTER 16 – IRRATIONALISM

1 Wilson (1970); Hollis and Lukes (1982).
2 Feyerabend (1975; 1978; 1987).
3 Brown (1978).
4 de Maistre (1965, p.207).
5 de Maistre (1965, p.108).
6 Burke (1969, p.183).
7 Burke (1969, p.156).
8 Burke (1969, p.171).
9 de Maistre (1965, pp.186-187).
0 de Maistre (1965, p.270).
1 de Maistre (1965, p.161).
2 Burke (1969, pp.136-137).
3 de Jouvenel (1957, p.190).

CHAPTER 17 – MATERIALISM

1 Marx (1978a; p.67).
2 Marx (1975, p.452).
3 Marx (1978a, p.64).
4 Abercrombie *et al.* (1980).
5 Marx (1978b).
6 Marx (1978b, pp.42-44).

CHAPTER 18 – RATIONALITY

1 Russell (1946, p.1).

CHAPTER 19 – RATIONALITY AND IRRATIONALISM

1 Burke (1969, p.285f).
2 Burke (1969, p.299).
3 de Maistre (1965, p.285).
4 Peters (1972, p.58).
5 Burke (1969, p.175).
6 Paine (1945, p.292).
7 Paine (1945, p.292).
8 Paine (1945, p.264).
9 Wild (1938, pp.211-225).
0 Russell (1947, p.145).
1 de Jouvenel (1957, p.230).
2 Paine (1945, pp.260-261).
3 Bolingbroke (1926, p.53).
4 Longford (1974, p.260).
5 Longford (1974, p.229).

CHAPTER 20 – IRRATIONALITY AND MATERIALISM

1 Ryan (1981).
2 Weber (1968, p.45).
3 Engels letter; cited in Lee and Newby (1983, p.116).
4 Gramsci (1971, p.168).

CHAPTER 21 – MYTH

1 Duncan, H.D. (1962; 1968; 1969).
2 Duncan, H.D. (1962, p.11); cited in Cleveland (1973, p.30f).
3 Reported in *Evening Post*, Wellington, New Zealand, 31st March 1970; cited in Cleveland (1973, p.35).
4 Shils and Young (1953, p.5).
5 Pethick-Lawrence (1953, p.324).
6 Cleveland (1973, p.34).
7 Bagehot (1965, p.100).
8 Weightman (1953, p.413).
9 Marx (1978a, p.150).
10 *ibid.*
11 Birnbaum (1955, p.15).
12 Pethick-Lawrence (1953, p.324).
13 de Laguna (1927, pp.345-346).
14 Farb (1968, pp.280-285).
15 Nyozekan (1952); cited in *Bartlett's Familiar Quotations* (14th Edition), p.913.
16 *ibid.*
17 Bullock (1968, pp.76-77).
18 Barthes (1976).
19 Paine (1945, p.256)

CHAPTER 22 – THE MONARCHY MYTH

1 Morrah (1958, pp.38-39).
2 Gretton (1930, p.101).
3 Guiness (1984b, p.34).
4 Gretton (1930, p.12).
5 James Stuart I (1918); Filmer (1949); Bolingbroke (1926, p.93).
6 Hobbes (1968).
7 Figgis (1965).
8 James Stuart I (1918).
9 Gretton (1930, pp.27-28).
10 de Maistre (1965, p.98); Longford (1974, p.260).
11 Hobbes (1968).
12 Bolingbroke (1926, p.83); Gretton (1930, p.18).
13 de Maistre (1965, p.116); Worsthorne (1977, pp.167-168).
14 Bagehot (1965, p.96).
15 Turner (1968, p.580).
16 Birnbaum (1955, p.18).
17 Morrah (1958, p.13).
18 Marx (1978b, p.12).

9 Pethwick-Lawrence (1953, p.324).
10 Martin (1937, pp.102-103); Woolf (1935, p.35).
11 Sampson (1971, p.230).
12 McInnes (1966, p.148); Brendon (1986).
13 Marx (1978b, p.9).
14 McInnes (1966, p.148).

CHAPTER 23 – RELIGION

1 Shils and Young (1953, p.75).
2 Figgis (1965, p.155).
3 Petrie (1933, p.25-26).
4 Enoch Powell; cited in Phelps (1977, p.16).
5 Nichols (1973b).
6 Morrah (1958, p.40).
7 Shils and Young (1953, p 69).
8 Bagehot (1965, pp.86 − 90).
9 Cited in McLachlan (1975, p.312).
10 Howard (1977, p.89).
11 Locke (1965).
12 Bolingbroke (1926, p.54).
13 cited in Figgis (1965, p.258).
14 Nicolson (1962a, p.195).
15 McLachlan (1975, p.312).
16 Laird (1959, pp.172-173).
17 McKinnon (1963, p.17).
18 *ibid.* (p.27).
19 Windsor (1975).
20 Russell (1957, pp.24-47).
21 Geertz (1968, p.403).
22 Central Statistical Office (1983, pp.150-151); (1987, pp.175-176).
23 Grigg (1978a, p.8).
24 Weightman (1953, p.411).
25 Shils and Young (1953, p.75); *cf.* Nicolson (1962a, p.27 f).
26 Rose and Kavanagh (1976, p.566).
27 *ibid.*
28 McLachlan (1975).
29 Langley (1978); *cf.* McLachlan (1975).

CHAPTER 24 – PSYCHOLOGY

1 Jones (1964); *cf.* Martin (1963, pp.177-179).
2 Jones (1964, p.228).
3 Masters (1973, p.78; p.99; p.47).
4 Archer (1935); cited in Masters (1973, p.132).
5 Ansbacher (1959, pp.376-382); cited in Sulloway (1980, p.363).
6 Peters (1958, pp.52-61).
7 Erwin (1984).
8 Popper (1969, pp.37-38).

CHAPTER 25 – SUMMARY AND CONCLUSIONS – MYTHS — no references

CHAPTER 26 – HISTORY AND 'PERSONS'

1 James Stuart I (1619; 1918, pp.307-308); cited in Howard (1977, p.24).
2 *Ecclesiasticus* 38:24-25.
3 Burke (1969, p.138).

CHAPTER 27 – LIBERTY

1 Scruton (1980, p.119).
2 Hogg (1947, p.46).
3 Windsor (1975).
4 Bocca (1959, p.14).
5 Berlin (1958, p.50).
6 Mill (1956, pp.8-9).
7 Hanson (1973).
8 Blumler (1971); Baistow (1973); Burnett (1981); Brunt (1984); Burchill (1984).
9 Callaghan (1982).
10 Bagehot (1965, pp.247-249).
11 Martin (1963, p.176).
12 Blumler *et al.* (1971).

CHAPTER 28 – EQUALITY

1 Firth (1891, p.301), quoted in Sabine (1963, p.483) and Hampton (1984, p.188).
2 Murray Brown (1969, p.204); Gorer (1966, pp.63-71).
3 Worsthorne (1977, p.180).
4 *ibid.* (p.168).
5 Hayek (1960, p.98); Butt (1977).
6 Wells (1969, pp.46-47).

CHAPTER 29 – JUSTICE

1 Miller (1976).
2 Hume (1741; 1948, p.319).
3 Einzig (1969).
4 Rawls (1972).
5 Grainger (1977); Levy (1983).

CHAPTER 30 – FRATERNITY

1 Tawney (1951, p.225).
2 *Galatians* 3:26.
3 Butler (1969, p.201).
4 Halsey (1978, p.11).
5 Titmus (1970).
6 Worsthorne (1977, p.179).
7 Worsthorne (1977, p.180).
8 Holden (1979, p.133).
9 Duncan (1970, p.209).
10 Stephen (1873; 1967, p.221).

11 Stephen (1967, p.15).
12 *Times* report, 29th July 1981, p.28a
13 Honderich (1980).

CHAPTER 31 – UTILITY

1 Bagehot (1965, p.614).
2 de Jouvenel (1957, p.21; pp.45-49).
3 Bagehot (1965, p.245).
4 Bagehot (1965, p.26).
5 de Jouvenel (1957, p.10).
6 de Jouvenel (1957, p.47).
7 Bell (1947).
8 Eliot (1948).
9 Eliot (1948, pp.42-43).
10 de Jouvenel (1957, p.82).
11 Bottomore (1964, p.147).
12 Eliot (1948, p.49).
13 Bolingbroke (1926, p.56); *cf.* Harris (1966, p.162).
14 Bolingbroke (1926, p.50).
15 Gretton (1933, p.63).

CHAPTER 32 – SUMMARY AND CONCLUSIONS – DEMOCRACY – no references

CHAPTER 33 – CONSTITUTIONAL CHANGES

1 J. Harvey and L Bather (1977), pp.213-237.
2 P. Norton (1982).
3 G. Marshal (1982), Review of P. Norton's *'The Constitution in Flux'* – *Times Higher Education Supplement*, 19th November, p.17; Ascherson (1985).
4 N. St John Stevas (1980) – *Open Letter to Conservative Constituency Party Chairman*; reported by K. Renshaw, 'Labour split poses dilemma for Queen' in *Sunday Express*, 5th October, p.1; Bogdanor (1983).
5 Bagehot (1965, pp.116-117).
6 Bagehot (1965, p.109).
7 Quoted in R. Harrison (1980), review of N. Gash (1979), *Aristocracy and People* in *Guardian*, 10th January.
8 Woolf (1935); Martin (1936; 1937; 1963); Black (1953); Blumler *et al.* (1971); Blumler and Nossiter (1975); Cleveland (1973); di Michele (1979); Brunt (1984); Nairn (1985); Birnbaum (1955); Mosley (1985).

CHAPTER 34 – REFORM

1 Grigg (1957); Muggeridge (1957; 1981).
2 Martin (1936); Gossman (1962, p.60).
3 Stewart (1952).
4 Crossman (1981, pp.249-250).
5 Hamilton (1975, pp.235-236).
6 Bagehot (1965, pp.105-106).
7 Adams (1944, p.13).
8 Jennings (1972, p.20).

 9 Marlowe (1973, p.41).
10 Thackeray (1929, p.320; p.312).
11 Bogdanor (1983, p.83).
12 Bogdanor (1983, p.123).
13 Bogdanor (1983, p.122).
14 Bagehot (1965, pp.108-109).
15 Bogdanor (1983).
16 Bogdanor (1982).
17 Blake (1971; 1984); Harvey and Bather (1977, p.50).
18 Bagehot (1965, p.207).

CHAPTER 35 – ABOLITION OF THE MONARCHY

 1 Hall (1939, p.31).
 2 Thackeray (1929).
 3 Bradlaugh (1874); Carnegie (1893); Martin (1936); Gossman (1962).
 4 Dudley Sommer (1960), *Haldane of Cloan: his life and times 1856 – 1928*,
   Allen and Unwin, London, pp 30-31; quoted in Martin (1963, p.180, n. 5).
 5 Holden (1980, p.41).
 6 Peabody (1970); Blaustein and Flanz (1977); McWhinney (1985).
 7 Lane (1981).
 8 Weber (1964, pp.328-341).
 9 Jones (1979, p.57).
10 Jennings (1945, p.94 ff.)
11 Jennings (1945, p.91).
12 Lords (1986).
13 Jones (1979).
14 Harvey and Bather (1977, pp.48-50).
15 Butt (1980).
16 Scruton (1980, p.56).
17 Butt (1980).
18 Barker (1928).
19 Cole (1920).
20 Laski (1917; 1919; 1921; 1925a; 1925b).
21 Barker (1928,p.178); cited in Birch (1964, p.108).
22 Cole (1920, p.108; p.115); cited in Birch (1964, p.109).
23 Laski (1963, p.59).
24 Hume (1948, pp.377-378; p.382).
25 Jennings (1945, p.94).

CHAPTER 36 – POLITICAL POSTSCRIPT

 1 Martin (1936, p.169).
 2 Esher (1934, p.433-434), quoted in Martin (1963, p.69).
 3 Jeremy Bentham (1843), *Works* IX, Bowring edition, Edinburgh, pp.1-2;
   cited in Gossman (1962, pp.47-48).
 4 Hardie (1979, p.77).
 5 Birch (1964, p.89); *cf.* Labour Party (1923).
 6 Weightman (1952); Hale (1971; 1972).
 7 Hanson (1973); *New Statesman* (1977); Tweedie (1979); Fowles (1982);

Evans and Milligan (1982); Mosely (1985); Burchill (1984; 1985); Brunt (1985); Brendon (1984, 1986); Nairn (1981, 1985, 1988a, 1988b).
8 Fenton (1977); Chappell (1986).
9 Harris (1988).
10 Hogg (1947, p.46).
11 Doring (1983).
12 Ascherson (1985).
13 Labour Party (1923).
14 Hale (1971; 1972).
15 Counter Information Services (1977): *Socialist Youth* (1981); *Militant* (1983).
16 Whitehead (1981).

CHAPTER 37 – AFTERWORD – no references

BIBLIOGRAPHY

Abercrombie, N., Hill, S., and Turner, B.S. (1980), *The Dominant Ideology Thesis*, George Allen and Unwin, London.

Adams, G.B. (1944), *Constitutional History of England* (2nd edition); revised by R.L. Schuyler; Cape, London.

Adamson, D. (1981), 'Is the Commonwealth being kept up past its bed-time?' in *Daily Telegraph*, 28th September, p.14.

Ansbacher, H.L. (1959), 'The significance of the Socio-Economic status of the Patients of Freud and Adler' in *The American Journal of Psychotherapy*, 13, pp.376-382.

Archer, W.L. (1935), *On Dreams*; T. Besterman (ed.); Methuen, London.

Arthur, G. (1935), *King George V* (1929), Cape, London.

Ascherson, N. (1985), 'Republicans who stay in the closet' in *Observer*, 6th October, p.9.

Ascherson, N. (1988), 'The State burgles our freedoms' in *Observer*, 24th January, p.7.

Atkinson, A.B. (1974), *Unequal Shares*, Penguin, Harmondsworth.

Atkinson, A.B. (1983), *The Economics of Inequality* (2nd edition), Clarendon Press, Oxford.

Atkinson, A.B., Maynard, A.K., and Trinder, C.G. (1983), *Parents and Children: incomes in two generations*, Heinemann, London.

Bagehot, W. (1965), *The English Constitution* (1867), introduction by R.H.S. Crossman, Fontana, London.

Bailey, D. (1984), 'Three loud jeers for the Hooray Henrys' in *Mail on Sunday*, 17th June, p.8.

Baistow, T. (1977), 'Loyal Fourth Estate' in *New Statesman*, 93(2411), 3rd June, pp.742-744.

Barber, L. (1986), 'The Duchess Entertains' in *Sunday Express Magazine*, 17th August, pp.14-16.

Barker, E. (1928), *Political Thought in England: 1848-1914* (2nd edition), Clarendon Press, Oxford.

Barker, E. (1945), 'British Constitutional Monarchy' in *Essays on Government*, Clarendon Press, Oxford, pp.1-19.

Barker, E. (1961), *Principles of Social and Political Theory*, Oxford University Press, London.

Barnett, C. (1966), *The Swordbearers*, Penguin, Harmondsworth.

Barthes, R. (1976), 'Myth Today' in *Mythologies*, Paladin, London, pp.109-159.

Bell, C (1947), *Civilisation*, Penguin, Harmondsworth.

Benn, S.I., and Peters, R.S. (1968), *Social Principles and the Democratic State*, George Allen and Unwin, London.

Berlin, I. (1958), *Two Concepts of Liberty*, Oxford University Press, Oxford.

Birch. A.H. (1964), *Representative and Responsible Government*, George Allen and Unwin, London.

rnbaum, N. (1955), 'Monarchs and Sociologists' in *The Sociological Review*, 3(1), pp.5-23.

shop, P. (1981), 'Democracy rules for the princess' in *Observer*, 11 January, p.4.

lack, D. (1980), *Inequalities in Health*. Department of Health and Social Security, London. Typescript, restricted circulation. Ref. Townsend, P. and Davidson, N. (1982).

lack, P. (1953), *The Mystique of Modern Monarchy*, Watts, London.

lake, R. (1969), 'The Crown and Politics in the Twentieth Century' in J. Murray-Brown (ed.), *The Monarchy and its future*, George Allen and Unwin, London, pp.11-26.

lake, R. (1971), 'The Case for the Queen' in *Spectator*, 7459, 12th June, p.808.

lake, R. (1984), *Monarchy*, Gresham Special Lecture Series, Gresham College, City University, London, 3rd July.

laustein, A.S., and Flanz, G.H. (1977), *Constitutions of the Countries of the World*, 15 vols., Oceana, New York.

lumler, J.G., Brown, J.R., Ewbank, A.T., and Nossiter, T.J. (1971), 'Attitudes to the Monarchy: their structure and development during a ceremonial occasion' in *Political Studies* 19(2), pp.149-171.

lumler, J.G., and Nossiter, T.J. (1975a), 'The Monarchy: Powers, Duties and Popular Feelings' in Audio Learning Cassette POA020, London.

lumler, J.G., and Nossiter, T.J. (1975b), 'The Monarchy: Its Significance, and a Comparison with Other Heads of State' in Audio Learning Cassette POA020, London.

occa, G. (1959), *The Uneasy Heads: A report on European Monarchy*, Weidenfeld and Nicolson, London.

ogdanor, V. (1982), 'The Royal Right to Refuse' in *Guardian*, 28th August, p.17.

ogdanor, V. (1983), *Multi-Party Politics and the Constitution*, Cambridge University Press, Cambridge.

olingbroke, Viscount (Henry St John) (1926), *Letters on the Spirit of Patriotism, and The Idea of a Patriot King* (1745); introduction by A. Hassall; Clarendon Press, Oxford.

ottomore, T. (1964), *Élites in Society*, Penguin, Harmondsworth.

radlaugh, C. (1874), *The Impeachment of the House of Brunswick* (4th edition), Watts, London.

rendon, P. (1984), 'Totem and Taboo' in *New Statesman*, 17th August, pp.8-10.

rendon, P. (1986), *Our Own Dear Queen*, Secker and Warburg, London.

ritish Field Sports Society (1981), *What the British Field Sports Society Does for You*, British Field Sports Society, London.

ritish Equestrian Federation (1980), *The Case for the Riding Horse*; foreword by the Duke of Edinburgh; British Equestrian Federation, Kenilworth.

ritish Tourist Authority (1971), *Research Newsletter* no 3, Winter; cited in Young, G. (1973), *Tourism*, Penguin, Harmondsworth.

rown, H. (1978), 'On being rational' in *The American Philosophical Quarterly* 15(4) pp.241-248.

Brunt, R. (1984), 'The Changing Face of Royalty' in *Marxism Today* 28(7), pp.7-12.

Bryan III, J., and Murphy, J.V. (1979), *The Windsor Story*, Granada, London.

Buckingham Palace Press Office (1983; 1986), *Overseas visits by the Queen when Sovereign*. Photocopy, March; August.

Bullock, A. (1962), *Hitler − a Study in Tyranny*, Penguin, Harmondsworth.

Burke, E. (1969), *Reflections on the Revolution in France* (1790); C.C O'Brien (ed.); Penguin, Harmondsworth.

Burnett, A. (1981), 'Wedding Thoughts' in *Independent Broadcasting*, November, pp.2-5.

Burchill, J. (1984), 'The royal family must go pure showbiz' in *Sunday Times*, 14th October, p.35.

Burchill, J. (1985), 'They bring out the worst in the British' in *Sunday Times*, 11th August, p.37.

Butler, J. (1969), *Sermons*, Bell, London.

Butt, R. (1977), 'Why the British need to have a Monarch' in *Sunday Times*, 5th June, p.14.

Butt, R (1980), 'The making of a new upper house' in *Sunday Times*, 31st July, p.14.

Callaghan, J. (1982), 'Many duties are humdrum, but she never shirks' in *Sunday Times*, 7th February, p.5.

Cameron, J. (1981), 'Cut to the Bone' in *Guardian*, 8th December, p.10.

Cannadine, D. (1977), 'The not so ancient traditions of Monarchy' in *New Society*, 40(765), 2nd June, pp.438-440.

Cannadine, D. (1983), 'The British Monarchy: 1820-1977' in E. Hobsbawm, T. Ranger (eds.), *The Invention of Tradition*, Cambridge University Press, pp.101-164.

Carnegie, A. (1893), *Triumphant Democracy*, Scribner, New York.

Carlyle, T. (no date), *Oliver Cromwell*; E. Sanderson (ed.); Hutchinson, London.

Cassels, A. (1969), *Fascist Italy*, Routledge and Kegan Paul, London.

Cave-Brown, A. (1987), *C: The Secret Life of Stuart Menzies*. Routledge and Kegan Paul, London.

Central Office of Information (1969), *The British Monarchy* (1st edition), Her Majesty's Stationery Office, London.

Central Office of Information (1975), *The Monarchy in Britain*, Her Majesty's Stationery Office, London.

Central Statistical Office (1983), *Annual Abstract of Statistics no 18*, Central Statistical Office, London.

Central Statistical Office (1983), *Social Trends 13: Participation in Religion*, Central Statistical Office, London, pp.150-151.

Central Statistical Office (1987), *Social Trends 17: Participation in Religion*, Central Statistical Office, London, pp.175-176.

Chappell, H. (1986), 'The Fergie Factor' in *New Society* 75(1213), 28th March, pp.533-534.

Clarke, G. (1974), 'Mr Short and the Left Wing in Dispute on the Queen's freedom of choice' in *The Times*, 11th May, p.2c.

Cleveland, L. (1973), 'Royalty as symbolic drama: the 1970 New Zealand tour' in *The Journal of Commonwealth Political Studies* XI, pp.28-45.

ole, G.D.H. (1920), *Social Theory*, Methuen, London.

ooke, A. (1977), *Six Men*, Penguin, Harmondsworth.

ooper, D.E. (1980), *Illusions of Equality*, Routledge and Kegan Paul, London.

opi, I.M. (1972), *Introduction to Logic* (4th edition), Collier MacMillan, London.

ounter Information Services (1977), *Highness: Jubilee Anti-Report*, Counter Information Services, London.

ounter Information Services (1979), *The Wealthy: Anti-Report no. 25*, Counter Information Services, London.

owling, M. (1971), *The Impact of Labour 1920-1924*, Cambridge University Press, Cambridge.

owling, M. (1978), *Conservative Essays*, Cassels, London.

rossman, R.H.S. (1971), 'The Royal Tax Avoiders' in *New Statesman*, 28th May, pp.721-722.

rossman, R.H.S. (1981), *The Crossman Diaries vol. 2*, David and Charles, London.

urran, J. (1973), *The Manufacture of News*, Constable, London.

aily Telegraph Editorial (1978), '*Qui mal y pense*' in *Daily Telegraph*, 30th March; cited in Warwick, C. (1983), *Princess Margaret*, Weidenfeld and Nicolson, London, p.152.

alton, E.H.J.N. (1962), *High Tide and After: Memoirs 1945-1960*, Frederick Muller, London.

anziger, D. (1988), *Eton Voices*, Viking, London.

avie, M. (1982), 'Fetters that bind Aussies to the Poms' in *Observer*, 21 November, p.16.

avie, M. (1988), 'Making our Palaces Pay' in *Observer*, 6th March, p.12.

öring, H. (1983), 'Who are the Social Democrats?' in *New Society*, 8th September, pp.351-353.

owd, E. (1984), 'Not Amused' in *Sunday Mirror*, 30th September, p.5.

ownes, S. (1981), *Information Letter*, October, The Jockey Club, Newmarket.

uke-Wooley, R.M. (1981), Letter to the author *re* the Hurlingham Polo Association, dated 2nd November.

uncan, A. (1970), *The Reality of Monarchy*, Heinemann, London.

uncan, H.D. (1962), *Communication and Social Order*, Bedminster Press, New York.

uncan, H.D. (1968), *Symbols and Society*, Oxford University Press, New York.

uncan, H.D. (1969), *Symbols and Social Theory*, Oxford University Press, New York.

uncan, N. (1980), 'The Queen should abdicate at 60' (Marplan Survey) in *NOW*, 8th February, p.14.

inzig, P. (1969), *Decline and Fall*, MacMillan, London.

liot, T.S. (1948), *Notes towards the definition of culture*, Faber, London.

rwin, E. (1984), 'The Standing of Psychoanalysis', in *The British Journal for the Philosophy of Science* 35(2), June, pp.115-128.

sher, R. (1934), *Journals and Letters of Reginald, Viscount Esher* vol. 11,

Nicholson and Watson, London; cited in Martin (1963, p.183, n. 5).

Farb, P. (1968), *Man's Rise to Civilisation*, Dutton, New York.
Fenton, J. (1977), 'Why they hate the Queen', in *New Statesman* 93(2411), 3r
    June, p.730.
Feyerabend, P. (1975), *Against Method*, New Left Books, London.
Feyerabend, P. (1978), *Science in a Free Society*, New Left Books, London.
Feyerabend, P. (1987), *Farewell to Reason*, Verso, London.
Field, F. (1973), *Unequal Britain (A Report on the cycle of inequality)*, Arrow,
    London.
Field, F. (1979), *The Wealth Report*, Routledge and Kegan Paul, London.
Field, F. (1981), *Inequality in Britain: Freedom, Welfare and the State*, Fontana
    London.
Figgis, J.N. (1965), *The Divine Right of Kings* (1896), Harper, London.
Filmer, J (1949), *Patriarcha*; P. Lastlett (ed.); Blackwell, Oxford.
Firth, C.H. (ed.) (1891), *The Clarke Papers* (including the Putney Debates)
    vol. 1, Camden Society Publications, London.
Flew, A.G.N. (1967), 'Ends and Means' in P. Edwards (ed.), *Encyclopaedia o*
    Philosophy vol. 2, Collier MacMillan, London, pp.508-511.
Flew, A.G.N. (1981), *The Politics of Procrustes*, Temple Smith, London.
Fowles, J. (1982), 'The Falklands and a death foretold', in *Guardian*, 14th
    August, p.7.
Frazer, J.G. (1970), *The Golden Bough: A study of Magic and Religion* (1922),
    MacMillan, London.
Fulford, R. (1948), *Royal Dukes*, Pan, London.
Fulford, R. (1970), *Hanover to Windsor*, Fontana, London.

Garthorne-Hardy, G.M. (1953), 'Democratic Monarchy' in *International*
    Affairs XXIX pp.273-276.
Geertz, C. (1968), 'Religion: Anthropological Study' in D.L. Sills (ed.),
    International Encyclopaedia of the Social Sciences vol. 13, Collier
    Macmillan, London, pp.398-406
George, N. St. (1981), *Royal Quotes*, David and Charles, London.
Gibbon, E. (1960), *The Decline and Fall of the Roman Empire*, abr. D.M.Low
    Harcourt Brace, New York.
Glasgow University Media Group (1976), *Bad News*, Routledge and Kegan
    Paul, London.
Glasgow University Media Group (1980), *More Bad News*, Routledge and
    Kegan Paul, London.
Glass, D.V., and Hall, J.R. (1954), 'Social mobility in London: a study in
    inter-generation changes in status' in Glass, D.V. (ed.) *Social Mobility*
    in Britain, Routledge and Kegan Paul, London, pp.177-265.
Goldthorpe, J., Llewellyn, C., and Payne, C. (1980), *Social Mobility and Class*
    Structure in Modern Britain, Clarendon Press, Oxford.
Gorer, G. (1966), *The Danger of Equality*, Cresset, London.
Gossman, N.J. (1962), 'Republicanism in 19th Century England' in
    International Review of Social History, VII, pp.47-60.
Grainger, J.H. (1977), 'The Activity of Monarchy' in *The Cambridge Quarter*
    7(4) pp.297-313.
Gramsci, A. (1971), *Prison Notebooks*; Q. Hoare and G. Nowell-Smith (eds.);

Lawrence and Wishart, London.

Greaves, H.R.G. (1948), *The British Constitution* (2nd edition), George Allen and Unwin, London.

Gretton, R.H. (1930), *The King's Majesty*, Faber and Faber, London.

Grice, E. (1979), 'Horses nibble away the green belt' in *Sunday Times*, 25th November, p.4.

Grice, E. (1981), 'Why the dole can led to suicide' in *Sunday Times*, 3rd August, p.3a.

Griffith, J.A.G. (1977), *The Politics of the Judiciary* (3rd edition), Fontana Collins, London.

Griffith, J.A.G. (1985), *The Politics of the Judiciary* (4th edition), Fontana Collins, London.

Grigg, J. (1957), 'The Monarchy Today' in *The National and English Review* 149(894), August, pp.61-66.

Grigg, J. (1969), 'A summer storm' in J. Murray-Brown (ed.), *The Future of the Monarchy*, George Allen and Unwin, London, pp.43-56.

Grigg, J. (1978a), 'Halting the drift from God' in *Observer*, 23rd July, p.8.

Grigg, J. (1978b), 'Prince, Church and State' in *Spectator* 41(7851), 30th December, p.15.

Guardian Editorial (1982), 'Referee without a rule book' in *Guardian*, 28th August, p.8.

Guinness, J., and Guinness, C. (1984a), *The House of Mitford*, Hutchinson, London.

Guinness, J., and Guinness, C. (1984b), 'Unity Mitford' in *Sunday Times*, 18th November, pp.33-34.

Hale, T.F. (1971), 'The Labour Party and the Monarchy' in *The Contemporary Review* 219, pp.73-79.

Hale, T.F. (1972), *The British Labour Party and the Monarchy*. Ph.D. dissertation, University of Kentucky, unpublished, University Microfilm International, British Library Microfilm 73-7346.

Hall, D.G.E. (1939), *A Brief Survey of English Constitutional History*, Harrap, London.

Halsey, A.H. (1978a), 'The Social Order' in *The Listener* 99, 16th February, pp.208-211.

Halsey, A.H. (1978b), *Change in British Society*. Oxford University Press, London.

Halsey, A.H., Heath, A.F., and Ridge J.M. (1980), *Origins and Destinations: family, class and education in modern Britain*. Oxford University Press, London.

Hamilton, W. (1969), 'The Crown, the Cash and the Future' in J. Murray-Brown (ed.), *The Monarchy and its Future*, George Allen and Unwin, London, pp.59-70.

Hamilton, W. (1975), *My Queen and I*, Quartet, London.

Hamilton, W. (1977), 'The case against the Monarchy' in *The Queen*, Penguin Special series, Penguin, Harmondsworth, pp.145-164.

Hampton, C. (ed.) (1984), *A Radical Reader*, Penguin, Harmondsworth.

Hanson, D. (1973), 'The Royal Wedding Project' in *New Society*, 26(576), 18th October, pp.140-141.

Harbury, L.D., and Hitchins, D.M.W.N. (1979), *Inheritance and Wealth inequality in Britain*, George Allen and Unwin, London.

Hardie, F. (1979), *The Political Influence of the British Monarchy 1868-1952*, Batsford, London.

Harris, L. (1966), *Long to Reign over us? The status of the Royal Family in the 1960s*, William Kimber, London.

Harris, K. (1983), 'The Compleat Consort' [Philip Mountbatten] in *Observer Review*, 2nd October, p.25.

Harris, R. (1988), 'Charles is warned by Tebbit' in *Observer*, 10th April. p.1.

Harvey, J., and Bather, L. (1977), *The British Constitution* (4th edition), MacMillan, London.

Hatch, J. (1977), 'Twenty-five years of Commonwealth' in *New Statesman* 9(2411), 3rd June, pp.734-735.

Hayek, F.A. (1980), *The Constitution of Liberty*, Routledge and Kegan Paul, London.

Health Education Council (1987), *The Health Divide*, Health Education Council, London.

Heatherington, P. (1981), 'Queen target for bomb at Sullom Voe' in *Guardian*, 12th May, p.1.

Hennessy, P. (1983), *States of Emergency*, Routledge and Kegan Paul, London.

Herbstein, D. (1981), 'The Royal Estate where just one tenant in 850 has a black face' in *Sunday Times*, 23rd August, p.4.

Heuston, R.F.V. (1964), *Essays in Constitutional Law*, Stevens, London.

Hibbert, C. (1964), *The Court at Windsor*, Longmans, London.

Higgins, G. (1969), '*Monarchie á l'Anglaise*' in J. Murray-Brown (ed.), *The Monarchy and its Future*, George Allen and Unwin, London, pp.87-96.

Hills, B. (1977), 'The Coronation is over — Carry on Suffering' in *Sunday Times*, 11th December, p.11a.

Hogg, Q. (1947), *The Case for Conservatism*, Penguin, West Drayton.

Hoggart, R. (1982), 'The Divisive Society' in *Observer Review*, 21st February, p.27.

Hobbes, T. (1968), *Leviathan* (1651); C.B. MacPherson (ed.); Penguin, Harmondsworth.

Hobsbawm, E.J. (1975), 'Fraternity' in *New Society*, 27th November, pp.421-423.

Holden, A. (1980), *Charles, Prince of Wales*, Pan, London.

Hollis, M., and Lukes, S. (eds.) (1982), *Rationality and Relativism*, Blackwell, Oxford.

Home, C.D. (1981), 'The Dilemma of the British Monarchy' in *The Times Royal Wedding Magazine*, 23rd July, pp.13-15; p.17; p.19.

Honderich, T. (1980), *Violence for Equality*, Penguin, Harmondsworth.

Hood-Philips, O. (1970), *Reform of the Constitution*, Chatto and Windus, London.

House of Commons (1972), *Report on the Select Committee on the Civil List* (appendix 13), H.C. 29 1971-72.

Howard, P. (1977), *The British Monarchy*, Hamilton, London.

Hughes, E. (1956), *The Life of Keir Hardie*, George Allen and Unwin, London.

Hume, D. (1948), *Moral and Political Philosophy*, Hafner, Darien, Connecticut.

Jennings, W.I. (1945), *The British Constitution*, Cambridge University Press, Cambridge.

Jennings, W.I. (1972), *The Queen's Government*, Penguin, Harmondsworth.

Johnson, F. (1973), 'The matter of the monarchy', in *Daily Telegraph*, 16th November, p.15.

Jones, E. (1936), 'The Psychology of Constitutional Monarchy', in *New Statesman and Nation*, 1st February, pp.141-142.

Jones, E. (1964), 'The Psychology of Constitutional Monarchy' (1936), in *Essays in Applied Psychoanalysis* vol. 1, International Universities Press, New York, pp.227-233.

Jones, W. (1979), 'The Monarchy and the House of Lords', in D. Kavanagh (ed.), *British Politics Today*, Manchester University Press, Manchester, pp.57-67.

Joseph, K. (1979), 'The Class War' (Gilbreth Lecture), in *Guardian*, 18th July, p.7.

Joseph, K., and Sumption, J. (1979), *Equality*, John Murray, London.

Jouvenel, B. de (1952), *The Ethics of Distribution*, Cambridge University Press, Cambridge.

Jouvenel, B. de (1957), *Sovereignty*, Cambridge University Press, Cambridge.

Keatley, P. (1984), 'Downing Street, the Palace, and the Third World', in *Guardian*, 21st January, p.17.

Kennedy, M. (1987a), 'Cover up over Queen's cousins denied', in *Guardian*, 7th April, p.1.

Kennedy, M. (1987b), 'Inside Story', in *Guardian*, 7th April, p.25.

Kent, N. (1950), *John Burns: Labour's Lost Leader*, Williams and Norgate, London.

Knight, S. (1984), *The Brotherhood*, Granada, London.

Knightley, P. (1980a), 'Richest Family in huge tax-dodge', in *Sunday Times*, 5th October, p.1.

Knightley, P. (1980b), 'Vesteys may face back-dated tax-claim', in *Sunday Times*, 12th October, p.1.

Knightley, P. (1981), The Vestey Affair, *MacDonald, London*.

Labour Party (1923), *Annual Conference Report*, pp.250-251.

Laguna, G.A. de (1927), *Speech: its Function and Development*, Humphrey Mitford, London.

Laird, D. (1959), *How the Queen Reigns*, Hodder and Stoughton, London.

Lane, C. (1981), *The Rites of Rulers*, Cambridge University Press, Cambridge.

Langer, S. (1957), *Philosophy in a New Key*, Harvard University Press, Cambridge, Massachusetts.

Langley, C. (1978), 'The Time Bomb under the Throne', in *The Times*, 4th July, p.16.

Laski, H.J. (1917), *The Problems of Sovereignty*, George Allen and Unwin, London.

Laski, H.J. (1919), *Authority in the Modern State*, Yale University Press, New Haven, Connecticut.

Laski, H.J. (1921), *Foundations of Sovereignty*, George Allen and Unwin, London.

Laski, H.J. (1925a), *A Grammar of Politics*, George Allen and Unwin, London.

Laski, H.J. (1925b), *The Problem of a Second Chamber*, Fabian Tract no. 213, Fabian Society, London.

Laski, H.J. (1963), *Introduction to Politics*, Unwin, London.

Lee, D., and Newby, H. (1983), *The Problem of Sociology*, Hutchinson, London.

Lenin, V.I.U. (1977), *The State and Revolution*, Progress Publishers, Moscow.

Levenson, H. (1981a), 'The network of nepotism that serves the rich', in *The Times Higher Education Supplement*, 10th April, p.12.

Levenson, H. (1981b), 'Uneven Justice — Refusal of Criminal Legal Aid in 1979', in *Legal Action Group Bulletin*, May, pp.106-100.

Levy, D.T. (1983), 'The Real and the Royal', in *The Salisbury Review* vol. 3, pp.17-20.

Linton, W.S. (ed.) (1851-1855), *The English Republic* (4 volumes), J. Watson, London.

Locke, J. (1965), *Two Treatises of Government*, Mentor, London.

Longford, E. (1974), *The Royal House of Windsor*, Weidenfeld and Nicolson, London.

Longton, J. (1984), 'Powell condemns Queen's bias', in *Guardian*, 21st January, p.1.

Lords (1986), 'Peers by Party Affiliation', in *The House [of Lords] Magazine*, 21st February, pp.20-23.

Low, R., and Lean, G. (1981), 'Shots at Queen — treason charge', in *Observer*, 14th June, p.1.

Luce III, H. (1969), 'Monarchy: the vital Strand', in J. Murray-Brown (ed.), *The Monarchy and its Future*, George Allen and Unwin, London, pp.129-134.

McLachlan, H. (1975), 'Religion and the Monarchy', in *New Humanist* 90, January, pp.312-313.

McClachlan, N. (1977), 'Thumbs Down Down Under?', in *New Statesman* 93(2411), 3rd June, p.735.

McGirk, T. (1984), 'The King who guards democracy', in *Sunday Times*, 19th August, p.6.

McGlaughlin, C. (1987), '19 millions are living in Poverty', in *Labour Weekly*, 8th August, p.1.

McInnes, C. (1969), 'Our own Kings', in J. Murray-Brown (ed.), *The Monarchy and its Future*, George Allen and Unwin, London, pp.137-150.

McKinnon, D. (1963), 'Moral Objections to Christian Belief', in A.R. Vidler (ed.), *Objections to Christian Belief*, Penguin, Harmondsworth, pp.9-29.

McKenzie, R., and Silver, A. (1968), *Angels in Marble. Working class conservatives in Urban England*, Heinemann, London.

MacMillan, H. (1972), *Pointing the Way 1959-1961*, MacMillan, London.

MacPherson, C.B. (1962), *The Political Theory of Possessive Individualism*, Oxford University Press, London.

McWhinney, E. (1985), *Constitution Making: Principles, Process, Practice*, Toronto University Press, Toronto, Ontario.

Magnus, P. (1967), *King Edward VII*, Penguin, London.

Maisky, I. (1962), *Journey into the Past*, Hutchinson, London.

Maistre, J. de (1965), *The Works of Joseph de Maistre*; introduction by Jack Lively, George Allen and Unwin, London.

Mann, H.H. (1939), *Why were they proud?*, The Pacifist Research Bureau, London.

Marlowe, J. (1973), *George I*, Weidenfeld and Nicolson, London.

Martin, K. (1936), 'The evolution of popular Monarchy', in *The Political Quarterly* vii, pp.155-178.

Martin, K. (1937), *The Magic of Monarchy*, Nelson, London.

Martin, K. (1963), *The Crown and the Establishment*, Penguin, Harmondsworth.

Marquand, D. (1962), 'All Monarchists Now', in *Spectator* CCVIII, 1st June, p.715.

Marx, K. (1975), 'Preface to "A Contribution to the Critique of Political Economy"' (1844), in R. Livingstone and G. Benton (trs.), *Karl Marx: Early Writings*, Penguin, Harmondsworth, pp.424-428.

Marx, K. (1978a), *The German Ideology* (1845-1846); C.J. Arthur (ed.); Lawrence and Wishart, London.

Marx, K. (1978b), *The Eighteenth Brumaire of Louis Bonaparte* (1852), Foreign Languages Press, Peking.

Masters, B. (1973), *Dreams about H.M. the Queen*, Mayflower, St Albans.

Michele, L. di (1979), 'The Monarchy and the Representation of Power: the Queen's Silver Jubilee 1952-1977', in *Annalia Anglistica Instituto Universitario Orientale Napoli* XXII(1).

Middleton, D. (1957), *The British*, Secker and Warburg, London.

Militant (1983), 'Why the monarchy must go', by C. Walder and G. Adams in *Militant*, 2nd September, p.12.

Mill, J.S. (1956), *On Liberty* (1859), Bobbs-Merrill, New York.

Miller, D. (1976), *Social Justice*, Clarendon Press, Oxford.

Milliken, R. (1981), 'Thatcher wins Summit battle over Namibia', in *Sunday Times*, 4th October, p.6.

Montgomery, J. (1957), *The Twenties: An Informal Social History*, George Allen and Unwin, London.

Milligan, S. (1982), 'Face to Face', in *Animal's Defender* [Journal of the National Anti-Vivisection Society], January/February, pp.1-3.

Moore, R. (1982), 'Spike blasts Royal "Hunting Junkies"', in *Sunday Mirror*, 31 January, p.1.

Morrah, D. (1958), *The Work of the Queen*, William Kimber, London.

Morrah, D. (1959), *Queen and People*, Central Office of Information, London.

Morrah, D. (1969), *To Be a King*, Arrow, London.

Mosley, C. (1985), 'Corgis with Everything', in *New Society* 73(1179), 2nd August, pp.162-163; *cf.* 'Happy Families', in Channel 4 TV Opinions series, 27th July, 7.30-8.00 pm, Panoptic Productions.

Mountbatten, P. (1980), 'One Aspect of Human Conflict': Annual Lecture, St George's House, Windsor.

Mountbatten, P. (1983), *A Question of Balance*, Sphere, London.

Muggeridge, M. (1957), 'Does England Really Need a Queen', in *Saturday Evening Post*, 19th October.

Muggeridge, M. (1981), 'The Monarchy provides a sort of *ersatz* religion', in

The Listener 105(2705), 26th March, pp.397-401.

Murray-Brown, J. (ed.) (1969), *The Monarchy and its Future*, George Allen and Unwin, London.

Nairn, T. (1981), 'The House of Windsor', in *New Left Review* (127), pp.96-100.

Nairn, T. (1985), 'The Glamour of Backwardness', in *The Times Higher Education Supplement*, 11th January, p.13.

Nairn, T. (1988a), 'The Burial of Popular Sovereignty', in *New Statesman* 115(2972), 11th March, pp.16-21.

Nairn, T. (1988b), *The Enchanted Glass: Britain and its Monarchy*, Century Hutchinson Radius, London.

Namier, L. (1955), 'Monarchy and the Party System', in *Personalities and Powers*, Hamish Hamilton, London, pp.13-38.

New Statesman (1977), Jubilee issue, 93(2411), 3rd June, pp.730-751.

New Statesman Profile (1977), 'Neither Dignified nor Efficient' [Philip Mountbatten], in *New Statesman* 93(2411), 3rd June, pp.740-741.

Nichols, P. (1973a), 'Paragons or hot potatoes in the Palace', in *The Times*, 14th May, p.12.

Nichols, P. (1973b), 'Prerogative without partisanship', in *The Times*, 15th May, p.16.

Nichols, P. (1973c), 'How Britain has kept the Magic of the Monarchy', in *The Times*, 16th May, p.18.

Nicolson, H. (1962a), *Monarchy*, Weidenfield and Nicolson, London.

Nicolson, H. (1962b), 'I would give the Monarchy a Hundred Years', in *Time and Tide* XLIII, 6th and 13th December, p.25.

Norton, P. (1982), *The Constitution in Flux*, Martin Robertson, London.

Nyozekan, H. (1952), 'The lost Japan', in Tsunoda *et. al.* (eds.), *Sources of Japanese Tradition*, Columbia University Press, London.

Orwell, G. (1941), *The Lion and The Unicorn: Socialism and the English Genius*, Secker and Warburg, London.

Page, J. (no date), *Monarchy: an Annotated Bibliography of Theories of Kingship*, The Monarchist Press Association, London.

Paine, T. (1792), *Address to the Republic of France*, 25th September, London.

Paine, T. (1945), *Selected Writings of Thomas Paine*; R.E. Roberts (ed.); Everybody's, New York.

Parker, T. (1983), 'Not a word against the Queen', in *New Society* 64(1070), 19th May, pp.261-262.

Peabody, A.J. (1970), *Constitutions of the Nations* (4 volumes), Nijhoff, the Hague.

Penguin Special (1977), *The Queen*, Penguin, Harmondsworth.

Peters, R.S. (1958), *The Concept of Motivation*, Routledge and Kegan Paul, London.

Peters, R.S. (1972), 'Reason and Passion', in R.F. Dearden, P.H. Hirst, and R.S. Peters (eds.) *Reason*, Routledge and Kegan Paul, London, pp.58-79.

Petrie, R.C. (1933), *Monarchy*, Eyre and Spottiswoode, London.

Petrie, R.C. (1952), *Monarchy in the 20th Century*, Andrew Dakers, London.

Pethick-Lawrence, F.W. (1953), 'The Coronation', in *The Contemporary Review* CXCII, pp.323-324.

Phelps, G. (1977), *The Story of the British Monarchy*, Nile and McKenzie, London.

Pine, L.G. (1962), *Ramshackledom*, Secker and Warburg, London.

Polanyi, G. and Wood, J.B. (1974), *How Much Inequality?*, Institute of Economic Affairs, London.

Popper, K. (1969), *Conjectures and Refutations*, Routledge and Kegan Paul, London.

Postgate, R. (1951), *The Life of George Lansbury*, Longmans Green, London.

Powell, E. (1986), 'The Plot that Bounced Back', in *Daily Mail*, 22nd July, p.6.

Priestley, J.B. (1962), 'Crown without Anchor', in *New Statesman and Nation*, 12th October, pp.485-486.

Rawls, J. (1972), *A Theory of Justice*, Oxford University Press, London.

Reid, I. (1981), *Social Class Differences in Britain*, Grant McIntyre, London.

Reith, J.C. (1975), *The Reith Diaries*; J. Stuart (ed.); Collins, London.

Rentoul, J. (1987), *The Rich Get Richer*, George Allen and Unwin, London.

Reynolds News Editorial (1887), 'Jubilee Juggernaut', in *Reynolds News* (1923), 19th June, p.1.

Ridley, F.A. (1957), 'Lord Altrincham and the Monarchy', in *The Freethinker* LXXVII(41), 11th October, pp.321-322.

Roscil, G. (1981), 'Delays put Queen away from bomb', in *Sunday Times*, 17th May, p.3.

Rose, D. and Vogler, C. (1988), *Social Class in Modern Britain*, Hutchinson, London.

Rose, R., and Kavanagh, D. (1976), 'The Monarchy in Contemporary British Culture', in *Contemporary Politics* 8(4), pp.548-576.

Rousseau, J.J. (1954), *The Social Contract*, Gateway, Chicago.

Routledge, P. (1985a), 'Pit hopes fail as union rejects "worse formula"', in *The Times*, 2nd February, p.1.

Routledge, P. (1985b), 'The Queen did not at any time say the mining strike was promoted by Mr Scargill', in *The Times*, 1st March, p.32.

Royal Commission on the Distribution of Income and Wealth (Chairman: Lord John Diamond) (1975), Report No. 1, Cmnd 6171, Her Majesty's Stationery Office, London.

Royal Commission on the Distribution of Income and Wealth (1976), Report No. 3, Cmnd 6383, Her Majesty's Stationery Office, London.

Royal Commission on the Distribution of Income and Wealth (1976), Report No. 4, Cmnd 6626, Her Majesty's Stationery Office, London.

Royal Commission on the Distribution of Income and Wealth (1977), Report No. 5, Cmnd 6999, Her Majesty's Stationery Office, London.

Royal Commission on the Distribution of Income and Wealth (1978), Report No. 6, Cmnd 7175, Her Majesty's Stationery Office, London.

Royal Commission on the Distribution of Income and Wealth (1979), Report No. 7, Cmnd 7595, Her Majesty's Stationery Office, London.

Royal Commission on the Distribution of Income and Wealth (1979), Report No. 8, Cmnd 7679, Her Majesty's Stationery Office, London.

Royal Commission on the Distribution of Income and Wealth (1980), *An A to*

Z of Income and Wealth: everyman's guide to the spread of income and wealth, Her Majesty's Stationery Office, London.

Russell, B. (1946), *Let the people think*, Watts, London.

Russell, B. (1947), *A History of Western Philosophy*, George Allen and Unwin, London.

Russell, B. (1957), *Why I am not a Christian*, Simon and Schuster, London.

Ryan, C. (1981), 'Beyond Beliefs', in *The American Philosophical Quarterly*, January, pp.33-41.

Sabine, G.H. (1963), *A History of Political Theory*, Holt, Reinhart and Winston, London.

Sampson, A. (1971), *A New Anatomy of Britain*, Hodder and Stoughton, London.

Saxe Coburg Gotha, Victoria (1911), *The letters of Queen Victoria: a selection from Her Majesty's correspondence and journal between the years 1886 and 1901* vol. 11; Earle Buckle (ed.); John Murray, London.

Scott, J. (1982), *The Upper Classes: Property and Privilege in Britain*, MacMillan, London.

Scruton, R. (1980), *The Meaning of Conservatism*, Penguin, Harmondsworth.

Secrest, M. (1984), *Kenneth Clark; a Biography*, Weidenfeld and Nicolson, London.

Shils, E. and Young, M. (1953), 'The Meaning of the Coronation', in *Sociological Review* 1(1) pp.63-81.

Shirer, W. (1960), *The Rise and Fall of the Third Reich*, Simon and Schuster, New York.

Simon, Lord (1982), 'The Influence and Power of the Monarchy in the United Kingdom', in *The Parliamentarian* (63), April, pp.61-65.

Simpson, C., and Knightly, P. (1981), 'Why all the fuss about those tapes?', in *Sunday Times*, 10th May, p.17.

Smith, A. (1926), *The Wealth of Nations* vol 1 (1776), Dent, London.

Smith, A. (1981), *Stitches in Time: the Commonwealth in World Politics*, Andre Deutsch, London.

Smith, S.A. de (1981), *Constitutional and Administrative Law* (4th edition); H. Street and R. Brazier (eds.); Penguin, Harmondsworth.

Smith, G. (1981), 'The lowdown on Polo', in *Sunday Times*, 26th July, p.32.

Socialist Youth (1981), 'The real role of the monarchy', in *Socialist Youth* (13), July / August, pp.6-7.

Sommer, D. (1960), *Haldane of Cloan: his life and times*, George Allen and Unwin, London.

Spender, J.A. (1923), *The Life of Campbell Bannerman* vol. 1, Hodder and Stoughton, London.

Stephen, J.F. (1967), *Liberty, Equality, Fraternity* (1873), Cambridge University Press, Cambridge.

Stuart, James I (1918), 'A Speech to the Lords and Commons of Parliament at Whitehall on Wednesday the xxi of March anno 1609', in *The Political Works of James I* (1619), Oxford University Press, London, pp.306-325.

Stewart, M. (1952), 'Labour and the Monarchy', in *Fabian Journal* vii, pp.17-22.

Stone, L., and Stone, J.C.F. (1984), *An Open Elite?*, Oxford University Press, London.

Sulloway, T. (1980), *Freud: Biologist of the Mind*, Fontana, London.

Sunday Telegraph Editorial (1984), 'Queen and Nation', in *Sunday Telegraph*, 22nd January, p.16.

Tawney, R.H. (1952), *Equality* (1931), George Allen and Unwin, London.

Thackeray, W.M. (1929), *The Four Georges*, Dent, London.

Thomas, C. (1979), 'Family and Kinship in Eaton Square', in F. Field (ed.), *The Wealth Report*, Routledge and Kegan Paul, London, pp.129-159.

Thompson, L. (1971), *The Enthusiasts: a biography of John and Katherine Bruce Glazier*, Gollancz, London.

The Times (1980), 'Survey findings show how far Britain's national morale has sunk', in *The Times*, 10th Septmber, p.4.

Titmus, R. (1970), *The Gift Relation, from Human Blood to Social Policy*, George Allen and Unwin.

Townsend, P. (1979), *Poverty in the United Kingdom*, Penguin, Harmondsworth.

Townsend, P. and Davidson, N. (1982), *Inequalities in Health*, Penguin, Harmondsworth.

Tracey, H. (1932), 'Who made MacDonald Prime Minister?', in *The Social Democrat* XLVIX(2230), June, p.1.

Tsunoda, R., de Bary, W.T. and Keene, D. (eds.) (1964), *Sources of the Japanese Tradition* (2 volumes), Columbia University Press, New York and London.

Turner, V.W. (1968), 'Myths and Symbols', in D.L. Sills (ed.), *Encyclopaedia of the Social Sciences* vol. 10, Collier MacMillan, London, pp.576-582.

Tweedie, J. (1979), 'Why can't we all live like the Shah and Princess Anne . . .?', in *Guardian*, 19th July, p.13.

Veitch, A. (1986), 'How you have been hearing only one side of the stories', in *Guardian*, 13th August, p.11.

Veitch, A. (1987), 'Report ban fails as facts emerge on health of poor', in *Guardian*, 15th March, p.1.

Walker, M. (1981), 'Wilson to testify over *coup* attempt', in *Guardian*, 31st March, p.2.

Wardroper, J. (1981), 'Those outrageous Spencer girls', in *Sunday Times*, 1st March, p.13.

Warwick, C. (1983), *Princess Margaret*, Weidenfeld and Nicolson, London.

Weaver, M. (1977), 'The Queen states her case', in *Daily Telegraph*, 7th July, p.12.

Webb, S., and Webb, B. (1920), *A Constitution for the socialist commonwealth of Great Britain*, Longmans Green, London.

Weber, M. (1964), *The Theory of Social and Economic Organisation*; T. Parsons (ed.); Collier MacMillan, London.

Weber, M. (1968), *Economy and Society: an outline of interpretative Sociology*; G. Roth and G. Wittich (trs.); Bedminster Press, New York.

Weightman, J.C. (1953), 'Loyal thoughts of an ex-republican', in *Twentieth Century* CLIII, June, pp.406-414.

222   *The Myth of British Monarchy*

Wells, H.G. (1939), *Travels of a Republican Radical in Search of Hot Water*, Penguin, Harmondsworth, pp.28-39.

Wells, H.G. (1944), 'A Republican's Faith', in *New Statesman and Nation*, 23rd December, p.421.

Wells, H.G. (1969), *Experiment in Autobiography*, Cape, London.

Whale, J. (1971), 'Mystery of the Monarch's Money', in *Sunday Times*, 18th April, p.12.

Whitehead, P. (1981), 'Windsor Soap Opera', in *New Socialist* (1), September / October, pp.71-72.

Wiener, M. (1981), *English Culture and the Decline of the Industrial Spirit 1850-1980*, Cambridge University Press, Cambridge.

Wild, K.W. (1938), *Intuition*, Cambridge University Press, Cambridge.

Wilson, B.R. (ed.) (1970), *Rationality*, Blackwell, Oxford.

Winchester, S. (1982), 'The commoner *versus* the peers', in *Sunday Times*, 22nd March, p.13.

Windsor, C. (1975) Port Moresby Speech (Reuter's report) in *Guardian*, 15th September.

Windsor, C. (1981a), 'Leading from the Front', in *Engineering Today*, 23rd November, pp.18-21.

Windsor, C. (1981b), 'Why we should think small', in *Sunday Times*. 22nd November, p.13.

Woolf, L. (1931), 'On a constitutional revolution', in *Political Quarterly* II, pp.474-477.

Woolf, L. (1935), *Quack! Quack!*, Hogarth, London.

World Tourism Organisation (1981), *Tourism Compendium*, World Tourism Organisation, Madrid.

World Tourism Organisation (1982), *World Tourism Statistics Yearbook* vol 35 (1980-1981), World Tourism Organisation, Madrid.

World Tourism Organisation (1986), *Yearbook of Tourism Statistics 1981-85* (2 vols), World Tourism Organisation, Madrid.

Worsthorne, P. (1977), 'The case for the Monarchy', in Penguin Special, *The Queen*, Penguin, Harmondsworth, pp.165-184.

Worsthorne, P. (1979), 'When treason can be right', in *Sunday Telegraph*, 4th November, p.16.

Wright, P. (1987), *Spycatcher*, Viking, New York.

Young, B.A. (1957), 'Foundation Stones and Things', in *The National and English Review* 147(898), pp.70-73.

Young, G. (1973), *Tourism*, Penguin, Harmondsworth.

Ziegler, P. (1978), *Crown and People*, Collins, London.

INDEX